22

W9-ABT-069

THE ZEN OF THERAPY

ALSO BY MARK EPSTEIN

Advice Not Given:
A Guide to Getting Over Yourself

The Trauma of Everyday Life

Thoughts without a Thinker:
Psychotherapy from a Buddhist Perspective

Going to Pieces without Falling Apart:
A Buddhist Perspective on Wholeness

Going on Being:
Buddhism and the Way of Change

Open to Desire:
The Truth About What the Buddha Taught

Psychotherapy without the Self:
A Buddhist Perspective

THE ZEN
OF THERAPY

Uncovering a Hidden Kindness in Life

MARK EPSTEIN, M.D.

PENGUIN PRESS
NEW YORK
2022

PENGUIN PRESS
An imprint of Penguin Random House LLC
penguinrandomhouse.com

Copyright © 2022 by Mark Epstein
Penguin supports copyright. Copyright fuels creativity, encourages
diverse voices, promotes free speech, and creates a vibrant culture.
Thank you for buying an authorized edition of this book and for
complying with copyright laws by not reproducing, scanning,
or distributing any part of it in any form without permission.
You are supporting writers and allowing Penguin to continue
to publish books for every reader.

LIBRARY OF CONGRESS CATALOGING-IN-PUBLICATION DATA
Names: Epstein, Mark, 1953– author.
Title: The Zen of therapy : uncovering a hidden kindness in life /
Mark Epstein, M.D.
Description: New York City : Penguin Press, 2022. | Includes index.
Identifiers: LCCN 2021013934 (print) | LCCN 2021013935 (ebook) |
ISBN 9780593296615 (hardcover) | ISBN 9780593296622 (ebook)
Subjects: LCSH: Buddhism and psychoanalysis. |
Psychotherapy—Religious aspects—Buddhism.
Classification: LCC BQ4570.P755 E674 2022 (print) |
LCC BQ4570.P755 (ebook) | DDC 294.3/3615—dc23
LC record available at https://lccn.loc.gov/2021013934
LC ebook record available at https://lccn.loc.gov/2021013935

Printed in the United States of America
2nd Printing

Designed by Amanda Dewey

To Arlene, Sonia, and Will

A monk asked, "What are the words of the ancients?"
The Master said, "Listen carefully! Listen carefully!"

CHAO-CHOU, *Recorded Sayings*, #220

AUTHOR'S NOTE

In order to protect privacy, I have changed patient names and other identifying details. But the specifics of the psychotherapy sessions have been rendered as closely as possible to how they occurred. All patients read and approved the material based on their sessions.

CONTENTS

Author's Note *xi*

Introduction *1*

PART ONE

INTO THE MYSTIC *15*

1. Inner Peace *17*

2. The Path of Investigation *39*

PART TWO

A YEAR OF THERAPY *53*

3. Winter *55*

· *Clinging* *61*

4. Spring *107*

· *Mindfulness* *113*

5. Summer *153*

· *Insight* *159*

6. Fall *207*

· *Aggression* *215*

PART THREE

THE GATE OF ONENESS *265*

7. Kindness *267*

Acknowledgments 291

Notes 293

Index 297

THE ZEN OF THERAPY

INTRODUCTION

The Buddha, before his enlightenment, was protected by his father from ever seeing old age, illness, and death after the unexpected passing of his mother a week after he was born. Upon marrying and fathering a child of his own decades later, he finally chanced upon a sick person, an old person, and a corpse and, reacting in horror, quickly replicated his childhood trauma by abandoning his own loving family and seeking freedom (or escape) through the available spiritual pursuits of his time. After spending the next several years in the forest searching for meaningful help, the Buddha seized upon the practice of self-mortification as the vehicle of his long-sought awakening. There was already a strong ascetic tradition in ancient India, and the aspiring Buddha, in his relentless search for inner peace, saw austerity as the surest method of detaching himself from his all-too-human body and mind.

Filled with disgust and self-loathing, like many a self-hating or shame-filled person of our own era, he tried, for a long time, to remove himself from himself by deliberately renouncing all forms of pleasure. He was better at this than anyone until, at the point of self-extinction (much like modern-day sufferers from anorexia who starve themselves, tragically and heroically, until their organs begin to fail), he had an inkling that something was wrong with his basic approach. An unbidden memory came to his mind of himself as a young boy sitting joyfully under a rose-apple tree while his father plowed the fields in the distance. He was taken by the memory but surprised by how uncomfortable it made him feel. He was afraid of something that the memory brought up, he realized, frightened of the joy he had once felt. Why? he wondered. Why had the memory come at this precise moment, and why did it make him feel afraid? An answer came spontaneously to his mind, an early example of the power of free association.

He had been seeking happiness and freedom outside of himself, he grasped, when, maybe, just maybe, it was already in him, the way it was under the rose-apple tree when he was a boy. This possibility nagged at him and he began to entertain it seriously. "Perhaps I've been going about this entirely wrong," he thought to himself. "Maybe I'm trying to tell myself something. Could the enlightenment I am seeking lie in this direction, toward the remembered joy of my childhood? That would go against everything I've been thinking, everything I have thought. That's why the joy frightens me: it's forcing me to rethink my entire orientation." Savoring the memory and brightened by his new understanding, the Buddha appreciated that with his body so emaciated, there would be no way of supporting such a joyful feeling. If he were going to take his realization seriously, he concluded, he had better find something to eat.

At this moment, a young woman named Sujata from a neighboring village approached him bearing a golden bowl of rice porridge. It was a case of mistaken identity. Sujata was actually bringing her offering to a local tree spirit who she believed had helped her conceive a baby. Her maid had been in the forest earlier and seen the withered Buddha languishing under the very banyan tree whose spirit her mistress had earlier propitiated, and she had rushed back to the village to excitedly give Sujata the news of her sighting. Sujata set out right away, thrilled to be able to thank the deity in person. Mistaking the emaciated Buddha for her venerated spirit, Sujata fed him, brought him back to life, and unknowingly gave him the strength to continue his quest. Sujata's milk-rice was so nutritious it is said to have sustained him for the next forty-nine days, a critical interval in which he did the internal work necessary for his enlightenment. I think of these forty-nine days as a kind of liminal period in the Buddha's life, a time of intensive therapy in which he was able to make sense of his past and reach into his future, becoming the person he was meant to be.

Sujata, of course, had no idea who the Buddha really was or who he might become. But, filled with gratitude after having recently given birth, she fed the hungry soul who had chanced into her neighborhood. There is no record of their conversation, but the Buddha is said to have held on to her golden vessel for a while, ultimately using it as a kind of talisman to verify that he was now on the right track. Tossing the bowl into a nearby river sometime later, he declared to himself, according to one ancient report, that if the bowl floated upstream against the current, it would be a sign that his change of heart was correct. It did float upstream, before sinking to the bottom and coming to rest on the bowls of three previous Buddhas who had all taken crucial nourishment at the same locale. The sound of the bowls' clanging woke a local naga, or serpent king, who lived at the bottom of the river, to the news that a new Buddha was in the making. This snake, to my mind, represents the underworld, the unconscious energy the Buddha was now empowering to use for his awakening.

I think of this chance encounter between Sujata and the Buddha as a metaphor for psychotherapy. The symbolism is overwhelming. The Buddha, like most people who come to therapy, had a sense that he was doing something wrong, that he was somehow getting in his own way. The coping strategy he had developed to deal with his own trauma was not really working; it was, in a sense, only perpetuating the very feelings of deprivation he was struggling to eliminate. Having left his own wife and child, with the mistaken thought that renunciation of worldly entanglement was essential for his spiritual progress, he could not proceed without reestablishing the connections he had divorced himself from. Those connections were both inner and outer. He needed to remember his childhood joy, and he needed to feed, so to speak, at Sujata's breast, two critical events that, in my way of thinking, were redolent of the trauma of his own mother's death seven days after he was born. Without the recovery of his relational nature, the Buddha could never have awakened; he would have worn himself out in a heroic quest of self-denial. Sujata, as the Buddha's "spiritual friend," gave of herself, new mother that she was, without ever knowing how meaningful her contribution would be. And the Buddha, propelled by his recovered memory and nourished by her grateful offering, finally set himself right.

At my best, I see psychotherapy in the same light. Many people who come to therapy are disgusted with themselves for one reason or another, much as the Buddha was in his own time and in his own way. This disgust can take many forms: shame, fear, anxiety, or feelings of unworthiness are common expressions of it, but the possibilities are endless. Some people even develop what is called a "reaction formation" and seem the opposite of disgusted. They come across as prideful or conceited and unwilling to admit their faults or self-doubts. But these individuals are often just propping themselves up, creating a false front to mask their vulnerabilities, and somewhere inside they are troubled because they know they are not being real.

Common to all of these variations is a difficulty with emotional life. Emotions are threatening. They move on nerve pathways that are faster than thought; they can take us by surprise and overwhelm our carefully constructed mental defenses.

Emotions, by their very nature, are out of our control. In our efforts to fit in, adjust, and comply with all of the demands that are placed on us as we mature, emotional life is often given short shrift. We learn to squelch feelings that get in the way of a "healthy" adjustment and deny those that challenge the identities we construct to get along in the world. Superficially, things might look okay but inside, as a result, are confusion and conflict. The self we present to the world and the self that dwells inside us are not always aligned.

In the story of the Buddha, his effort to close himself off from his inner experience was made manifest by his embrace of asceticism. But we do not have to be ascetics to be at odds with ourselves. The tendency to deny, or be defensive about, one's true inner experience is widespread. Freud called it "resistance" when he encountered it in his patients, and he came to understand that one way to overcome it was to make it the primary object of therapeutic scrutiny. Exposing one's resistance to a therapist is what allows it to gradually peel away. In a similar vein, the Buddha, in the aftermath of his awakening, taught his followers to make peace with their own minds. The Buddha needed Sujata to help point him in this direction. Many of us need therapy.

The heart of this book is a year's worth of selected psychotherapy sessions. Early in my life I had a chance encounter with Buddhism that grabbed me, fed me, and shaped the way I came to practice psychiatry. This early encounter helped me the way Sujata helped the Buddha: it set me on the track that has guided me ever since. This was the most important influence on my work, but it was never something that I could describe easily. How exactly does Buddhism show up in my day-to-day sessions? What seeps through from my meditative experiences in conversations with my patients? In this book I have tried to examine, in the incidental details of a given hour, how my Buddhist background influences the way I practice therapy. The result is a cross section of life in my office, a pointillist view that, if successful, conveys a picture of how the concerns and conflicts of ordinary life can be seen in a spiritual light.

I had a telephone conversation with my ninety-five-year-old mother the other day that offered another window into all of this. In a way, it was reminiscent of many of the therapy sessions I have structured this book around, but it was not a therapy session, it was a conversation with my mother, and it therefore posed a different, although related, set of challenges. I call my mom every Sunday and mostly we talk about what's new with my family, what she might have read lately in *The New Yorker*, or what is of interest in today's *New York Times*. I am rarely of any help with the Sunday crossword puzzle but we manage to find other things to talk about. Since shortly after my father passed away more than a decade ago, she has lived alone in a supportive apartment complex outside of Boston, populated by a host of other elderly retired people who, before COVID, ate dinners together and shared activities. While her mind is as clear as ever, her body has become more fragile over the years and she has had to spend increasing amounts of time in the more contained and confined environment of the community. She often chafes against its constraints, but for us, her four children, the place has been a godsend.

"I have a question for you," my mother interjected about fifteen minutes into my recent call. "I have a new friend here who I like a lot. We have much in common except for the fact that two of her three children have died. That's something I can't imagine. She says she is spiritual but not religious." My ears perked up. A new friend; I hadn't heard about a new friend in a long time! And "spiritual but not religious." "Like me!" I exclaimed, interrupting her. "Yes, 'like your son.' That's what she said. She has read your books." There was the briefest pause. "What does that mean, 'spiritual but not religious'?" she asked.

For a moment I was stunned. What does she mean what does that mean? After all these years of my involvement with mindfulness meditation and Buddhism, was she still as clueless about this as she sounded? It was true that she had never been curious about my pursuits, but she is a smart woman and I have given her copies of all of my books. But, inside, I knew that because her new friend was interested, she could now make room for something that had heretofore had little relevance for her. My mother has always had good friends—most of whom have died by now—and she has always been a good friend to her friends. I decided to get over myself and try to answer her question.

At first I fumbled around. I thought of her friend having lost her children—I'm not sure whether they died in adulthood or childhood—and I imagined she had some inkling of life continuing in some form after the death of the body. That would be one way of making her "spiritual": an openness to the life of the soul as distinct from the life of the body. I tried to formulate this for my mom and sent her a link to a book about reincarnation that I thought her friend might appreciate. "If that were the case, after thousands of years you'd think there would be some evidence of it," my mother replied, dismissing my first explanatory attempts.

I tried another tack. "You know those meditation retreats I've been going to for forty years," I said. "That's what they are about. At first you are just alone with your everyday thoughts and concerns, but after a while you start to see other things about yourself you didn't know were there." I was on slightly firmer ground here, and I went on. "You think you know who you are, but other more mysterious things start to poke through." What other things? I wondered to myself. How could I make this make sense to my mom? Silence, stillness, spaciousness, love? Would she take any of that seriously? I wanted to speak to her of the soul, in contradistinction to the ego, but I became tongue-tied and retreated to a more defensible position. "Something happens there," I said, referring back to the meditation retreats. "You get beyond yourself. You see all your usual thoughts and preoccupations, but they come and go, and sometimes you touch places you didn't know were there, and that gives you a sense of being part of something greater, of something that might not die when the body dies, of something more meaningful, something that helps you understand your real purpose." I crowded everything into one sentence, and I knew while I was talking that I was not getting through.

"Well, I still don't get it," she sighed.

Later that evening I forwarded my mother an article from that week's *New York Times* entitled "Taking Ayahuasca When You're a Senior Citizen." I hoped that the *Times* would do a better job of explaining "spiritual but not religious" than I had in its depiction of how this mind-expanding plant substance was being used for therapeutic purposes. The story began with a now seventy-four-year-old venture capitalist who was four years old when his father disappeared from their Budapest home in 1942 without saying goodbye. The boy blamed himself for his father's disappearance, attributing it to his being a "bad boy," and never saw him again, his father presumably killed by the Nazis. The ayahuasca journey brought him into contact with his deceased father, who assured him he had been watching over him for his entire life from the other side. He communicated to his son that he had been certain he would get away from the German authorities and so there had been no need to wake him to say goodbye. This conversation, in his psychedelic imagination, relieved the man of a burden he had been carrying for his whole life. The article quoted the author Michael Pollan as follows: "What psychedelics seem to be particularly good for is jogging us out of our grooves of habit and allowing us to acquire a fresh perspective on familiar things. And as you get older, you get mired in habits."

The article closed with another example. A seventy-year-old man journeyed to Peru for multiple ayahuasca ceremonies. "I knew that my childhood, while it wasn't abusive, was very very cold," he said. "It had very little approval or affection in it. What I saw that night was: picture an upside-down pyramid. That point of the pyramid was the first thought. The first thought was loneliness and need for affection and approval. And the pyramid going up from that was my whole life. So my whole life was based on that one moment, seeking affection and approval." As in the first case, this vision freed the man from his exclusive identification with a single aspect of his personality. He could see his loneliness not as an intrinsic aspect of his character but as a contingent and relational outgrowth of a specific set of circumstances, not as the definition of who he was.

Later that night, I read the article aloud to my wife after telling her of my conversation with my mother. She remembered a related experience of her own, without drugs, in which, while listening to a lecture I had dragged her to by a spiritual teacher, she had the realization that *her* mother's constant worrying— about getting places on time, cleaning things up, buying the right shoes, being healthy—did not mean that worry had any intrinsic value. My wife had long ago rejected her mother's overt ways of fretting, and to all appearances she was nothing like her mother, but in the free-floating mindset that the lecture encouraged she discovered a grain, or kernel, of belief still operating in her subconscious that suggested that worry was a prerequisite for optimal functioning. Somewhere deep inside she still believed that things would unravel without it. This assumption, she realized, was based entirely on her mother's mode of being in the world. In some way, it was a means of staying close to her mother, but once she saw it clearly, it lost its power over her. Worry was not intrinsic to my wife's way of being, nor was it necessary. She could live without it. There were other ways of honoring her mother!

She recognized this as a "spiritual" realization although there was certainly nothing overtly religious about it.

That evening I read an article that a writer friend had forwarded to me earlier in the day about the relationship between poetry and Zen by the poet Gary Snyder. It was written in 1991 but had somehow resurfaced on the internet. My friend thought I would appreciate it as much as she had. The very beginning of the article seemed to articulate what I was trying to say to my mother.

> *Although the term meditation has mystical and religious connotations for many people, it is a simple and plain activity. Attention: deliberate stillness and silence. As anyone who has practiced sitting knows, the quieted mind has many paths, most of them tedious and ordinary. Then, right in the midst of meditation, totally unexpected images or feelings may sometimes erupt, and there is a way into a vivid transparency. . . .*

> *No one—guru or roshi or priest—can program for long what a person might think or feel in private reflection. We learn we cannot in any literal sense control our mind. Meditation cannot serve an ideology. A meditation teacher can only help a student understand the phenomena that rise from his or her own inner world—after the fact—and give tips on directions to go. . . . Within a traditional Buddhist framework of ethical values and psychological insight, the mind essentially reveals itself.*

My mother told me the following week how much her friend had appreciated the book I had sent the link to. "He must really understand me!" she reported her friend exclaiming, but my mom said nothing about the ayahuasca article. Yet the conversation stayed with me. "Spiritual but not religious" was something I believed in; it was another way of talking about the "vivid transparency" that Snyder described. The mind essentially revealing itself is something that makes sense to me; it is something I believe therapy can help make happen. While I am not sure the phone call with my mother opened up anything new for her, it put me in touch with something of relevance for this book. I remembered visiting Ram Dass, a Harvard psychologist turned psychedelic pioneer whom I was lucky to befriend in my early twenties, after not seeing him for many years. He had had a stroke in 1997, and this was a year or two afterward. I had published a couple of books by then and had been a functioning psychiatrist for more than a decade.

"So," he teased me, "are you a *Buddhist* psychiatrist now?" "I guess so," I replied sheepishly. Ram Dass had known me when I was a college student; I knew that for him I was still indelibly about twenty-one years old even though I was by then already in my midforties. There was a long pause before he said anything more. His stroke made it difficult for him to find words. "Do you see them as already free?" he finally said in an uncharacteristically serious and penetrating tone, the words stretching out over time. It took me a minute to understand what he was asking. "Already free? Do I see my patients as already free?" But then I understood. He was talking about the mind revealing itself, about the vivid and transparent thing hidden within the twisted shards of our individual personalities. Did I see that freedom in my patients?

While it took Ram Dass to express it for me, I recognized the truth in what he was saying. I do see my patients as already free. The seed is in them already, just as the Buddha's joy under the rose-apple tree was there within him. My challenge in being a therapist has been to stay true to this vision even when my patients, like my mother, object. Therapy can help people make room for this possibility or, more precisely, to get their own feel for it. As Ram Dass liked to say in his later years, "We are all walking each other home."

. . .

I have divided this book into three parts: Part 1, "Into the Mystic," gives background to my efforts to reconcile Buddhist thought with my Western training in psychiatry and psychotherapy. It begins with a description of my first encounter, as a Harvard Medical School student on a research expedition in India, with an esoteric Tibetan Buddhist form of yoga and then describes the thinking behind my efforts to integrate meditation and therapy. Although I immersed myself in Buddhism before learning to be a psychiatrist, for many years I was careful not to let my spiritual leanings overtly intrude into my work as a therapist. I was content to use my training in mindfulness as a private resource, letting it guide me in the way I listened to my patients but hoping that the Buddhist influence would be invisible to them. But as I became more open about the spiritual aspects of my thinking, I found that many of my patients wanted this to be included in our work. I came to see that the divisions between the psychological, the emotional, and the spiritual were not as distinct as one might think, and that one way of looking at therapy was as a two-person, interpersonal meditation in which whatever arises is worthy of investigation. Thinking about therapy in this way has prompted the writing of this book.

Part 2, "A Year of Therapy," is a record of my attempt, over a year's worth of selected therapy sessions, to examine how this actually looks in practice. It is, in essence, a chronicle of personal inquiry in which I have held up a mirror to my own internal processes to try to zero in on the ways in which a therapy relationship can also be a spiritual friendship. The therapy sessions are grouped according to the four seasons in which they took place and are described as closely as possible, with privacy constraints in mind, to how things actually unfolded in the office in real time. Following the report of each session, I have presented my own thoughts about it, sometimes explaining more about a given patient's issues but more often exploring the thinking behind my own words and behavior. Certain themes emerge in each of the seasons: clinging as the fundamental way we perpetuate our suffering in the winter, mindfulness as the antidote in the spring, insight into the self's insubstantial nature in summer, and aggression as both the stumbling block and the gateway to compassion in the fall.

Part 3, "The Gate of Oneness," contains my final conclusions. I learned from this year of self-scrutiny and, with gratitude to all of my patients for reading over their sessions and my commentaries, emerged with a firmer grasp on how the Zen of therapy is made manifest. I will not attempt a summary here but will allow it to come in its own time.

My intention in what follows is twofold: to show that meditation does not have to be a solitary intrapsychic endeavor but can also work interpersonally, and to demonstrate that emotional life, rather than being a distraction, can serve as a critical doorway to spiritual understanding. There is a crosscurrent of dialogue here: one between myself and my patients and another between Buddhist thought and psychotherapeutic action. Out of these conversations I hope that one important thing will emerge. Spiritual life, if it is to go into the territory of personal freedom, must be individually configured. One way or another, a person's real-life issues must be brought into awareness to serve as grist for the spiritual mill, and a therapist, as spiritual friend, can help make this happen. This is the essence of my own attempt to bring together the worlds of Buddhism and psychotherapy.

I have chosen to be matter of fact in my descriptions. While the patient material is, of course, interesting (most therapists are by nature one part gossip and another part voyeur), I have tried to take readers into my own thinking in order to show how a Buddhist understanding can enhance a therapeutic relationship. In doing this, I have reached into the poetry of the Zen Buddhist tradition of East Asia. I think this is because of the way that the artists and artisans of China and Japan seamlessly integrated Buddhist thought into their already established creative pursuits. While my study of Buddhism has been mostly grounded in the practice of insight meditation, I have found the lyricism of the Zen poets to be most aligned with the sensibility I am describing in this book. To my way of thinking, therapy, like the poetry of medieval Japan, is an art form of our time and place, one that can reach new depths by way of a creative synthesis with Buddhist thought and practice.

Years after his encounter with Sujata, the Buddha had a conversation with Ananda, his close friend and personal attendant, that reflected how important he thought friendship was. Of course, there was no such thing as psychotherapy in the Buddha's time, but I take this conversation to be another indication of therapy's potential to channel the Buddha's wisdom. Ananda began by rather exuberantly declaring to the Buddha, as if he had just had an important realization, "This is half of the holy life, lord: admirable friendship, admirable companionship, admirable camaraderie." The Buddha, as he often did in his conversations with Ananda, admonished him in return. "Don't say that, Ananda. Don't say that," he exclaimed. "Admirable friendship, admirable companionship, admirable camaraderie is actually the whole of the holy life."

This is the territory I set out to explore in this book: the whole of the holy life. In the context of psychotherapy, how can friendship, companionship, and camaraderie actually emerge?

PART ONE

INTO THE MYSTIC

It is too clear and so it is hard to see.

*A dunce once searched for a fire with a
lighted lantern.*

Had he known what fire was,

He could have cooked his rice much sooner.

THE GATELESS GATE

One

Inner Peace

I first tried to meditate during the summer of 1973, between my sophomore and junior years of college, when I was working as a research assistant for a cardiologist at Boston City Hospital. This physician, Dr. Herbert Benson, a specialist in the treatment of high blood pressure, or hypertension, was the first to publish a scientific paper about the relaxation benefits of Transcendental Meditation, made popular by the Beatles several years earlier. His coauthor, Robert Keith Wallace, was a student of Maharishi Mahesh Yogi, the Indian guru who popularized TM, and together Benson and Wallace were among the first to show that meditation had measurable physiological effects. According to their studies, meditation slowed the body's metabolic rate, reducing both oxygen consumption and carbon dioxide output, inducing what they called a "wakeful hypometabolic state." In essence, they suggested that meditation flipped the nervous system into neutral, allowing the body to rest, digest, recuperate, and recharge. They christened these bodily effects "the relaxation response" (the antidote to the stress-induced fight-or-flight response) and suggested that its regular elicitation might actually lower blood pressure as well as relieve stress. Meditation was given scientific credence by their research. It was a real thing, not just someone's wishful thinking, and it had the potential to become an important tool of modern medicine. This research became the basis for *The Relaxation Response*, a popular book Dr. Benson published in 1975 that was among the first to suggest the health benefits of meditation.

I was intrigued by this work and met with Dr. Benson at the behest of my father, who had recently taken over as chairman of the department of medicine of which Dr. Benson was a part. I think it was an effort on my father's part to keep me in the medical fold despite my burgeoning interest in what he considered a rather esoteric pursuit. I had become intrigued by Eastern thought in general and Buddhism in particular in my first years of college and regularly perused the spiritual bookstores then popular in Harvard Square. At the university itself Eastern spirituality was looked down upon, but I had stumbled upon two graduate students, one in the religion department and one in psychology, who quietly encouraged my nascent interests. Diana Eck, who went on to become a distinguished professor of religion, the first female "master" of a Harvard house, and the author of a comprehensive book on the Indian holy city of Banaras, was my section person in a freshman world religion class, and Daniel Goleman, who later wrote *Emotional Intelligence* and who had already been to India to learn about meditation, was my section leader for a second-year class in psychophysiology. They each, in their own discreet ways, supported my pursuits, while being careful to shield their own spiritual leanings from the greater Harvard milieu. Meditation was not yet something I had tried for myself, however; I was still in an exploratory phase, suspicious of cultish atmospheres and without any formal instruction. I had read books about meditation but had never tried it myself. That Dr. Benson's influences were Hindu and not Buddhist meant little to me at the time.

In the year or two since publishing his research on meditation,

Dr. Benson had broken away from the Maharishi. He concluded that there was nothing special in Transcendental Meditation's approach, that a generic form of meditation could work just as well as the expensive training offered by the guru and his disciples, and that it was up to him to bring meditation into the medical armamentarium. Dr. Benson decided that the Sanskrit mantra at the heart of TM's approach was not essential and that the simple act of alertly concentrating one's attention, using whatever word, phrase, or prayer a person chose, could evoke an identical physiological response. For the patients in his hypertension clinic, he used the blandest word he could think of: "one." (Only later did he realize all of its potentially sacred meanings.) Needless to say, his appropriation of TM's technique earned him the enmity of the guru and his followers. At the same time, despite the widespread media attention given to his research, his mainstream academic colleagues treated him as a rather marginal figure because of his embrace of meditation. It might be okay for the Beatles, but a Harvard cardiologist should know better; that was the general consensus. They pressed him on the quality of his research and upbraided him for drawing sensational conclusions from preliminary findings. As a result, despite his growing fame, Dr. Benson was a rather isolated figure when I met him. He felt misunderstood and inappropriately judged by both his medical and meditative peers.

None of this concerned me, however. I was happy to have a prestigious summer job with someone who was open to my abstruse interests. I knew that Dr. Benson was doing my father a favor by taking me on, but I surprised him in our first meeting by talking at length about the placebo effect, a subject I had explored and written about during the previous semester in my psychophysiology course. Placebos have been confounding modern medicine for generations. Pills that have no active ingredients, given as part of a routine doctor-patient interaction, regularly produce meaningful, and scientifically documented, improvement in a variety of illnesses more than one-third of the time. Having grown up in a family in which academic medicine was king, and with a budding interest in the mind's pervasive influence on the body, I was taken with the placebo effect and thought Dr. Benson might be also. He was. He put me to work in the medical library exploring and reviewing fifty years of relevant clinical research. Was there something that could be cultivated in the doctor-patient relationship that might be important for healing? Did the physician's concern for the patient or the patient's faith in the doctor make a difference in a person's recovery? Might the placebo be somehow eliciting the relaxation response? Or was the relaxation response itself a manifestation of the placebo effect? Whichever way we looked at it, was there a key here to unlocking the body's ability to heal itself? I set out to analyze all of the pertinent studies in the medical literature.

Meditation was not a big part of my summer experience. Dr. Benson was using it in his clinic for patients with borderline high blood pressure but I was not involved in that work. I was back and forth to the library and only peripherally aware of Dr. Benson's other activities. I wondered about meditation though. I remember sitting, one sweltering August afternoon, at my paper-strewn desk in the back room of Dr. Benson's confined hospital suite and finally trying out his technique. "One, one, one," I repeated as my breath went in and out of my nostrils. "One, one." Nothing in particular seemed to happen. It felt like a radical thing to interrupt my work to sit there with my eyes closed, but at the same time the exercise seemed empty to me. I liked the idea in principle—the possibility of quieting my body's tensions with a trick of the mind appealed mightily to me—but I did not feel engaged by the technique. I tried it a few more times and then put it back on the shelf. While some people found the simplicity of Dr. Benson's instructions and their scientific credibility to be helpful, I was put off. Even if there was such a thing as the relaxation response, and even if I could be sure I was eliciting it, the whole approach felt too mechanical to me. Somewhere in me I knew that the relaxed hypometabolic state Dr. Benson envisioned could not be the be-all and end-all of what meditation was about.

In thinking about it now, I can see how my research into the placebo effect helped explain why this approach to meditation seemed so constrained. Science was of several minds about the placebo effect. Some researchers wanted to get rid of it altogether because it was impossible to know whether a new drug had anything to offer if it was no better than a placebo. Others, taking the phenomenon more seriously, wanted to tease out its active ingredient. What molecules, what neural pathways, were being stimulated by something as innocuous as a sugar pill? Yet others saw the placebo effect as inextricably bound up with the doctor-patient relationship, not as something that could be isolated from it. Something mysterious happens when we turn our illness over to a caring physician, they concluded. Could the very act of trusting someone to heal us stimulate healing? Is there something in the human touch or in the caring human interaction or in human kindness that has beneficial medical results? In the article that I cowrote with Dr. Benson that summer, published shortly thereafter in *The Journal of the American Medical Association*, we came down on the latter side. The placebo effect, whatever it is derived from, is a neglected asset in the care of patients, we concluded. Modern medicine could benefit from taking it more seriously.

For some people, the very medicalization of meditation, the assurance that science has proven its validity, creates a positive placebo effect. It helps them believe meditation is real. For these people, Dr. Benson's efforts to tease out the active ingredient in meditation and give it to them in a stripped-down form was a real gift. But for me the opposite was true. I was drawn to meditation for the same reason I was interested in placebos. The placebo effect points to the body's capacity to heal itself, helped along by some combination of trust, faith, and human empathy. Meditation seemed to be promising something similar for the mind. Given the right conditions, the mind could realize its own potential, healing itself through a combination of self-awareness, mindfulness, insight, and compassion. In turning meditation into a standardized medical treatment, something was being sacrificed, akin to what is lost when one's kindly country doctor is replaced by a harried technician or a robot. I saw how readily meditation in the stripped-down version could be adapted for the West, but, at the same time, I felt the lack of the ancient wisdom I was increasingly in search of. I did not fault Dr. Benson for his critique of Transcendental Meditation and I was not looking for a return of the Sanskrit phrase or the guru, but I knew I was searching for an approach more grounded in the traditions long associated with it, not one that was wholly divorced from them. As much as I appreciated the burgeoning science of meditation, I was also in search of its art. I completed my report on the placebo effect, praising it for what it implied about the mystery of healing, submitted my paper for publication, and returned to my studies. It was another year before I meditated again.

My karma with Dr. Benson was not over, however. Our placebo article received a good deal of media attention and became the basis for his next bestseller, *The Mind/Body Effect: How to Counteract the Harmful Effects of Stress*. I observed how he dealt with both the press and the medical establishment, and took note of what a fine line he had to walk in talking publicly about such esoteric topics. We had a special relationship; he showed me that it was possible to work within the Western medical system but still be open to ancient Eastern wisdom, and he encouraged me to follow in his footsteps. (And I am sure the recommendation he wrote for me was instrumental in getting me into medical school!)

In return, I maintained a dialogue with him over the next seven years as I turned toward Buddhist meditation, bringing him news from the front lines of a "spiritual" counterculture he was wary of engaging with too overtly. The mid-1970s marked the beginning of my engagement with mindfulness, the core Buddhist meditation technique, and I was fortunate enough, the very next summer, to connect with many of its first American ambassadors. By the time I entered medical school in 1977, I had befriended and sat numerous silent vipassana retreats with Joseph Goldstein, Jack Kornfield, Ram Dass, and Sharon Salzberg and traveled with them throughout India and Southeast Asia to meet many of their Eastern teachers. "Vipassana" is the ancient word for "insight," and this form of meditation, of which mindfulness is an essential component, is also known as "insight meditation."

In the meantime, Dr. Benson's books continued to break through to the mainstream, and Dr. Benson, always interested in esoteric reports of how the mind affected the body, was privately reading the exotic journals of a turn-of-the-century French explorer of Tibet named Alexandra David-Neel. She described witnessing Tibetan Buddhist monks nakedly meditating in subzero temperatures and warming themselves with a special practice of yoga and meditation called gtum-mo. Buddhism, in its time in Tibet, had merged with a shamanic tradition that had long preceded it there while keeping alive practices that dated from Buddhism's heyday in medieval India. David-Neel was one of the first Western explorers to document the result. Dr. Benson, as part of his inquiry into how the mind could affect the body, wanted to know if I knew anything of these practices, and, while I did not, in one of my periodic meetings with him I told him that in September of 1979 the Dalai Lama would be passing through on his first American visit and if we could secure a meeting, we could ask him ourselves. I had been to his palace in exile in India two years before, and I knew that he was scheduled to visit the Insight

Meditation Society, the retreat center in western Massachusetts founded by my mindfulness teachers on the grounds of a former seminary. The Dalai Lama liked scientists, and Dr. Benson liked to associate with spiritual leaders. It seemed to me like a match made in heaven.

Using our Harvard Medical School credentials, Dr. Benson reached out to the Office of Tibet to ask for an appointment. He heard back some time later that it would indeed be possible. I was present for the conversation and remember the somewhat awkward moment when the Dalai Lama, while acknowledging the veracity of some of David-Neel's reporting, recoiled at the idea of Western scientists measuring his meditating monks. Nevertheless, Dr. Benson persisted. He told the Dalai Lama of his success with the transcendental meditators and pressed him to see if we could come to India to document this esoteric Tibetan practice. These meditations are for private spiritual purposes, the Dalai Lama responded, not for public display. They have always been shrouded in secrecy so as not to make people think that so-called miracles are more important than the healthy mental development that is the real goal of such pursuits. But then he abruptly changed his mind. "For skeptics, you must show something spectacular," he said, "because, without that, they won't believe."

It took a year and a half to arrange but in the spring of 1981, during my final year of medical school, the Dalai Lama and his personal physician hosted Dr. Benson, me, and an associated team of investigators in the Indian hill station of Dharamsala, where he has resided in exile since his 1959 flight from his homeland. I managed to string together several months of independent study and receive medical school credit for my participation. Accompanied by Jeffrey Hopkins, a professor of Tibetan studies at the University of Virginia who served as our interpreter, we took measurements from three senior monks, proficient in gtum-mo, who were in long-term retreat in cabins scattered in the local hillsides. With a film crew in tow, we hiked into the mountains toting our laboratory equipment. While the monks did not raise their core body temperatures over the normal 98.6 degrees Fahrenheit, they did show a remarkable, and for most of us impossible, ability to deliberately raise the peripheral temperatures of their arms and legs to that of their core. This in itself was a major finding even if it did not reach mystical proportions. We hypothesized that the monks must have found a way to voluntarily open up their distal blood vessels, those that supply the arms, legs, fingers, and toes. Ordinary people are not capable of willfully dilating their capillaries in such a way, and the temperatures of their hands and feet are consistently much lower than their interior. This was further demonstration of the power of the mind to influence the body, and it grounded and authenticated David-Neel's observations. In one ironic twist, however, we found that one of the monks on retreat had dangerously high blood pressure. His meditative prowess had not protected him from the potential ravages of hypertension.

Dr. Benson and I parted ways after this trip, however. Or it might be more accurate to say we diverged in the midst of this trip. He found me to be more interested in talking with the monks about the psychology behind gtum-mo than I was in taking their temperatures. He was right! My idea of our research extended to investigating what these monks were doing in their meditations. These were highly accomplished men who had spent years developing themselves spiritually. They were Buddhist monks in long-term retreat in stone huts with earthen floors, practicing meditations I knew nothing about. What were they doing? With an interpreter present, I had an unparalleled opportunity to probe these monks' minds, not just their rectal temperatures. I was not about to forgo the opportunity, and the scientific stance necessitated by our research project struck me as in contradiction to all I had learned from the study of the placebo effect. Having now spent four years in medical school, I knew how tempting it could be to turn ailing people into objects of medical investigation, treating and following them with blood tests, X-rays, and invasive procedures rather than attending to them as people. The monks were not our patients, of course, and we *were* there to take their temperatures, but this did not mean, I told myself, that we had to ignore who they were as individuals. Nor did we have to overlook the art of their experience by focusing exclusively on our dedication to science. My initial discomfort with Dr. Benson's approach to meditation— trying to extract the active ingredient and thereby removing it from its philosophical context—found new expression in my uneasiness with the limited scope of our project.

But I am not sure that this by itself is an adequate explanation for our diverging paths. We had known each other and collaborated for seven years by this point and worked hard to put together this entire expedition. Dr. Benson had been my champion as I made my way through Harvard, and he had done the same for my friend Daniel Goleman, willingly serving on his PhD thesis committee and adding the weight of his Harvard Medical School credentials when much of Goleman's psychology department was opposed to meditation research. By the time we met up in New Delhi in February of 1981 to begin the trek to Dharamsala, however, I was beginning to strike out on my own. I was finishing medical school and heading for a career in psychiatry. I wanted to write more expansively about Tibetan medicine, psychology, and meditation and planned to use my time in the Tibetan community to that end. Dr. Benson, on the other hand, was in the prime of his professional life and focused primarily on his research and its clinical applications.

In addition, I had come to India a month before, while Dr. Benson had flown in for just several days. It was his first trip to Asia, while I had been there before. In the month before meeting up with him, I had been in the holy city of Vrindavan, the birthplace of the Hindu god Krishna, at the opening of a new ashram of Ram Dass's recently deceased Indian guru. I was staying in the temple with a number of friends and with some of the principal Indian disciples. Much of my time there was spent in their company singing devotional songs, meditating, hanging out, drinking tea, and celebrating, India-style, the opening of the temple. K. C. Tewari, a sparkling, wise, and joyful devotee, the "Indian father" of my friend Krishna Das, could not believe that I was (almost) a doctor because of how young I looked. "Dr. Boy," he called me, laughing, as we sang, meditated, and talked on and on about spiritual longing.

I had immersed myself in a sacred environment before meeting up with Dr. Benson. I was Dr. Boy now and excited to continue my investigations. I was curious about the esoteric Tibetan practices and surprised that Dr. Benson seemed not to be. The tension between our two agendas was emblematic of the two worldviews, the scientific and the spiritual, that I was trying to navigate, and it was a foreshadowing of issues I would subsequently confront in my career as a therapist. Where did my allegiance lie, with the East or with the West, and was it actually possible to blend the two?

Dr. Benson returned to America after a couple of days, satisfied with the measurements we had obtained, while I stayed in India for another several months exploring the philosophy and psychology behind gtum-mo. Every morning for the next six weeks I shadowed the Dalai Lama's personal physician, Dr. Yeshi Dhonden, sitting by his side as he saw patients in the small courtyard of his home just down the street from the Dalai Lama's palace in exile. He diagnosed by feeling his patients' pulses and looking at their first morning's urine, stirring, shaking, and smelling it until he was satisfied with his analysis. In the latter part of the day, I hung around with our translator, Jeffrey Hopkins, and a European monk named Georges Dreyfus, an old friend of

Jeffrey's soon to become a professor of religion at Williams College. They had endless conversations about the Tibetan Buddhist concept of emptiness—it is a "nonaffirming negative," I remember them repeating over and over, although it took me a long time to understand what they were talking about. Their conversations made about as much sense to me as Dr. Dhonden's urine examinations, but I was fascinated by the whole environment and eager to find out more.

I learned that the heat yoga that the monks were practicing was one aspect of the Six Yogas of Naropa, an ancient high-level meditation practice handed down over the centuries by meditation masters to their disciples, part of what Tibetan Buddhism calls Highest Yoga Tantra. From the point of view of Highest Yoga Tantra, difficult emotions do not need to be suppressed or eliminated, as some more elementary meditations strive to do. Their energies can, instead, be used for enlightenment. By moving the attention from a complete immersion in the feeling to the observation of it, the emotions could be harnessed for spiritual purposes. The mind is a terrible master but a wonderful servant, this approach proclaimed. Evocative paintings of wrathful or erotic deities adorning the Tibetan temple walls made this point with graphic emphasis. Anger, no longer an obstacle to meditative attainment, was portrayed in these paintings as an instrument of insight. Desire, no longer viewed as an obstructive impediment, was embodied as a vehicle of empathy. Ambition, no longer for personal aggrandizement, was represented as the intention to help others. As if to highlight the connection between the personal and the spiritual, the four esoteric stages of Highest Yoga Tantra were named for four stages of falling in love. Looking, smiling, embracing, and orgasm are the closest one comes in regular life to the joyous celebration, and spontaneous loss of ego, uncovered in successful meditations of this type. In everyday life, these feelings are fleeting but the monks practicing heat yoga learned to prolong such exalted states for extended periods of time. The heat in their bodies was a reflection of their changing inner reality; it was a by-product of a process of mental and emotional transformation, not their primary intent.

Some weeks after Dr. Benson left Dharamsala, I had a private meeting with the Dalai Lama. He was supportive of my interest in Buddhist psychology and urged me to continue my pursuits. He wrote a letter of introduction for me to take to other Tibetan monasteries and teachers in India, and he clarified one important question for me. Was meditation trying to get rid of the self that Western psychology thought was so important? I was hoping it was. I was unsure of myself, uncomfortable in my own skin, and had always found Buddhist thought appealing because of the way it downplayed the importance of the ego. I was ready to declare the self to be unreal and be done with the whole thing. "No," he said. "Our human birth is a great privilege. It's just that the self that we take to be so real is never as real as we think it is. Self-lessness means seeing things for what they are," he declared, "identifying as nonexistent something that never did exist in the way we imagine it." This was the "nonaffirming negative" I had already heard so much about in the endless discussions of empti-ness I had listened to. He used the analogy of someone wearing sunglasses to illustrate his point. The sunglass wearer does not mistake the distorted color for reality even though things appear rosier when seen through their lenses. We are like a person wear-ing sunglasses who has forgotten they are on, taking what we see for granted rather than understanding that we are laying a scrim over it. The self exists, but not in the way we ordinarily take for granted, he seemed to be saying. We have to put it to good use rather than trying to shore it up or, alternatively, tear it down.

He then inquired about my own career ambitions, and asked if I would visit the local monastic college, the Institute of Buddhist Dialectics, to talk with the monks in training about the kind of education I had received. They had a traditional monastic curriculum, heavy in Buddhist philosophy but short on Western arts and sciences. I was taken aback. I had come to Dharamsala to learn from the Dalai Lama; I was not anticipating that he would be interested in me. But this inquiry was a preview of an important reformation that the Dalai Lama later initiated in the training of Tibetan Buddhist monks. He insisted that they be schooled in Western science as well as in Buddhist philosophy, and he enlisted me as an early advocate of that perspective. It was a bit ironic. After feeling frustrated with our research because of its insistence on the scientific method, here I was talking it up for the monks. I gave an overview of my medical school education to a classroom full of young monastics and emphasized that the relationship could go both ways. Just as the outer science of the West could be integrated into the monastic curriculum, the inner art of the Buddha could do much to enrich Western psychiatry and medicine.

Upon my return to Boston three months later, I found Dr. Benson still disappointed that I had not adhered to a more traditional stance in our research. The bloom had faded in our relationship. We soon published our gtum-mo findings in the prestigious British scientific journal *Nature*, however; it was the first documentation of conscious control over this aspect of the involuntary nervous system ever reported. I began my medical internship right after graduation and by the following year had moved to New York City to begin a new life, having resolved, once and for all, never to completely forsake my spiritual worldview, even as I began my training in psychiatry. Dr. Benson and I did not collaborate again and did not see each other until my father's memorial twenty-seven years later when we had a friendly conversation that, after so many years, meant a great deal to me.

While Dr. Benson and I went our separate ways, the Dalai Lama remained a perennial presence as I became a working psychiatrist. I never again met with him privately but I was at a conference with him in Newport Beach in October of 1989 when news came that he had won the Nobel Peace Prize. I was on a panel with him in Toronto several years later and reached out to him when my first book, *Thoughts without a Thinker*, was in press, in 1994. The editor of that book thought it would be a coup if I could get the Dalai Lama to write the foreword to it. I was skeptical but agreed to try. I wrote to him through all the avenues I could remember but heard nothing. My friend Robert Thurman, professor of religion at Columbia and a friend and sometime translator for him, told me discouragingly how many such requests came his way, but offered to bring the manuscript with him on a visit to Dharamsala in case there was an opportunity to ask. The book went to press without a foreword but at the very last minute a fax (there was no email in those days) from the Dalai Lama's office came through to my editor with three short paragraphs attached. It began like this:

The purpose of life is to be happy. As a Buddhist I have found that one's own mental attitude is the most influential factor in working toward that goal. In order to change conditions outside ourselves, whether they concern the environment or relations with others, we must first change within ourselves. Inner peace is the key.

As thrilled as I was to receive his endorsement for my book, it took me some time to appreciate what he had written. His words initially seemed like platitudes, off the cuff, superficial, maybe even churned out by an assistant. "Inner peace," while a worthy goal, did not seem very far from Dr. Benson's relaxation response. In my new role as a psychotherapist, I was suspicious of the nascent wellness movement and of the new age drive for inner peace and reluctant to see happiness as the ultimate purpose of life. I worked with a lot of people drawn to Eastern thought who were hoping to leapfrog over their personal issues by using meditation to calm their minds, the way I was hoping to get rid of my self when I first spoke with the Dalai Lama. I realized that a spa treatment is often what people want from meditation—and that it was often being sold as such—but I could tell from my own meditations that relaxation, while an occasional benefit, was not always accessible on demand. For me, meditation had come to mean being with my own mind no matter what state it was in. In this way, it was closer to psychotherapy than I had initially thought. Freud's daughter Anna, herself a practicing psychoanalyst, had said that a therapist has to sit equidistant from id, ego, and superego, not presumptuously taking any particular side. This was a good description of the meditative attitude as well. I liked imagining myself inside a triangle, whether on the meditation cushion or in my therapy office, maintaining a neutral position even while being buffeted from every possible direction.

Gradually, though, over time, it dawned on me that relaxation and inner peace were not the same thing at all. I had naively equated them but in so doing had missed the deeper point of the Dalai Lama's foreword. My burgeoning understanding came on two fronts. On the Buddhist side, I continued to benefit from the Dalai Lama's input. I attended numerous teachings he gave. I took a notebook, and all of my scribbling circled one central theme. The more I listened, the more I understood that when the Dalai Lama spoke of inner peace he was talking about nonviolence rather than relaxation. Not only nonviolence in the outer world but also nonviolence in one's inner world. Just as he had not urged me to jettison my sense of self, he was neither encouraging an empty mind nor recommending meditation simply as a form of rest and repose. He was asking us to use meditation to look into our minds and examine our behavior, to listen to the way we spoke to ourselves and thought about others, and to explore the attitudes we held in our most personal and private thoughts. From his perspective, inner peace is possible only when one has made peace with one's own mind, when one's own inner violence has been dealt with. This requires honesty and an internal ethic that is endlessly challenging. Inner peace comes not from turning off the mind, but from deliberately confronting one's own innermost prejudices, expectations, habits, and inclinations. This went to the heart of my objection to the medicalization of meditation that I first felt in Dr. Benson's hospital suite. Meditation as stress reduction, as a way of calming the mind, does not address its mission to challenge, confront, befriend, and change one's innermost mental attitudes.

As I worked as a therapist and my thinking evolved, the work of the great British child analyst Donald Winnicott, an influential, but at times overlooked, figure in the psychotherapy world, began to speak to me with a renewed vigor. Like the Dalai Lama, Winnicott also stressed the importance of nonviolence. For Winnicott, the father of the phrase "the good-enough mother," the willingness to recognize and tolerate anger was intimately related to one's ability to love. In this regard he was very much in line with the paintings of Highest Yoga Tantra adorning the Tibetan monastery walls. Anger was an obstacle to love when it could not be acknowledged, he wrote. In order not to be a victim of one's anger, it was important to be able to recognize it with a compassionate attitude. He pointed out how ruthlessly infants treat their mothers and how much hatred—in herself and from her children—a good-enough mother is able to endure and accept. He extolled mothers for their altruism, for their natural ability to cast aside selfish reactions for the benefit of their children, and, in popularizing the phrase "good-enough," made room for the inevitable failures that, rather than derailing a good relationship, make it real. Winnicott had the same matter-of-factness about human nature that I also appreciated in the Dalai Lama. They each stressed an inherent goodness that could shine through when people looked at themselves, not with rose-colored glasses, but with honesty and humility. Inspired by their common approach, I delighted in the fact that the English translation of the Tibetan word for the heat yoga we had studied, gtum-mo, was "fierce mother." Somehow the two worlds were lining up! I used this parallel in my own work with patients, helping them to first acknowledge and then curb their most destructive impulses. That my own inner work involved the same processes only made it more urgent.

The Dalai Lama had a special way of introducing people to this possibility, words that I have written over and over in the notebook I took to his teachings. "Everyone has the potential for Buddha nature," he would say. "Within each of us is a pure body of perfect spontaneity waiting to be discovered." I found this phrase delightful. "A pure body of perfect spontaneity"! What could he possibly mean? Freud loved free association but knew how difficult it was to achieve. He focused on the obstacles that came up when people attempted it, and outlined the defenses that blocked the freedom he had quite possibly found in himself. The Dalai Lama seemed to suggest that the defensiveness that first intrigued and eventually frustrated Freud did not always have to have the last word. "We call this pure body a natural quality: the innate mind of clear light," he would say. "The clear light mind does not come from an original primordial god or Buddha, it comes from ordinary beings diligently working with their own minds." In putting it this way, he was challenging those who did not believe in their own potential just as he had impressed me years before by taking my young self seriously. Enlightenment did not come from some faraway place outside of one's self, he insisted, it came from within. In his talks he often elaborated on this. "Narrow, self-centered, self-important, cowardly people keep the cause of suffering—self-centeredness—close to their hearts. They complain all the time, thinking, 'Me, me, me, poor me,' cherishing the very forces of their downfall. Mocking the self-cherishing attitude helps it go away. And opening to the suffering of others helps destabilize it." This notion of finding, and then mocking, the self-cherishing attitude was, for me, the big takeaway. The art of meditation lay in uncovering this tendency. This became the central, but unstated, principle of my clinical work. When I was able to help make it a reality for my patients, I knew I was doing the right thing.

While the Dalai Lama, like most Tibetan monks, had no experience with psychotherapy and no schooling in psychodynamic thought, he encouraged me to use my own training, and my own mind, to explore meditation from the inside and then put it to use. For me, this meant not only taking formal instruction from Buddhist teachers but also using my therapy training to make my own sense of the meditative experience. I felt, in the Dalai Lama's words about the "self-cherishing attitude," an approach that fit together with much of what I most valued in psychotherapy. How did meditation take on self-centeredness, really? Was it just by following a regimen of mental gymnastics, just by applying a technique the way Dr. Benson prescribed the relaxation response for his patients? Or was a more creative process necessary, one in which one's own self-centeredness and violence are confronted and pacified en route to a greater understanding of how much we all need each other? When I studied the traditional Buddhist maps of meditative progress, I was enthralled but dissatisfied. They outlined the various stages of meditation with great precision but said little about what a given individual might actually face while reaching for that pure body of perfect spontaneity the Dalai Lama insisted was waiting to be found. There were no case studies, few firsthand reports of the inner struggles a contemporary person might face while engaging with their own mind. In learning to meditate, albeit from some of the best teachers I could find, I came to appreciate that once I understood the basics, I had to teach myself how to do it. I had to take what I had learned, in terms of the formal techniques, and then make it real from the inside. Only then could I begin to appreciate what meditation could and could not accomplish.

Dr. Benson's collaboration with the Dalai Lama faded away sometime after our relationship broke up. I heard rumors about why but never got a complete story. But that early encounter with Tibetan Buddhism was pivotal in my own development. While I am still at a loss to fully understand the heat yoga we so carefully documented, the Dalai Lama's teachings have made a deep impression on me. In encouraging me to question my self-centeredness and recognize the violence it encodes while at the same time taking me seriously as an individual, he gave me a glimpse of the vision that Buddhism holds for each of us. We matter, each and every one of us, even while we do not need to be obstructed by our own self-regard. And a pure body of perfect spontaneity, while not necessarily linked to the concrete medical benefits of lowered blood pressure, is something within everyone's reach. I now understand that meditation has the potential to help us deal with the worst and bring out the best in ourselves. While the Dalai Lama never said anything so concrete, his inspiration helped me rise above the Western emphasis on mental *illness* to encompass an appreciation for the possibilities of mental *health*. That I could aim in this direction while working as a psychotherapist gave me a vision and purpose that has sustained me through many decades of work.

Over the years, meditation has moved from the fringes of the culture into mainstream psychology and medicine. Dr. Benson's initial research and his subsequent elaboration of it at Harvard Medical School played no small part in this. TM and mindfulness, derived respectively from the meditative traditions of Hinduism and Buddhism, have been successfully integrated into sports, business, education, medicine, and psychotherapy. The emerging field of cognitive neuroscience has helped to make mindfulness popular by mapping much of meditation's promise onto what we are beginning to understand about the brain. But the mindset of the West threatens to reduce our ability to truly benefit from this integration. We want a quick fix with demonstrable results. We want to see changes in our brains. We want the experts to show us what to do and even, if we are lucky, to do it for us. In its absorption by the wellness movement, meditation threatens to become more like cosmetic dermatology than the ongoing self-examination that is its own kind of higher education.

As instrumental as Dr. Benson's research was in helping meditation gain acceptance in the West, our culture's effort to tease out and promote its active ingredient as a tool of modern medicine diminishes what meditation has to offer. It might not be useful to separate the placebo effect from the heart and soul of the doctor-patient relationship, and it might not be helpful to strip meditation away from its broader spiritual agenda of nonviolence and inner peace. Meditation is a tool that helps us explore hidden aspects of our individual experience. It is not something that anyone can do for us, and only its formal outlines can be taught. If it is going to be of any help, we have to actively engage with it as an art rather than subjecting ourselves to it solely as a science. A goal-oriented approach, whether it is to calm the mind, relax the body, or achieve some kind of transcendental experience, is antithetical to meditation's greater purpose. For me, the trust and intimacy of the psychotherapeutic relationship was to become instrumental in helping to bring this greater purpose into focus.

Two

The Path
of Investigation

As indicated in the preceding chapter, I discovered meditation before deciding to become a psychiatrist, before medical school, before knowing very much about the Western approach to psychotherapy, before being in therapy myself, and before seeing any of my own patients. In particular, despite my time with Dr. Benson, whose take on meditation was derived from TM, with the Dalai Lama, whose expertise lay within the Tibetan Buddhist tradition, and with Ram Dass, who was primarily inspired by his Hindu guru, I was drawn to vipassana, or insight meditation, as introduced to me by some of the first American teachers of that Buddhist tradition: Joseph Goldstein, Sharon Salzberg, and Jack Kornfield. Insight meditation is built around mindfulness, the clear and single-minded awareness of whatever is happening to us and in us at the successive moments of perception, but it uses mindfulness as a stepping-stone for the investigation of the self. One of its core principles is that much of what we consider self is a construct and that the effort that goes into maintaining its image ultimately encloses us in a prison of our own making.

Insight meditation, it turns out, derives its power from the rather peculiar fact that we see ourselves most clearly when we are doing nothing at all. The mind does not stop even when we cease all physical, or digital, activity. Without our regular lives to distract us, we can't help looking more deeply into our own psyches. What do we see? At first, we mostly see what we already know. The mind's incessant activity. Everyday thoughts and worries. Leftover neurotic tangles. Angers, fears, longings, cravings, and resentments. Social media anxieties. But there are also memories, many of them painful, some of them not. These memories come floating up from somewhere just as things begin to settle down. That friend who betrayed us or the one who was unexpectedly kind. The teacher who saw something special in us. A parent's recurrent rage or a peaceful moment with a grandparent. First love and its subsequent disappointments. Sex. Many of these memories speak to the trust upon which our relational selves are based, while others contain hints of trauma. Some of them are what therapists call "screen memories"; they contain clues to our identities, to the emotional events that helped form us. Seemingly random, their persistence suggests hidden meanings to be explored.

Why is one of my first memories that of my mother promising that I could watch *The Mickey Mouse Club* when I got home from nursery school? Did I need to be bribed to come home or was I just attracted to Annette Funicello? Why does this memory continue to come up? There is ample time in meditation to ponder such questions, but clear answers are rarely forthcoming. What emerges most saliently is the feeling of the memory, the visceral sense of the scene and one's place in it. I have a feel for myself in the nursery school playroom, the tune of *The Mickey Mouse Club* playing in my head and, as a result, some kind of familiarity with myself at the age of four. I am hard pressed to say why this is important, but I know that it is. There is tenderness in the memory, tenderness toward the little boy whose enthusiasm I can still summon.

Insight does not stop there, however. As compelling and important as these recovered memories are, they are stepping-stones rather than resting places on the path of investigation. While they provide an invaluable sense of continuity, they also give access to how incidental the building blocks of the self actually are. When I remember myself in nursery school, I am relieved to feel the connection with my four-year-old exuberance, but I also recognize how flimsy the backbone of my identity is. My self-concept is based on this? If I trace myself back to my beginnings, I find . . . Mickey Mouse? Vipassana illuminated this for me, connecting me to my history in a deep and meaningful way, while pointing out the randomness of the material that formed me. The self is constructed on a very insecure foundation. We emerge from nothingness and cobble ourselves together out of the arbitrary and unbidden experiences that come our way. My wife, describing the simultaneous horror and wonder of pregnancy, likes to say that she made a baby out of tuna fish. What could be more strange than growing a human being inside one's body? Meditation lets us see something similar. It shows us how we are continually constructing a self out of the raw material of our everyday experience. Like the blind man and the elephant in the Indian parable, we grope in the darkness, telling ourselves a story out of whatever bits and pieces we manage to touch.

In the classical schemas of Theravada Buddhism, that which is practiced in Burma, Thailand, and Sri Lanka, there are, broadly speaking, two types of meditation. The first is concentration, in which attention is consistently focused on a single object, such as the breath or a sound, prayer, or mantra. Anything else is treated as a disturbance or interruption. When the mind is distracted from the central object, the meditator is instructed to dismiss the interference and return attention to the central object. This is what people generally think of as the whole of meditation, but it is really only a fraction. The other major type of practice is mindfulness, in which impartial attention is given to everything there is to observe: to changing objects of contemplation. In this type of meditation there is no such thing as a distraction. Whatever arises—thoughts, feelings, memories, emotions, and sensations, even consciousness itself—can become an object of mindful awareness. Seasoned meditation involves the interplay of concentration and mindfulness; both are cultivated from the start. It is very difficult to stay mindfully attentive to rapidly changing elements of experience, for instance, without the buildup of sufficient concentration, so most meditators in the Buddhist traditions are using both techniques at different times, oscillating between the two modes of attention.

But from the perspective of insight, both of these strategies are entry-level practices rather than ends in themselves. They are designed to guide the meditator toward a deeper understanding. Insight, in this context, means seeing through the fixed nature of things, in particular the fixed images we have of persons, beliefs, identities, expectations, and "selves." The word for insight, "vipassana," has the original meaning of "seeing by dividing." It means seeing analytically, taking things apart, and looking beneath their superficial appearances. With continual, mindful attention to the ever-changing flux and flow of experience, the mind/body that we naturally see as "me" and "mine" begins to lose its solidity. Those addictive thoughts that reinforce our sense of separateness—of judgment, criticism, and clinging—of "I like this" or "I don't like that"—are seen as temporary, porous, and incidental rather than necessarily "right" or "correct." The sense that we are each isolated in our own minds and bodies, fundamentally cut off from each other and from the world in which we are embedded, starts to give way and a greater sense of interconnectedness emerges. Compassion arises for those—including oneself—who are hampered by a more primitive, and self-centered, way of thinking, and this combination of compassion and insight-derived wisdom is said to be the fruition of the path of investigation, a reconfiguration in which selfish desires and concerns are diminished and altruistic ones brought to the fore.

By the time I completed my medical training and began to learn about Western psychiatry and its psychoanalytic tradition, I was already deeply familiar with this way of thinking. One of the first things I discovered was that there was really no playbook for how to be a therapist. As with meditation, it had to be figured out from the inside. There was no script to follow when sitting with a patient, no "right way" to handle things, only a set of ethical guidelines and a trust that listening "with a third ear" would help shape a useful response and serve a useful purpose. Each person, each visit, and each issue required an improvisatory spirit that kept me on my toes, much as I had felt when practicing mindfulness on my first silent retreats. I have had wonderful teachers, supervisors, and therapists, but, even in my first days, while still in training, once the door closed and I was alone with my patient, no one knew what I might do or say, least of all myself.

This put me in an interesting position from the start. I recently read the book of a Western-trained Japanese psychoanalyst who had traveled to Switzerland to study Jungian analysis. Through his work there he came to appreciate the Zen Buddhist tradition of his own country that had previously been of little interest to him. Therapy made Zen make sense to him because of its shared emphasis on "non-doing."

In my situation, because I had immersed myself so deeply in spiritual life before medical school, I tended to look at everything I was learning about therapy through the prism or lens of Buddhist thought. Buddhism made therapy make sense to me. I came to see that Western psychotherapy has the potential to be a vehicle of awakening just as meditation can be. It is another way of uncovering and confronting the egocentric preoccupations that keep us from living a more fulfilling life. That the meditator's attention was directed inwardly and the therapist's externally did not make their postures any different. I found that I could maintain an allegiance to both mindfulness and insight while conversing with my patients, and this gave me a great deal of confidence in the power of psychotherapy to transmit something spiritual.

While living in Sicily in the early 1920s, D. H. Lawrence wrote a poem called "Snake" that describes a version of this process perfectly. I was unaware of the poem until a friend mentioned it recently but, since then, many people have told me that they studied it in school. My friend who alerted me to it, for instance, said that she first read it in the fifth grade and that it made a deep impression on her, even then. For me, the poem was revelatory, coming as it did after many years of my own attempts to integrate Buddhism and therapy. Lawrence wrote the poem in conventional everyday language, describing a brief sighting of a golden snake while he was fetching water from his backyard well. But he had a poet's self-awareness, similar (if not identical to) that which is cultivated in meditation. He observed not just the serpent but also his own mind. And he was brought up short by what he saw in himself, in much the same way that insight, whether it comes from meditation or from psychotherapy, pulls us into conversation with the implicit violence of our own egos. Here, in its entirety, is Lawrence's famous poem:

Snake

A snake came to my water-trough
On a hot, hot day, and I in pyjamas for the heat,
To drink there.

In the deep, strange-scented shade of the great dark carob tree
I came down the steps with my pitcher

*And must wait, must stand and wait, for there he was at the
trough*
   before me.
*He reached down from a fissure in the earth-wall in the gloom
And trailed his yellow-brown slackness soft-bellied down, over
   the edge of the stone trough
And rested his throat upon the stone bottom,
And where the water had dripped from the tap, in a small clearness,
He sipped with his straight mouth,
Softly drank through his straight gums, into his slack long body,
Silently.*

*Someone was before me at my water-trough,
And I, like a second-comer, waiting.*

*He lifted his head from his drinking, as cattle do,
And looked at me vaguely, as drinking cattle do,
And flickered his two-forked tongue from his lips, and mused
   a moment,
And stooped and drank a little more,
Being earth-brown, earth-golden from the burning bowels of
   the earth
On the day of Sicilian July, with Etna smoking.*

*The voice of my education said to me
He must be killed,
For in Sicily the black, black snakes are innocent, the gold are
   venomous.*

*And voices in me said, If you were a man
You would take a stick and break him now, and finish him off.*

*But must I confess how I liked him,
How glad I was he had come like a guest in quiet, to drink at
   my water-trough*

And depart peaceful, pacified, and thankless,
Into the burning bowels of this earth?

Was it cowardice, that I dared not kill him?
Was it perversity, that I longed to talk to him?
Was it humility, to feel so honoured?
I felt so honoured.

And yet those voices:
If you were not afraid you would kill him!

And truly I was afraid, I was most afraid,
But even so, honoured still more
That he should seek my hospitality
From out the dark door of the secret earth.

He drank enough
And lifted his head, dreamily, as one who has drunken,
And flickered his tongue like a forked night on the air, so black,
Seeming to lick his lips,
And looked around like a god, unseeing, into the air,
And slowly turned his head,
And slowly, very slowly, as if thrice adream,
Proceeded to draw his slow length curving round
And climb again the broken bank of my wall-face.

And as he put his head into that dreadful hole,
And as he slowly drew up, snake-easing his shoulders, and
    entered further,
A sort of horror, a sort of protest against his withdrawing into
    that horrid black hole,
Deliberately going into the blackness, and slowly drawing
    himself after,
Overcame me now his back was turned.

I looked round, I put down my pitcher,
I picked up a clumsy log
And threw it at the water-trough with a clatter.

I think it did not hit him,
But suddenly that part of him that was left behind convulsed
*   in undignified haste,*
Writhed like lightning, and was gone
Into the black hole, the earth-lipped fissure in the wall-front,
At which, in the intense still noon, I stared with fascination.

And immediately I regretted it.
I thought how paltry, how vulgar, what a mean act!
I despised myself and the voices of my accursed human education.

And I thought of the albatross,
And I wished he would come back, my snake.

For he seemed to me again like a king,
Like a king in exile, uncrowned in the underworld,
Now due to be crowned again.

And so, I missed my chance with one of the lords
Of life.
And I have something to expiate:
A pettiness.

Every time I read this poem I am filled with awe. "I missed my chance with one of the lords of life," Lawrence moaned. How many chances have I missed, I wonder, overtaken by my own ego/ albatross? Yet Lawrence was present for the entire drama, himself included. He saw himself seeing the snake and simultaneously saw his mind reacting to the scene. He was witness to his inner conflict—his wonder at the snake's majesty versus his "educated" desire to destroy the dangerous threat—and he was helpless, in the unfolding spectacle, to prevent the "voices" of his "accursed education" from taking control. He saw his ego as it rose up to steal the show, coercing him into a destructive act that proved his manhood but ruined and debased the grandeur that had been momentarily granted him. But he learned from watching himself. He came face to face with the vulgarity and pettiness of his ego, a meditative accomplishment if there ever was one. For it is only by observing the ego dispassionately, over and over and over again, that its nature can be significantly revealed. Without direct experience of how limiting its small-mindedness can be, there is no motivation to grow beyond it.

Lawrence bringing his pitcher to the water-trough was like any of us sitting down to meditate. We never really know what we are going to find. The pitcher, like the bowl of rice porridge offered to the Buddha, is a stand-in for the kind of attention we cultivate in meditation, the attention that encourages us to be fascinated by even those things that most disturb us. And the snake, like the serpent king the Buddha awakened at the bottom of the river after tossing his bowl, represents the latent energy that is mobilized by this awareness. I like the word "beholding" to describe meditative contemplation. I was once told that James Joyce used that word to describe the only way to look at a work of art: bringing the object too close is like pornography, and distancing oneself from it too much is like criticism. Lawrence, waiting, holding his pitcher, was beholding the entire garden scene, the way a young monk in the Buddha's time was instructed to "sit cross-legged and place his mindfulness before him." But his ego got the better of him and he put his pitcher down, replacing it with a log. This tendency to abandon the neutral and watchful stance and replace it with a critical and judgmental one is widespread, even among those well schooled in a spiritual ideology. It is easy to see one's basic instincts as dangerous or destructive and to attempt to side-step or eradicate them the way the Buddha, in his ascetic days, first tried to do. But this robs us of the power, energy, and raw material of our human nature, all of which need to be recruited for the purposes of awakening. As I have found, psychotherapy is a useful ally in this approach. While therapists and their patients can get bogged down in the instinctual turmoil and personal history that memories, dreams, and reflections often summon, this is not a given. There is much to be learned from the lords of the underworld, the uncrowned and exiled kings of the unconscious.

In the Zen Buddhist tradition of East Asia, the process of awakening is described not by way of a snake, but through the taming of an ox. A series of ten illustrated poems describe the way in which the mind, represented by the ox, is found, seen, caught, tamed, ridden, forgotten, transcended, and eventually accepted as a useful, if ultimately illusory, tool for helping others. The famous verses highlight how unruly the untamed mind can be, what an effort it is to maintain a disciplined stance of self-observation, and what a relief it is to no longer be at the mercy of one's thoughts and feelings. Here are a few of my favorites:

4. Catching the Ox

Last desperate effort, got him!
Hard to control, powerful and
    wild,
The ox sprints up a hill and at
    the top
Disappears into the misty
    clouds.

5. Taming the Ox

Don't lose the whip, hold onto
    the rope

Or he'll buck away into the
  dirt.
Herded well, in perfect
  harmony
He'll follow along without any
  constraint.

8. Ox Transcended

Whip, rope, self, ox—no
  traces left.
Thoughts cannot penetrate the
  vast blue sky,
Snowflakes cannot survive a
  red-hot stove.
Arriving here, meet the ancient
  teachers.

This series of verses, describing how difficult it is to tame the mind, gives an extremely useful overview for those setting out to explore meditation, but it does not offer much in the way of psychological guidance for all of the issues someone is likely to face in trying to bring meditative awareness into real life. My patients are not living the lives of twelfth-century Japanese monks, nor are they focused exclusively on meditative contemplation. They are raising children, pursuing careers, having relationships, and doing creative work, struggling with parents, partners, employees, friends, and their own destructive urges. In trying to bring a measure of understanding to their hectic lives, they have sought therapy, looking for meaning in the midst of time that speeds past, interrupting the breakneck pace of everyday life for a measure of pause and reflection.

The Zen traditions of China and Japan were always reaching for creative ways of illuminating a person's true nature. I cannot help but marvel at the ancient wisdom of the traditional Zen koans that encapsulate the paradoxes of a true understanding. Here is one that seems appropriate for what follows:

> A monk asked, "What is the substance of the true person?"
> The Master said, "Spring, summer, autumn, winter."
> The monk said, "In that case, it is hard for me to understand."
> The Master said, "You asked about the substance of the true person,
> didn't you?"

This particular one speaks to me of impermanence, of the way our true nature, from birth to death, is reflected in the changing seasons. Through poetry, painting, and spiritual teachings, Zen sought methods of pulling back the curtains of ego so that a deeper intuitive understanding could dawn. Often, the vehicle was close observation of the natural world whose contours mirrored, in some intuitive way, the inner landscape of the observer. Meditative contemplation, turned inside out, allowed the tiny particulars of a given moment to describe the endless process of becoming that we are all part of. As Lucien Stryk put it in his introduction to a compilation of Zen poetry, "Foreground, background, each was part of the process, in poetry as in painting, the spirit discovering itself among the things of the world." In my own way, I have tried to do something similar in this book, focusing on the tiny particulars and mundane bits of conversation of a given psychotherapy session the way the Zen poets zeroed in on the flavor of their immediate surroundings. With the seasons as a backdrop, I have tried to re-create the flow of therapy as it unfolded in a given year: winter, spring, summer, and fall, coming and going as patients came and went from my care.

> *On the rocky slope, blossoming*
> *Plums—from where?*
> *Once he saw them, Reiun*
> *Danced all the way to Sandai.*

Can blossoming plums grow out of the rocky slope of psycho-therapy? Can the spirit discover itself in a therapist's office, and, if so, might we, like the Zen monks of old, dance each other home?

PART TWO

A YEAR
OF THERAPY:
Winter, Spring,
Summer & Fall

*We all hope that our patients will finish
with us and forget us, and that they will
find living itself to be the therapy that
makes sense.*

D. W. WINNICOTT

Three

Winter

began this project—chronicling the mercurial nature of a series of psychotherapy sessions—to answer a vexing question. How does my involvement with Buddhism affect my work as a therapist? Meditation has taught me, changed me, and shaped my life. But how do I use it—or, more to the point, how does it use me— in my interactions with patients? It is rare that I give any formal meditation instruction for example, and were it not for my books, many of my patients would not necessarily be aware of my Buddhist leanings. I know meditation has taught me how to sit still and listen nonjudgmentally, but are these the only ways it has contributed to my process? What am I offering my patients that is different from what a non-Buddhist therapist gives? And, if something is getting through, what is it and how is it coming across?

One would think this would not be such a difficult thing to figure out. I spent years writing about the parallels between the two psychologies: comparing, contrasting, and translating the ideas of one into the language of the other while seeing clients and attending regular silent meditation retreats. But I have never felt that I was an expert in either tradition, nor have I been motivated to formulate, let alone trademark, a hybrid between the two. I reacted with horror at the advent of "mindful psychotherapy" and have always been careful neither to cloak myself in spiritual garb nor to dismiss the accumulated wisdom of contemporary psychoanalytic thought. Mindfulness as a substitute for traditional psychotherapy strikes me as shortsighted, throwing the baby out with the bathwater, and blending the two traditions, just as they are getting to know each other, has always seemed premature. Most such attempts have cobbled together superficial elements of each to the detriment of both.

But, despite these qualms, I know that Buddhism has been and remains a major influence in my work. Having evolved my own style as a therapist, I have come to trust myself to find my way with the people who come to see me. For this book, I set myself the task of probing my own process more deeply. Can I explain what Buddhism is bringing to the table? I have always wanted it to come through me wordlessly. Is it? Or are my words important too? What are people getting from me that makes a difference in their lives?

I realized, as I began to contemplate all this more directly, that I did not have satisfactory answers at the ready, and that in many ways this "not knowing" has been a deliberate choice on my part. I have always wanted to let Buddhism be in the background of my work, figuring that if I had gotten anything from it, it would emerge naturally in the context of helping people through the ordinary struggles of their everyday lives. I have wanted meditation to be *in* me and *of* me, to be something that I embody rather than something that I give too much literal instruction about. Better to just trust in the process and not attempt to make a religion out of it, I have always thought. Acting on a combination of faith and accumulating experience, I have allowed myself for many years only a modicum of self-examination on this particular topic.

But now that has changed. I have always been happy to work in the moment, to trust sessions to reveal themselves and to let them disappear when they were done. I rarely take detailed notes, nor do I try to remember specifics of a patient's history that I do not spontaneously recall when they are in the room with me. But to probe the question I had set, I decided to turn the lens back on myself, to hold my method—such as it had become—up to the light, to pull the curtain back on my work in the office and mindfully—so to speak—examine it more carefully. What makes what I do Buddhist? Can I find it in the details of my daily sessions? And might I be able to articulate it more precisely once I have looked more closely at my actual interactions?

I challenged myself over the course of a single year to write down, as accurately as I could recall, the details of at least one session every week (or every other week) when something interesting caught my eye, when I had the sense that the Buddhist element was in play. Sometimes this influence was overt: people might ask me about meditation technique, or I might spontaneously bring something I had learned from Buddhism into the conversation. And sometimes it was only a feeling: I might find myself reaching beyond traditional analysis to help someone grasp an alternative perspective on whatever issue was troubling them. I had to force myself to persevere with the project, and I rarely read over anything I had written until most of the year had passed, but I stayed with it, accumulating a semi-random sampling of a year's worth of psychotherapy in my New York City office. My choices were, on one level, arbitrary. I made no effort to chart the progress of any particular patient but focused instead on my own feelings of having contributed something of value in whatever encounter I chose to record. In the course of this chronicle, therefore, many patients are introduced but make only a single appearance, while only a few reoccur. Rarely are any issues resolved or settled, but there are nonetheless often hints of movement, of growth, and of opening. These were the interactions that came to grab my attention and that, as the year progressed, became more and more interesting to me. What was happening in those moments? Nuanced, subtle, and fleeting, they were also, at times, magical.

Because of the chance nature of my choices, the major through line in this record is my own process of investigation and discovery. I did not know that I would be chronicling the final year of face-to-face, in-person psychotherapy before the onset of COVID-19, and while that was certainly not my agenda, there is, already, a certain historical quality to the material that follows. Be that as it may, in presenting an assortment of a year's worth of cases, a sense emerges of both the breadth of a typical therapist's workload and the ordinariness of much of the subject matter. With the advent of quarantines, social distancing, and sheltering in place, there would certainly have been a shift in our topics of conversation but most of people's underlying issues would undoubtedly have remained the same. The specific details of my patients' lives, compelling though they often are, are not the point of this endeavor, however. Psychotherapy as a spiritual experience is what I wanted to explore.

While I was interested in how and when I tried to teach elements of Buddhist meditation, I came to see that this instruction, by itself, did not explain what I was after. Meditation introduces a new sensibility to people. It can be practiced as a technique, but ultimately it is something that one internalizes and adapts to one's own circumstances, to one's own self. The meditative awareness, as I perceive it, encourages people to accept their neuroses, their conflicts, their shortcomings, and their troubling emotions but not to be caught by them. It asks people to look beyond their usual defenses, their usual preoccupations, and into the still, silent center of the personality where we are who we have always been. Meditation is about seeing through one's presumed identity, one's identifications, in order to become a truer version of one's own unique self.

Am I ever able to make this a reality for the people who come to work with me? I do not think so. No one can do it for another person; we each can do it only for ourselves. And yet, something important transpires when a meditative sensibility is filtered through the psychotherapy experience. In traditional Buddhism, the analogy is often given of fingers pointing at the moon. I always have had difficulty with this example. What are the fingers supposed to represent, and what is the moon? But in writing this book, I have come to understand it better. The moon is our true nature. We have to find it ourselves. But words, conversations, dialogues, teachings, and even a good psychotherapy can, like the fingers, help point the way. In what follows, I have tried to take the gloves off and show my hand, so to speak. If this encourages some people to seek out their own moon, I will be very happy.

CLINGING

A monk asked, "What is meditation?"
   The Master said, "It is not meditation."
   The monk said, "Why is it 'not
meditation'?"
   The Master said, "It's alive, it's alive!"

CHAO-CHOU, Recorded Sayings, #100

Jack · 12/5/18: 11:30 a.m.

Jack wants to know whether he will ever be healed. He is the child of Holocaust survivors whose parents met in a displaced persons camp at the war's end before he was born. His father was a cattle farmer on the Polish border of Germany who was swept up at the very beginning of the war and confined to a series of labor and death camps after his first wife and two sons were summarily killed. His mother, from an educated background in Lithuania, lost her original family, a young child among them, to the gas chambers and survived multiple brutalities inflicted upon her in the camps. Jack, now in his sixties, was born in South Africa after the war and remembers the unbearable and unreachable sadness of his parents. "Was I a good boy today?" he would ask them repeatedly, as if his behavior were the cause of the suffering he intuited but could never reach. His parents rarely spoke of their ordeal in front of him nor did they talk about the prior families they had lost.

"When will I ever be healed?" Jack asks me again. He is not really asking for a timetable but he is expressing the impossibility of ever being free of his parents' pain, although they are by now long deceased. He has just met a cousin of his mother, still living in South Africa, who has given him new information about her. She had lived in a beautiful house in the center of Vilnius, her father a lawyer, and had gone to a prestigious gymnasium. As she and her family were being herded out of the ghetto and into a concentration camp, they knew they were heading toward their deaths. His mother, then a beautiful young woman in her early twenties, was spared, but she was the only member of her immediate family who was not put to death in the camps.

Jack has been in therapy with me for a couple of years, navigating the aftermath of a divorce, a major job change, a new marriage, and his children's progress toward adulthood. But behind all of these life events lies the incomprehensible nature of his parents' pain. He would dream of dark alleyways, of long hallways punctuated by locked doors, and of being unable to find his way home. There is an ache in him that will not go away.

I am moved by Jack's wish to be healed but know that there is no way to erase his childhood quest to relieve his parents of their suffering. Nor is there any remedy for his parents' inability to provide him with the joyful interpersonal environment he craved. The Holocaust is etched too deeply into everyone's psyche for any of that to be possible. Somehow I have to convey to him that his healing does not depend on getting rid of the traumas that have been handed down to him. I take a leap and invite him to jump too.

"You're already healed," I pronounce. "You don't need healing; you are the healer. Imagine what it must have been like for your mother and father to have another child after everything they went through." Jack looks at me as if I am crazy, and I have to repeat myself two or three times for him to take me seriously. I explain how young children take in their parents' sadness, whatever its source, and assume they are the cause of it. Children can't help being self-centered and they often take responsibility for trouble in a marriage, for a parent's depression, or even for abuse they suffer at the hands of adults. Therapists call this "introjecting," and one of the tasks of therapy is to make these introjects conscious so that a person does not have to live under their sway. Jack has introjected his parents' trauma and made it his own.

In response to Jack's pleas, I tell him about the Buddhist bodhisattva of compassion, Kuan Yin, whose Chinese name means "she who hears our cries." Bodhisattvas are altruistic enlightened beings who stay in the world to help others find their way. Jack had never heard of Kuan Yin but he is interested. In Tibet, Kuan Yin changed sex and was turned into the thousand-armed Avalokiteśvara, whose multiple hands reach out to pluck suffering beings from their fates. "You are like that bodhisattva," I tell him. "You heard your parents' cries and came to them. Your very birth was already an act of compassion. That's what makes you the healer."

Jack seems a bit startled as he leaves, a little perplexed and unnerved, but I have a good feeling about the conversation. I surprised him and, throwing him off balance, have the sense that something has shifted.

. . .

This was the first session that I wrote down, before having a clear vision of what my project would entail. It was a rare, but not unique, example of my invoking an explicit Buddhist theme in the midst of a therapy session, and I think that is what grabbed my attention. The mention of Kuan Yin was spontaneous; I did not know whether Jack was familiar with her, and, when he was not, I needed to explain her to him. This took some time and threatened to overwhelm the session, taking him away from his feelings and into his intellect. But I wanted to turn around Jack's longstanding sentiments of never having been enough. If he could imagine himself, even for a moment, as the healer, I hoped this would begin to offset his unquestioning identity as someone who needed to be healed. His slightly off-balance reaction to our interchange suggested some degree of success. Instability is sometimes a sign of new possibilities.

In thinking about this conversation with Jack, I can see that it exemplified something essential about my approach. Buddhism teaches that the principal cause of suffering is clinging. The awakened mind, the enlightened mind, is a mind that, in the words of the Diamond Sutra, "clings to naught." As a therapist, I have trained myself to always look for and focus on my patients' clinging, however it might manifest. Sometimes it shows itself in intimate relationships, when someone holds on in a needy way; sometimes it shows itself in therapy, when people can't stop blaming their parents for ruining their lives; sometimes it is revealed when people repeatedly blame themselves in a punitive way for not being perfect; and sometimes, as in Jack's case, it comes in the form of repetitive plaintive thoughts that take on a life of their own. However it manifests, clinging is the common denominator, and an effective therapy, whether it be from a Buddhist or a psychoanalytic perspective, succeeds when it undermines this all-too-common tendency.

There is a famous painting by an eighteenth-century Japanese Zen master that speaks to the universality of Jack's predicament, even while the particulars of being a child of Holocaust survivors are outside the experience of most of us. Its imagery is a marvelous depiction of both clinging and its release. A monkey squats in a field with both hands tightly covering his ears, while a cuckoo, its mouth open in flight, soars in the background. Hakuin, the Zen master, drew the image sometime between his sixtieth and eightieth year, in the period after he attained enlightenment. Beneath the picture, he wrote a small poem in calligraphy. In translation it reads:

Even when not listening,
lift up one hand—
The cuckoo!

Hakuin is the originator of the well-known Zen phrase "What is the sound of one hand clapping?" a koan, or riddle, with no rational answer whose contemplation is meant to help someone reach an understanding beyond conceptual thought. Only Hakuin never phrased his question that way. It was always simply "What is the sound of one hand?" and his painting and poem provide the clues to its answer. The monkey in the picture is resolutely stuck in his own habitual thoughts. There he is in the field, his hands clenched over his ears, listening only to himself. "Monkey mind" is an image in Buddhist cultures for the relentless and repetitive thinking that clogs our everyday lives and obscures the pure mind of spontaneity that hides within. The cuckoo, revered in Japan as the harbinger of all of the ease, relaxation, and warmth of the coming summer, is emblematic of that natural underlying freedom. A cuckoo sings while in flight, hence its open beak, its song invisible to the crouching monkey, who is listening only to himself. Jack, like many of us, was stuck on a mournful thought that had long bedeviled him: "When will I ever be healed?" With this thought so preoccupying him, he was unable to take flight, to see the greater picture or hear the sweeter sound. My intervention, invoking Kuan Yin, was an attempt to get Jack to lift up one hand, to get the flow moving, to unstick him from his repetitive thoughts. Could he hear what I was saying? Could he open himself to another way of imagining things?

One of the classic images associated with this particular koan is that of a drowning man lifting one hand above his head in a last-ditch attempt to be saved. The drowning man is a symbol of those of us, like Jack, lost in suffering but yearning to be free. It is the bodhisattva, the spiritual friend par excellence, who reaches down to grasp the outstretched arm of the sinking spirit, offering something more helpful to hold on to. In some way, I was evoking all of that for Jack. The psychotherapy office, while far from the natural world so beloved by Zen poetry, is a place to lift up one's hand, even if one is not fully listening.

In subsequent sessions with other patients, I would sometimes think back to this encounter with Jack because of the way it so personified what I have come to think of as the essential principle of a Buddhist therapy: find the clinging. I was working intuitively when I had this conversation, but it grabbed my attention because of this point. Conventionally trained Western therapists are very attuned to the ways in which childhood experience determines adult behavior, and this perspective can be enormously useful. But Buddhist psychology adds another dimension. We all cling in one way or another, but as Hakuin reminds us, if we are searching for freedom, we must learn to lift up our hands. Early trauma like Jack's cannot be healed by simply pointing out its origins. Understanding that he was not the cause of his parents' anguish will not relieve him of the burden of it. But by working diligently to offset his mind's tendency to repeat itself, Jack can become compassionate toward his childhood predicament rather than identifying exclusively with the pain of it. This was the deeper message I was trying to convey.

Unsolvable trauma is unsolvable but it is not unresolvable.

In the next series of sessions, as my project got underway, this notion of finding the clinging was often paramount. What could I do to surprise, unsettle, and enliven my patients' inner lives? While not necessarily religious, these interventions, when successful, could certainly feel spiritual.

Willa · 12/5/18: 4:00 p.m.

Willa, a photographer, often dreams of my wife, a sculptor, whose work she is familiar with. Many times I am in the dream too. Willa comes to a party, or into a house, where there are lots of people, including my wife and me. She skirts the edge of the gathering and inevitably sees my wife in some kind of central position, colorfully dressed with people surrounding her. Then Willa, like Jack, is off into a labyrinth of hallways, closed doors, and dead ends. I have been cautious when these dreams come up, mostly interpreting them, if I do at all, in terms of how Willa looks up to my wife as an artist and how my wife must represent her own unrealized creative aspirations. Willa was molested by her father when she was an adolescent and has carried a great deal of shame since then. He was an accomplished pianist whom she looked up to, and their secret encounters, never acknowledged by either parent, left her tense and bewildered. When Willa first came to see me, she had dreams of crawling around on her hands and knees searching for something lost under a radiator. Her dreams screamed powerlessness and humiliation.

Today Willa tells me, after five or ten minutes of pleasantries, that she has had another dream about us. "It was like a revelation," she says softly after describing a bit of the scene. "I realized that I was in love with you." This is a very different report. Willa's face is open, her eyes alight and her gaze direct. Her only hesitation comes after the fact, when she begins to speak of trans-ference, how this must be transference, how she and her husband often speak of transference in couples therapy. Her husband often gets upset when Willa does not pay him enough attention. They know this is transference . . . he is relating not only to her but also to a projection from childhood he puts on her. She must be doing something similar, she thinks, projecting some earlier rela-tionship onto the one with me.

Therapists are trained to be sensitive to moments like this. For many, transference, and the information it reveals about child-hood relationships, is the whole shebang. When patients acknowl-edge the love they have for their therapists, there is an opportunity to probe deeply into their pasts. What early feelings are being resurrected by the current relationship? What does this tell us about the inner conflicts they are wrestling with, about the nature of their erotic lives? But in listening to Willa this afternoon, I am reminded of something Freud once wrote about the "unobjection-able positive transference" that he considered benign. He re-frained from interpreting it, in fact, believing that it was part of what made therapy work. I take my cue from Freud and don't say much about the dream. But I feel something lifting in Willa, a toxic sludge on her heart that had her, in other dreams, crawling around on the floor. In dreaming of love, and talking about it so unabashedly (I think to myself), is she actually freeing herself from the objectionable burden her father put on her?

Sexual abuse like the kind Willa experienced robs a person of innocence. Instead of discovering erotic life in a natural way with a peer, sexuality was forced upon her. Any pleasure she might have found in the awakening of her sensuality was contaminated from the beginning with confusion and shame. In talking about her dream, Willa spontaneously brings up a Reiki massage she once had. In Reiki, which is a Japanese "energy healing" popular in alternative circles, the therapist hardly touches the body; she mostly holds the patient's head and clears "energy blocks" by tapping into a universal underlying positive energy and channeling that energy through her hands. The energy blocks are thought to be concrete reflections of the patient's clinging. In referencing the massage, Willa is confirming what I feel when she tells me her dream. Something is releasing in her emotional body. She is experiencing a simple, natural, and unobjectionable love without guilt over replacing my wife or shame about experiencing something forbidden. I say a couple of things about this but do so very lightly. In my mind, I picture Hakuin's cuckoo flying through what is now a rapidly darkening early winter sky, a visual metaphor for the mind that clings to naught.

. . .

This session happened later the same day as Jack's and left me with a similar feeling. Both Willa and Jack were tarnished by early traumas that threatened to overwhelm their adult lives, but the flavor of each therapeutic encounter suggested that those traumas did not have to be the defining element of their identities. Some greater energy was poking through, surprising and relieving them at the same time. While many Western therapists, schooled in the vagaries of transference, would be tempted to analyze away Willa's profession of love, possibly tying it to the abuse she suffered at the hands of her father, I resisted such a reductionist approach.

Willa's love reminded me of D. H. Lawrence's snake. There it was, the forbidden thing, the uncrowned king of the underworld. What could be more challenging? Certainly our "education" would compel us to throw a log at such feelings, to make them retreat into the rocky slope of transference. But to do so would rob them of their majesty, sentencing us to Lawrence's state of vulgarity and pettiness. I think Freud was correct when he termed such feelings "unobjectionable" and "positive." While he was not known for his spiritual side, Freud would have appreciated what Hakuin did with similar material. He made a painting called *Swallow Among the Waves* and wrote a haiku to accompany it that reads as follows:

> *For all people*
> *crossing the ocean*
>   *of life and death*
> *how enviable is*
> *the flight of the swallow*

Hakuin's verse again uses a bird's flight—the swallow instead of the cuckoo—to symbolize the natural freedom of a mind that clings to nothing. Willa's forthright statement of affection reminded me of Hakuin's flight of the swallow just as Jack's instability upon leaving my office made me think of the sound of one hand. By the close of both sessions, the lightness I associate with the release of age-old psychic attachments was palpable. I found this buoyancy incredibly inspiring and resolved to look for it in subsequent sessions. I had known to challenge Jack's conviction about himself and had trusted myself not to overanalyze Willa's love, but now I had a sense of the reasoning behind my actions. What other forms was clinging taking in my patients' lives, and how might I meet it therapeutically?

Mitch · 12/6/18: 11:30 a.m.

Mitch tells me about stresses in her relationship with her new girlfriend, Ingrid. "There's too much transference in our relationship," she says. Everyone is talking about transference it seems! Ingrid has a depressed mother who has recently been institutionalized, not for the first time, and Ingrid has been very needy in the aftermath. It was her birthday last week and she wanted Mitch to spend the day with her, to go to a museum in the morning to begin the day. Mitch was not interested in the museum and asked to meet her afterward. This prompted an angry response from Ingrid that Mitch is still trying to process.

The previous weekend they had gone to a friend of Mitch's for a party, and Ingrid had been nervous about going. She didn't know anyone there, doesn't like big dinners, and hates having to make conversation with people she doesn't know. Mitch had arranged in advance for Ingrid to sit next to her at the dinner, and Mitch had had a wonderful time. But as soon as they left the party, Ingrid had said how difficult it was for her. "Why couldn't she just keep it to herself? Why did she have to wreck the evening?" Mitch wants to know. Ingrid was upset that she couldn't even tell Mitch what she was feeling without being criticized for it. Plus, Ingrid likes to go to bed by ten o'clock while Mitch likes to stay up till two. Ingrid gets upset with Mitch for not going to sleep with her at night. Mitch gets upset with Ingrid for not being able to compromise. She feels that Ingrid makes a lot of demands on her but that when she asks anything of Ingrid, it is always taken as an affront. "Where is the joy in this relationship?" Mitch wants to know.

First I warn Mitch about her habit of measuring and comparing and demanding reciprocity. She is not a lawyer but her method of examination is very legalistic. In her way of thinking, she gives so much and Ingrid gives so little. I tell her about the Buddhist concept of "kingly" giving, where one gives without expectation of receiving a reward. Buddhists have a hierarchy of giving where kingly giving beats out "beggarly" or "friendly" giving because there is no thought of "what will I get in return?" Then we speak of Ingrid's mother's depression. Mitch realizes that Ingrid's mother may have come to Ingrid in despair to seek closeness and that Ingrid may be doing much the same thing, using sadness to initiate closeness. This is an important thought and potentially helpful. Perhaps it's the closeness that Ingrid is seeking, rather than solace for her sadness. Maybe that's the way she has learned to ask for attention. Mitch remarks on how much fun they have when they go ballroom dancing or out to the movies or the theater. Clearly, there are pathways open to their shared joy.

We hypothesize that Ingrid turns separation into abandonment and then seeks connection through sadness. Mitch takes it personally when she does this and then gets angry and feels unappreciated. I want Mitch not to take it personally but to be clear with Ingrid that although she cannot fix Ingrid's sadness, she can bring her joy nonetheless. Mitch is halfway persuaded and agrees to try. She expresses astonishment that the time is already up, and she is reluctant to leave the office.

. . .

This was a session in which I was trying to inculcate a meditative sensibility in Mitch, not by giving her literal instruction, but by talking about a very common way that clinging manifests in couples: difficulty with separation. Ostensibly, her partner Ingrid is the one who has to learn to lift one hand. When feelings of abandonment are triggered, she gets locked in and upset. Her early trauma, a consequence of her mother's recurrent depression, set her up to have difficulty, but she was not the one seeking treatment. What could Mitch do to help?

Trivial separations create big problems that threaten to override the mutual joy the relationship affords both of them. I had one basic suggestion: Mitch could take it all less personally. In saying this, I did not mean to imply that Mitch should not confront Ingrid about the ways she exaggerates things. She does turn separation into abandonment, and I am pretty sure she has trouble knowing the difference.

But Mitch gets stuck in her own way of thinking. This is her version of clinging. When criticized for her lack of sensitivity, she gets defensive and creates a counteroffensive. She is the one doing all the giving, and what does she get in return? A lot of her mental space is taken up by the performance of calculations. Measuring things like this is one of the ego's great preoccupations. There is so much self-justification involved that we rarely get any distance from our minds when it is operating. This kind of thinking is one of the prime targets of meditation, and it is more common off the cushion, when the events of real life provoke it, than it is in the relative calm of the meditation hall. My comments about kingly giving were intended to help Mitch gain perspective on this particular kind of self-righteousness that brings to mind the pettiness of Lawrence's snake poem. How will Ingrid ever begin to take responsibility for her abandonment fears if her partner meets them with such legalistic zeal?

Issues in relationships take many forms, of course. Mitch and Ingrid have real joy when they are together, and I have hope for them. But this is not always the case when I hear other people's stories. The next session turned out to be a good example of this.

Anne · 12/7/18: 3:00 p.m.

Anne comes for a special session; she is someone I know well, having seen her regularly through her twenties and thirties. Now she comes only occasionally, usually when something is going wrong in a relationship. That is the case today. She has been going out with Brian for several months and their conversations are wonderful. They talk easily and spend lots of time together. But there is nothing going on physically between them. Once, at the movies, they held hands for a bit, and the other day she talked to him about it and they kissed, but it didn't go anywhere. He then spent the night and they talked for a good part of it but still . . . nothing. Finally they had a conversation and he said, "You want me to be your boyfriend and I don't want to be."

Anne is upset. "What is wrong with me?" she cries. "What can I do?" "Anne," I say, "get out. He is not giving you what you want. Get out." This is hard for her to hear. She is convinced the problem is in her. This is familiar territory in our discussions. Anne has a knack for finding extremely attractive and talented men who are so preoccupied with their careers that they retreat from the kind of ongoing physical and emotional intimacy she wants. She idealizes their charisma but then blames herself when the relationships falter. I remind Anne that she has trouble leaving these kinds of unsatisfactory relationships. She holds on tighter as her dissatisfaction grows. Some of this can be traced to her childhood. Her father was a brilliant lawyer but he was mentally ill and deteriorated as he got older, divorcing his wife and absenting himself from his adolescent children. Anne was angry with him and unable to retain much of a relationship. The combination of her adolescent rage and his decompensated mental state made it impossible. I remind Anne that some of her attachment to Brian might be coming from her unmet needs for her father. But Anne's version of the monkey mind makes it hard for her to hear me. Maybe she is not pretty enough or sexually experienced enough or accomplished enough, she wonders. No amount of reassurance from my side can convince her that she is off base. A good deal of her clinging is to try to wring the reason for rejection, the real reason, out of Brian. "What is wrong with me?"

Of course, we could say the flaw is in her self-esteem. She lost her father, watched him decompensate, and had to strike out prematurely on her own, the illusion of independence masking a feeling of inadequacy, as if her father's decline were somehow her failing. She knows all this but still . . .

I frame the problem for her as one of conflict over deploying healthy aggression. Brian is not giving her what she wants or needs. That is the obstacle she is trying to overcome. She deserves better. Her aggression should protect her, make a clear boundary, rather than attacking herself after failing to dislodge his resistance. She should not keep overriding herself and setting herself up for rejection and disappointment. She should get away. But Anne's aggression turns round and round on itself. Sometimes she lashes out at herself, and sometimes, in the privacy of her thoughts, she argues endlessly with Brian. She is not using her aggression for what it is good for: to protect herself and to cut through her own unhealthy attachment. I speak to her of the Buddha's Eight-fold Path. What is Right Action in this circumstance? Come on, Anne! Cut your losses and get rid of this guy.

. . .

This is a session in which I was not hesitant to be prescriptive and to give advice. In fact, while I framed the issue for Anne as one involving healthy aggression, I was also enacting my own aggression in the way I spoke with her. This happens in therapy sometimes. The missing quality in the patient is somehow made manifest by the therapist, either as an internal feeling or, as in this situation, in an actual behavior. In one way of thinking, I was simply modeling healthy aggression for Anne by telling her to leave Brian, but in another way of thinking, my reaction was giving me information about Anne's unconscious conflict around anger. I was trying to do the work for her because, for some reason, she was blocking herself. The outward display of this was in her clinging to a boyfriend who could not give her what she needed, but on an inner level there was something else going on. The more I thought about it, the more I focused on how threatening Anne's anger must be to her. She was scared of how furious she could become, and she masked this fear in various unhelpful ways, sometimes by criticizing herself mercilessly and sometimes by clamping down resolutely on the men she desired. Anne had reason to fear her aggression, I presumed. Perhaps she unconsciously attributed her father's breakdown to her own adolescent rage. I resolved to try to help her more with this in the future rather than just stepping in and trying to do the work for her.

don't understand why they don't hold her accountable!" Opal says of her two grown stepchildren. "Why don't those girls hold their mother responsible for all the pain she has caused them?" Opal has been married to their father for more than twenty years and has seen the two girls through their tumultuous adolescence and into their adulthood. They were recently home for a Thanksgiving dinner and were splitting time between their father's and mother's houses. Opal has never felt welcomed by them or appreciated by them even though she has provided the love and stability their father had never known in his first marriage. Opal lived through her husband's divorce and was witness to all of the destruction his ex-wife brought upon the family. "They just have a blind acceptance of her," she laments. "I don't know why." "You do know why," I contend. "She is their mother. It's primal."

I explain to Opal what another patient has told me. This patient is a child psychiatrist who works with abused kids and their foster families. "Those children cling to the biological parents the harder they are abused," she has told me. "It's counterintuitive. The state seeks to protect those kids from their parents, to separate them, but the children need them, and we have to figure out a safe way for them to retain contact." These two girls are not going to reject their mother, I tell Opal, "and they are not going to privilege you over her, no matter how good you have been for their dad."

"I have to get rid of my expectations," Opal says, pulling on what she has learned from Buddhism. "Your expectations are valid," I retort. "You don't have to invalidate them. You just have to know that they are not realistic." There is an important pause. "I latch on to them too hard," Opal says. "It takes me down a bad path. I made a real home here," she says wistfully. "It's never acknowledged by the girls." Opal is at an all-important juncture in her spiritual and psychological work. In seeing how she latches on to her expectations "too hard," she now has the potential to stop. It's not *what* she is thinking that matters, it's how she relates to her thoughts that will make all the difference.

· · ·

This last phrase is one that has been supremely important to me over the years. I have versions of it written down in the backs of inspirational books and in notebooks smuggled into meditation retreats and have repeated it in my own writings and talks. It is the central lesson of mindfulness because it implicitly addresses the way we cling. For years, when I would hear Joseph Goldstein or Jack Kornfield say something similar, I would run to write it down because it sounded so on point, only to find I had written similar things over and over again years before. Each time I heard it, it seemed so profound! There is so much in life that we cannot control no matter how we try. Circumstances, events, feelings, even our own thoughts! But we *can* take responsibility for how we relate to what happens. We can grimace with our hands over our ears or we can lift one hand. By now, this has become a refrain in my mind, one that often returns to guide me in my life and in my work with patients.

Mindfulness shines its light on everything indiscriminately. We cannot control much of what happens to us but we can learn to relate to it differently. Opal's wish to be acknowledged by her stepchildren is totally understandable, as is their unwillingness, or inability, to give her what she feels she deserves. This is not as simple a situation as Anne and Brian's. Opal cannot just break up with her stepdaughters because they are not meeting her very legitimate needs. Her first inclination, realizing that her expectations are in her way, was to try to wipe out the expectations. This is akin to the Buddha's first efforts in his search for enlightenment. Just eliminate the whole desire. Get rid of the body, too, while you're at it. But that use of aggression, turned back on the self, is self-defeating, and not in a good way. It just perpetuates the discomfort. I am hopeful that Opal can find her version of the Buddha's middle path in this situation, not holding on too tightly to an imagined but impossible closeness while not pushing away her legitimate hopes for a less conflicted relationship with her husband's children.

I am aware that I have chosen neither to analyze Opal's need for closeness with her stepchildren nor to explore her feelings of jealousy of them, her anger at her husband, or her own insecurities. It is quite likely that another therapist would have moved in one or all of those directions. I was much more focused on helping her cultivate an attitude of forgiveness for the entire situation. Nothing is perfect, certainly not after a divorce.

Lakshman · 1/3/19: 9:30 a.m.

Lakshman has just returned from a Christmas visit to Hawaii
to be with Ram Dass, a spiritual teacher who has been important to both of us, and someone who has been his friend for many
years. While there he had a conversation with him about his (Lakshman's) relentless objectification of women. Wherever he goes,
he rates all of the women he sees as "fuckable" or not. Sitting in
a crowded subway car, he entertains himself with this game. He
brings it with him to the therapy office, too, always commenting
on the looks of the women who precede him. "Where is that cute
girl?" he will often ask me if the patient from last week does not
emerge on cue. Lakshman is a smart and sensitive man and he
knows there is a problem here. The #MeToo movement has
driven the point home. Friends have told him he has to watch his
language. Women who know him have confided that he can make
them uncomfortable. Lakshman has a good sense of humor but
he tends to repeat himself. If I have to go to the bathroom before
we begin, he always says, "I'll start without you." When I give
him a bill at the end of the month, he always says, "That's a fine
howdy-do!" These comments have an edge of one-upmanship to
them, disguised as they are by his wit. Their repetitive nature,
word for word over the years, makes his obsessive evaluation of
women seem of a piece. He is a creature of habit and he makes
no attempt to disguise his prurient wishes.

Ram Dass told him several things. First he said, "Love the thoughts." Love the thoughts?! Lakshman cannot quite understand. He *does* love the thoughts; he doesn't want to give them up, but he is also ashamed of them. Ram Dass seemed to be addressing this guilty mix. To love the thoughts, he has to stand outside of them, or outside himself, a bit more. He has to observe himself observing the women (the way D. H. Lawrence observed himself observing the snake) instead of being completely caught in his game. And in loving the thoughts there is a potential for compassion for himself, lonely and aging man that he is. Perhaps some of his need to compulsively objectify is to provide a cover for himself, for his own deteriorating maleness and deepening needs, or just as someone who envies women yet desires their attention. As the one who rates the women's looks, he maintains a critical distance, a superior position that compensates for the intensity of his longing.

Then Ram Dass said something more surprising. "See yourself as a soul," he suggested. "After a while, you might start seeing them as souls too." This is interesting to Lakshman, and to me. I wouldn't have thought to start with seeing *himself* as a soul. But I grasp the intent immediately. Lakshman sees himself as deprived. At the same time, he has an inflated sense of himself, of what his lovemaking could do for these women, but in his heart of hearts he does not see himself as a soul. More like an egomaniac with low self-esteem. Like most of us, he is exclusively identified with his current body and mind. Sense pleasures are his drug of choice. He is a wonderful cook and a collector of art and an appreciator of fine things and he does not want to die. To see himself as a soul would distance him from all of that, just as loving his thoughts might. Ram Dass is helping Lakshman to unpack himself from his most basic identifications, to relieve him of his clinging. "I get pleasure from those thoughts," Lakshman admitted to Ram Dass. "I don't really want them to stop." Ram Dass did not try to disabuse him of this. "The thoughts give you pleasure but seeing souls will bring you happiness," he responded. Will Lakshman put any of this into practice? I don't think so, not really, although he was clearly touched by the interaction. But the report of the conversation gives me some added ammunition. Lakshman loves Ram Dass. And now, courtesy of him, I have a wedge I can use for a while with Lakshman, before the advice loses its sheen and becomes just another trope for him to ignore.

• • •

I did not know it at the time, but this bit of therapy between Ram Dass and Lakshman was to stay with me throughout the coming year. "Love the thoughts" and "see yourself as a soul" were phrases that often recurred in my head as I worked, clues in my own investigation of my method. I was glad that I wrote the session down because I might have let it fade away and forgotten those two little axioms. Ram Dass had been an important mentor of mine in my twenties. He was fired for giving psychedelics to students a long time before I arrived at Harvard, but he had remained close to several teachers of mine in the psychology department and often stayed with them when he was not in India, giving me an opportunity to get to know him.

During my years in college and medical school, when I was working with Dr. Benson, I took informal meditation classes with Ram Dass in the carriage house of one of my professors. I learned a lot from him, although I do not have many specific memories. "You are not who you think you are" is the phrase I remember most clearly from him. I loved the slight irony of the pronouncement. If I wasn't who I thought I was, then who was I? I absorbed a whole way of being from Ram Dass, and he, like the Dalai Lama, was to remain a lodestar for me over the next forty years, coming in and out of my life every decade or so but remaining someone for whom I had enormous respect. I thought his conversation with

Lakshman was very moving, and it made me wish that, in my own way, I could give such pointed advice. It was not my style to issue those types of pronouncements, but I appreciated where they were coming from. And I was proud of Lakshman for being able to take such guidance from Ram Dass and relay it to me. The work we had done together over the years had made him more receptive to such input.

Margaret · 1/8/19: 6:00 p.m.

Margaret begins the session by asking me unexpectedly, "What direction should you face when you meditate?" No one has ever asked me that before, I tell her. It's not like Mecca. "Come on," she says. "You're Mr. Meditation." I insist that it doesn't matter, that the thought of which direction to face has never crossed my mind. "We can google it," I suggest. And we do. Google says the direction to face is inward. We laugh. "Should you sit still with no thoughts?" Margaret asks. "Is that meditation? My stepson was asking me." I tell her that it is not possible to sit for very long with no thoughts and that's not the point anyway. Thinking is one of the things the mind does best, and it does not stop just because we think it should. In meditation we see how our thoughts grab us, though, how they keep pulling us into their worlds, how we cling to them and give them the last word.

Most of the time thoughts just happen on their own, I tell Margaret. We can learn to watch them the way we might watch the clouds in the sky, without immediately thinking of them as "me" or "mine." "But clouds are pretty," Margaret rejoins. "My thoughts are not." "There can be dark clouds too," I say. "Bad weather. 'What an idiot I am.' Those kinds of things." "Yes," Margaret murmurs. "Those are my kinds of thoughts." We talk about how hard it is to simply observe these thoughts without believing them wholeheartedly. They are so personal. And they have been around for a very long time, their persistence a remnant of how traumatic it was to be repeatedly yelled at and hit by her mother. But it is precisely the most personal thoughts that meditation has its eye on. Those are the ones we cling to the hardest. We are deeply identified with them, but in and of themselves they have no substance. Margaret reminds me that therapy has helped her admit to and face the traumas of her past. She now understands where those self-punishing thoughts come from, and that has been an enormous help. They haven't entirely been put to rest, but investigating them in therapy helped her understand how difficult her childhood had been. She suddenly notices the clock and gathers herself up hastily. "Oh, it's time!" she says. "I have to get out of here."

· · ·

I know from other sessions that Margaret can be a very harsh critic of herself. Our conversation, jocular at first, had come around to this tendency once again. The dark clouds of negative, self-punishing thoughts were lurking just over the horizon, waiting to make an appearance. In psychodynamic language, such thoughts are the province of what is called "the superego." According to Freud, the superego splits off from the ego early in life and takes on the role of inner critic. Its job is to keep us in line, to enforce the rules that check our most primitive impulses, and to make us a civilized part of society. But the superego can be primitive too. Its tendency, pronounced in someone like Margaret who suffered a lot as a child at the hand of a single mother who could not control her temper, is to objectify the self, to see it unidimensionally, in one particular way, as lousy, no good, inadequate, unworthy, or insufficient. "How, in Freud's view, has our virulent, predatory self-criticism become one of our greatest pleasures?" asks psychoanalyst Adam Phillips in a recent examination of how people cling to their inner critics. "How has it come about that we so much enjoy this picture of ourselves as objects, and as objects of judgement and censorship? What is this appetite for confinement, for diminishment, for unrelenting, unforgiving self-criticism? Freud's answer is beguilingly simple: we fear loss of love."

In encouraging Margaret to observe her self-critical thoughts without automatically believing them, I was endeavoring to rob this superego of some of its authority, to relieve her of this kind of pernicious clinging. Ordinarily, many people like Margaret give the superego's voice free rein. It is one of those subliminal sounds, like the background hum of the refrigerator, that, when we close the door to our room or stare at ourselves in the mirror, we just accept as reasonable, valid, and true, as the explanation for all of the love we have been denied.

The Buddha did not have the concept of the superego, of course, but his critique of the way we cling—he called it igno-rance or delusion—is completely in line with Freud's point of view. Like Freud, the Buddha saw how insecure most of us are, how we hold on to people and pleasures for reassurance while simultaneously judging ourselves for our faults. If Freud is correct in his analysis—that we over-identify with this judgmental voice because of a fear of loss of love—then the Buddhist conviction of a pure body of perfect spontaneity at the heart of our inner ex-perience is a powerful antidote. If the love we are seeking, the love we were deprived of, is actually present within, then our whole cosmology needs to be turned inside out. While even the awakened mind can be objectified, it is not easy. Bodhidharma's definition of enlightenment, "lots of space, nothing holy," is my favorite version. I am hopeful that as Margaret teaches herself to meditate, by looking inward she will relieve her superego of some of its authority and begin, as Ram Dass counseled Lakshman, to see herself as a soul.

Again, I notice that my tendency is not to be satisfied with an analysis of how, when, and why such a punitive superego took hold but to plant the seeds of an alternative. That there even *is* an alternative is a miracle in itself. I remember Ram Dass telling me that I am not who I think I am. Margaret is not who she thinks she is either.

Debby · 1/24/19: 4:30 p.m.

Debby, a retired nurse practitioner who once specialized in home births, has just come back from Calcutta, where she was assisting the nuns in Mother Teresa's organization. She has been there several times in the past five years, finding the work of tending to the destitute with a minimum of basic supplies unexpectedly fulfilling. I used to see her regularly but now she just checks in every year or so. She begins the session by holding up her left hand to me. "See, no wedding ring," she says. "Are you still married?" I say, somewhat alarmed. She reassures me and then directs the conversation back to her recent time in Calcutta. She tells me how visiting doctors sometimes critique the medical care the nuns are offering there to the indigent. "This is not about the finest medical care in the world," she tells them. "This is about love; seeing everyone as Jesus." I can feel the heat in what she is saying. "I didn't know anything about suffering," she continues, talking to *me* now, no longer recounting her conversations in Calcutta. "These people come with nothing, huge swollen sores. I work on them, I'm cleaning their wounds, and they are biting down on their dhotis to stifle their pain. When I am done, they are so gracious, they look up at me with these beautiful faces."

Debby then tells me how she has been missing love and affection from her husband and has finally confronted him about it.

He told her he has been mad at her for not working at a steady job and is worried about money. She comes from nothing and is not worried. In her view, they have plenty. "I'm sixty years old," she says. "I'm not going back to work." He could feel their worlds dividing but told her explicitly that for the sake of their children and grandchildren that he wanted to stay together. She was insulted by his reasoning. If that was his only motivation for staying together, it wasn't good enough for her. This is when she took off her wedding ring. "I want my own room," she told him. Debby is entering uncharted territory. I am quiet. We will see what transpires.

. . .

Debby could see everyone as Jesus when she was working side by side with the nuns in Calcutta, and I was immensely moved to hear her talk about it. But she had more difficulty at home. This is not surprising. Domestic life is much more challenging than a life of pure service. I heard from Debby again some time after this session and my first question to her was whether she was still married and wearing her wedding ring once again. "Oh yes," she said with a laugh. "It's everything to our kids that we manage not to kill each other." I smiled and asked if I could quote her on that.

In retrospect I was glad that I did not jump in and try to dissuade Debby from impulsively quitting her marriage. It is a big temptation, as a therapist, to try to make these decisions for people, or at least to covertly guide them one way or another. But I really did not know what was best for her and trusted that she would figure it out. It was much better that she came to it on her own.

Violette · 1/29/19: 12:30 p.m.

Violette is a relatively new patient, a twenty-nine-year-old theater actor who reached out to me after sitting several silent
vipassana retreats at the center where I also practice. I have
met with her twice before but am still getting to know her. I greet
her warmly but mispronounce her first name, calling her Violet.
She corrects me, says that happens often, people always make
that mistake, most times she doesn't say anything but then it
always bothers her so she is trying to do the right thing even
though it is embarrassing to correct me. I apologize and say her
name properly. She then tells me that she did not think she performed well with me the previous week. "Performed?" I question
her. She gives me some context as to why she used the word. An
actor since junior high school, Violette graduated from one of the
most prestigious drama schools in the country, and has already
worked with a number of the most cutting-edge young directors
in New York, but she is thinking seriously of leaving acting to
write and produce her own work. Acting has lost its sheen for
Violette, and she has recently experienced several episodes of
intense performance anxiety before going onstage. A previous
psychiatrist prescribed a beta-blocker for her (beta-blockers like
propranolol are drugs that block the release of adrenaline so that,
even if the mind is anxious, the body does not respond with a
pounding heartbeat or a rise in blood pressure), but she does not

like to need drugs and assumes that her body is trying to tell her that it's time for a change. She is under intense pressure, however, from a close friend to continue a collaboration they have already begun in which Violette would have to commit to another year of performing.

Violette has been married for three years and wants to have a baby, but after a year of not using birth control she has not conceived. "A year is not that long," I say reassuringly, but Violette tells me that she has already begun an infertility workup. So far, everything looks fine with her, but her husband, an obstetrician who is just finishing a grueling fellowship, has not yet made time to get his sperm tested. His work schedule makes it too difficult, and Violette is reluctant to stress him further. I suggest she find out whether the fertility clinic is open on the weekend; then he should have less of an excuse. He gets Saturdays off unless one of his patients is in labor. The conversation veers to sex. Her husband wants sex more often than she does, but while he is very supportive of her work, he is not that tuned in to her creative endeavors. Violette is at a crossroads in her life; she is reaching for greater meaning than acting has given her, and she would like to feel more of a connection with her husband while she figures things out. As far as the sex goes, Violette would like more closeness. That could include sex, she assures me, but it shouldn't have to only be sex. She has not mentioned this to her husband yet though.

I tell Violette about some books and podcasts I like about couples and sex and begin to talk to her about the importance of making more room for her own wants and needs. I point out that her concern with performance, expressed at the beginning of the session, might be a factor when she is intimate with her husband. A certain kind of selfishness is necessary in sex, I say, it's not just about submission to the demands of the other. Her own arousal will be arousing to her partner. The sex therapists, in cases where one or both people are having difficulties, often forbid intercourse as a first intervention in therapy, taking it off the table, so that people can have less of an agenda and be less focused on outcome when they are having sex. I show her my favorite Buddhist book about tantric sex, *Passionate Enlightenment* by Miranda Shaw, in which female arousal is described as the most sublime, the closest one comes in regular life to the bliss promised by the Buddha's enlightenment. She is intrigued. "I didn't feel like I was performing today," she tells me with a backward glance as she puts on her winter coat.

. . .

The superego is present in this session too. Violette's concern over performance is a sign of this. I am touched by her comment as she leaves the office, hopeful that I have succeeded, for a moment anyway, in relieving her of the perfectionistic pressure she puts on herself. Mindfulness has been a great help to me in countering this tendency myself. One of its great revelations is that it is impossible to be perfect at it. People try, the way they try to be perfect at sex, but inevitably they come up short. It is impossible to be present in every moment, to completely surrender to the sensations of the breath, or to be aware that you are thinking from the inception of a thought. We are constantly falling off the horse and having to get back on. The willingness to be imperfect, to be flawed, is one of the first gifts that meditation offers.

I was giving a fair amount of advice in this session—from suggesting a day for Violette's husband to go to the doctor to taking the book on tantric sex off my shelf—but it was all with the hope of freeing Violette to be more herself. Talking about sex with a young woman is a delicate thing. Who am I to give advice? But there was something in Shaw's book that has always been important to me that I know I was trying to communicate. In the esoteric Buddhist literature, female sexuality is said to embody one's highest spiritual intelligence. In its fullest form, it represents *being* rather than *doing*. Violette's desire to please and her perfectionism worked against her *being*.

Again, I noticed my reluctance to analyze solely from a traditional psychodynamic perspective. I wanted the session itself to *be* an alternative. In recognizing how much more enlivening therapy could be when she was not performing, Violette was letting me know that she understood what I was after.

Sally · 1/30/19: 11:30 a.m.

Sally, a talented media professional in her late thirties, has just returned from a winter vacation in the Caribbean where she and her partner were unfortunately caught, two nights ago, by a tornado that tore through the island. They were forced to take cover in the basement of their hotel for five hours but were able to return to New York the next day. She is still a bit shaken. Her parents, who live out west, were aware of the situation through texts but have not called. In fact, she has not heard from them since Christmas. She is waiting for them to reach out—testing them, I think—and feeling upset when they do not. The conversation veers to how important her weight, her looks, and her professional success have always been to her mom.

While her mother has long felt competitive to her, her father has been an important source of support and closeness, but recently he has moved more into the background. "Why not call them yourself?" I ask. I am reminded of the Buddhist concept of "injured innocence," when someone you love blames you for something you didn't do or hurts your feelings for no apparent reason. The feeling that wells up, of "how could they do that to me?" is thought to be the best opportunity for zeroing in on the feeling of "self" that we cling to, to our own detriment. It is one of the ways of confronting the self-cherishing attitude that the Dalai Lama talked about as the primary obstacle to inner peace.

I told Sally this and relayed my favorite statement from Adam Phillips about how the violent nostalgia for what went wrong in our childhood often is the hardest thing to let go of. Buddhism, in its teachings about injured innocence, says see it clearly but don't get caught up in an over-identification with being wronged. Holding a grudge against one's family situates identity in a backward direction and keeps us stuck in an outmoded concept of ourselves. Sally has moved on in her life, come to New York, and gotten married. She doesn't need her parents in quite the same way as she imagines she still does.

. . .

The passage from Adam Phillips I was referring to is from a book of his entitled *Missing Out*, published in 2012. It is one of my favorites and is something I almost know by heart, having quoted it so often. I find it very useful in drawing parallels between therapy and meditation because it takes one of therapy's current fixations and turns it on its head, in a manner consistent with what I perceive to be a Buddhist understanding. The fixation I refer to has to do with a tendency to blame one's parents, as Sally was doing, for their failures to be adequately attentive or loving when we were children or, in many cases, for their continuing failures when we are adults. Not that there isn't often reason to find fault, but the obsession with it can keep people nursing old grievances instead of helping them accept, with compassion, the hands, or the parents, they were dealt.

The heart of Phillips's argument is as follows:

We have been taught to wish for it, but the wish to be understood may be our most vengeful demand, may be the way we hang on, as adults, to our grudge against our mothers; the way we never let our mothers off the hook for their not meeting our every need. Wanting to be understood, as adults, can

be, among many other things, our most violent form of
nostalgia.

This kind of demand is another form of clinging. From a meditative perspective, the feeling of injured innocence is very important. Few people emerge from childhood intact; there is almost always a sense of something missing, of some kind of failure in the family. Often this failure is internalized and a person feels empty or impoverished, an absence where there could have been more of a presence. Usually, along with the empty feeling, there is also anger at the perceived perpetrator: at one's mother, in Phillips's formulation. This mix of feelings regularly comes up in therapy and, although it is not often talked about in psychodynamic language, it surfaces in meditation also. Learning to "hold" such difficult feelings in meditative awareness, without clinging and without condemning, is a crucial aspect of the work. The investigation of the self that meditation encourages rests on making room for such feelings and recognizing how easy it is to get hung up on them. Phillips's phrase "our most violent form of nostalgia" has helped me enormously in putting a brake on my own tendency to indulge in such notions. Maybe Sally will find it useful too.

Violette · 2/5/19: 12:30 p.m.

Violette tells me about preparing for a dinner party she gave last weekend. But first she thanks me for my suggestion about going to the fertility clinic on the weekend. The office was open, her husband went, they had porn films on the TV in the treatment room, and he left his sperm there to be analyzed. After the appointment he went food shopping for the dinner party but came home frazzled; it was pouring out, it took half an hour for the Uber to pick him up when he was done, and he was out in the cold rain waiting. "I hope we never have to have another dinner party," he said upon his return. He is thirty-four years old. Earlier in the morning, the smoke alarm in their apartment had gone off, and her husband had gotten upset with her about it. He had been up delivering a baby the night before and was counting on getting extra sleep. "He pulled the thing out of the wall to stop it from beeping," Violette says. His violence had frightened her. Violette had felt responsible for the alarm—she should have changed the batteries already—and for her husband's trauma from the shopping. "How can I make it up to him?" she wonders. She has one idea. "I could reorganize the closets. He gets so upset when he can't find anything in the morning."

I steer the conversation back to the dinner party. I want to hear more. Later in the day, as she was cooking, several people canceled at the last minute. She got upset and threw something—a kitchen utensil—against the kitchen wall. This is *her* violence, I point out; her husband does not have a monopoly on it. Her action woke her husband up. He became contrite and apologized for his earlier cantankerous behavior. The dinner party went well and the next day, after cleaning up, they lay down together and cuddled. I suggest that she and her husband go together to replace the smoke alarm instead of making it solely her responsibility. "There must be a hardware store near you," I say. "We can go to Target," she replies.

. . .

This session encapsulates the important relationship between perfectionism and anger en route to the Dalai Lama's ideal of nonviolence and inner peace. Meditation aims to free us from our own inner violence, but in order to be free of it, we have to be able to recognize it when it appears. Violette was good at seeing it in her husband, but her instinctive response was to repress her reaction and instead to see her *husband's* anger as a sign of *her* failures. Her anger broke through, however, when she threw the spatula against the wall, and this was a positive breakthrough, in my eyes. Getting angry meant she was no longer perfect, and it also meant she and her husband had to find a way to resolve the situation between them, just as they did with the visit to the fertility clinic. In the back of my mind I knew that Violette would also need to take possession of her aggression and use it productively if she was going to make the career changes she wanted to make. She would have to deploy that aggression and risk disappointing the friend who wanted her to continue with their joint project. Separation and connection are hard to reconcile!

Within the context of her marriage, where Violette, in being so supportive of her husband, was prone to taking on too much responsibility, the most important word in her conclusion, "We can go to Target," was "we."

Winnicott, my psychoanalytic hero, had something to say about this kind of situation. He was writing about parents' concerns about children's lies, but his insights go well beyond lying.

If development proceeds well the individual becomes able to deceive, to lie, to compromise, to accept conflict as a fact and to abandon the extreme ideas of perfection and an opposite to perfection that make existence intolerable. Capacity for compromise is not a characteristic of the insane. The mature human being is neither so nice nor so nasty as the immature. The water in the glass is muddy, but is not mud.

"Capacity for compromise is not a characteristic of the insane." I love that! And "the water in the glass is muddy, but is not mud" . . . It took me a while to understand what he meant by that, but now I think I do. Violette does not have to be stuck (in the mud of her perfectionism); she can let herself be muddied up by her complicated feelings. This is an important aspect of therapy, not just for Violette, but for many of my patients. The perfectionistic ideal, driven by an over-intrusive superego, does not make room for things as they are. People have complicated and conflicted feelings. Only the insane among us believe there is no room for compromise.

Rachel · 3/6/19: 10:30 a.m.

Rachel, a divorced mother of a sixteen-year-old girl, has been in a loving relationship for the past several years. She and her boyfriend do not live together but they spend a lot of time in each other's company and their relationship has been a happy one. They had a fight the other day, however. Rachel was in the kitchen washing dishes and preparing dinner when her boyfriend called. On most occasions she picks up the phone right away, but this time her hands were full and she let the call go to voice mail. Later, when FaceTiming with him, she could tell he was upset, but he would not, even when asked directly, say why. She pressed him, however, and he eventually conceded that his feelings were hurt when she didn't pick up. "What are you, twelve years old?" she responded immediately, shocked. "I was busy in the kitchen," she added. Recovering somewhat, and with an intuition about what she might hear, she asked him what was going through his head when she didn't answer the phone. He resisted her question at first, before finally, sheepishly replying, "Do you really want to know?" Then he came out with it. "I thought you were with another man."

Rachel had a hard time believing he was serious, and she must have laughed before seeing the pain in his face. "I am so devoted to him," she tells me, "it makes no sense. What is this about?" She reassured her boyfriend, who seemed to realize how far from reality his thoughts had strayed, but she was still perturbed by the time she came to see me a couple of days later. She is questioning herself. "Am I being too selfish? Am I not giving him enough? Is that where this is coming from?" But she is also, just below the surface, worried about his lack of trust in her. Is his jealousy going to override what has been so good between them? What does this portend?

I am very straightforward with her. "He has to deal with this," I tell her. "It's not about anything you are doing wrong." I tell her what I have learned from reading Freud about this kind of thing. He encapsulated it in his concept of the Oedipus complex. For a long time I had not taken Freud seriously on this issue. The Oedipus complex seemed rooted in a chapter of psychoanalysis no longer relevant to present-day concerns. But, over time, I have come to appreciate how important it is to take people's early psychosexual histories seriously. The roots of their clinging can often be found there. Freud put it this way . . . or at least this is my understanding of it: Children, from about the age of five, are already sexual beings. They are aware of genital feelings and experience arousal. They are vaguely conscious of their parents' exclusive intimate relationship and long to be part of it, but they are at one very specific disadvantage: they are not genitally equipped to compete effectively or to satisfy the parent they are attracted to. Feelings of sexual inadequacy, so common in many adults, can be literally—or figuratively—understood in these terms. In naming the complex after Oedipus, Freud emphasized the conflicted nature of a young boy's sexual longing for his mother because Oedipus, in the Greek myth, unknowingly marries his mother and murders his father.

• • •

For Freud, tensions around this triangular relationship were primary. He tended to see many of his patients' issues through its lens. In my experience Oedipal conflicts have only rarely turned out to be the pivotal issue for people I have worked with. And yet the issue that Rachel was faced with, of her boyfriend's jealousy, was most efficiently understood through Freud's paradigm. Rachel's boyfriend could not believe that he was enough for her, that she actually was satisfied by him and with him. He needed her reassurance and he needed her to faithfully pick up the phone when he called. In my formulation, he was endeavoring to stave off debilitating feelings of inferiority that surfaced immediately when she was unavailable, feeding the need to cling to her all the more tightly. Right away, as if regressed to a childhood place, he imagined her with another lover. Rachel's spontaneous cry, "What are you, twelve years old?" was off, in my view, by six or seven years.

Was there anything Rachel could do to help this situation? The most important thing, I told her, was not to take responsibility for her boyfriend's feelings but to help him see that they were natural reflections of his (both healthy and unhealthy) attachment to her. We all carry our early relationships inside of us; psychoanalysis made hay out of this fact in its concept of transference. When we are fortunate enough to find someone to love, these early relationships, hidden in our unconscious, are unlocked. When they are understood as reflections of the past, the energy they contain can infuse and enrich one's current relationships. When taken as present-day fact instead of archaic fantasy, though, they can be incredibly destructive, the horse carrying the rider far from where he really wants to go. Imagine how easy it would be for Rachel to be suffocated by her boyfriend's jealousies. Lucky for her, he was willing to learn from the experience. I encouraged her to get him to talk more openly about his fears and fantasies. He now had the chance to whittle away at his childhood view of himself, as many of us need to do. And Rachel did not have to use his jealousy as a means of criticizing herself. Clinging takes many forms, and she was as vulnerable as the next person to holding on to a perfectionistic ideal for herself that would be impossible to meet.

Lakshman · 3/7/19: 9:30 a.m.

Lakshman is back with a complicated tale of having to go to the emergency room because of chest pain. Long story short: He had an arrhythmia, not a heart attack, but it was not clear until he was hospitalized, via ambulance, in the ICU. The arrhythmia was life threatening. His heart stopped for twelve seconds and he started to "go under." He now has a pacemaker and is in remarkably good humor about the whole ordeal. But he has one complaint. "My libido is gone," he says ruefully. "Now when I'm on the subway I'm looking at everyone wondering who would make a good accountant." Lakshman doesn't quite know who he is anymore.

Four

Spring

When I first began speaking about my work in public many years ago, I needed a way to convey that meditation and psychotherapy were not as different as many people seemed to think. I came across an interview with the artist and composer John Cage, and it gave me huge inspiration. I was familiar with Cage's work but not really knowledgeable about it. I knew that he was the dancer Merce Cunningham's long-term collaborator; that he was influenced by Buddhism; that he often used an ancient Chinese divination tool, the *I Ching*, in his compositions; that he had once composed a musical piece of four minutes and thirty-three seconds of silence; and that he collected mushrooms. He had been on the faculty at Naropa Institute during the summer of 1974 when I was first introduced to both Buddhism and the New York City art world, and he had, since then (it was now sometime around 1986), achieved the status of éminence grise in the downtown culture in which I was more or less immersed. But I was not familiar with his music, his writings, his history, or with the fact that foraging for mushrooms involved the same arts of noticing that also inspired his music. I did not know that his famous silent concert—the one of four minutes and thirty-three seconds' duration—had taken place in an outdoor amphitheater in the Hudson Valley that was anything but totally silent. The sounds of nature, and the sounds of the audience, became the music of the performance, while the pianist sat quietly, opening and closing the cover of the piano keys at prescribed intervals. His so-called silent concert opened his audience to the music that was already surrounding them. The interview I found, in a little newspaper called *Inquiring Mind*, the Berkeley journal of the vipassana community of which I was a part, brought me up to speed. It also gave me a way of thinking about how therapy might be understood from a spiritual—or at least a Cageian—perspective.

Buddhist contemplation is a kind of therapy, after all; its whole orientation is toward relieving people of needless and self-inflicted psychological suffering. And psychotherapy, like meditation, is, at base, an inquiry into the nature of the self. The more you examine your experience, the more mysterious, and elusive, the self becomes. This is an enriching, if also a sobering and humbling, realization, one that insight meditation encourages and that psychoanalysis, after a century or more of self-examination, has been forced to admit. Freud famously proclaimed that the best he could do for people was to take them from a state of neurotic misery and return them to one of common unhappiness, while the Buddha promised freedom from both, but when it came right down to it, both men sensed salvation in a clear-eyed and realistic appraisal of the human condition, enhanced by a healthy dose of uncertainty. Their methods, of free association on the one hand and mindfulness on the other, were remarkably similar in that both were looking to bypass the unchecked ego's demands for control and security so as to access something more basic and true. John Cage, in his approach to making music, seemed to embody this very principle, and he was able to articulate it in a fresh, humorous, and original manner. Cage's journey paralleled my own in several interesting ways.

In 1951 Cage went to Columbia University to hear a series

of lectures on Zen Buddhism by a visiting professor named D. T. Suzuki. (A generation later, in the summer of 1974, I went to Naropa, where I heard a panoply of lectures on Buddhism by similarly distinguished teachers, John Cage among them.) Cage went for two years to Suzuki's classes. (I returned to Naropa for two subsequent summers.) Suzuki's lectures were in the philosophy department, but an assortment of people, including the painters Philip Guston and Agnes Martin, the psychoanalysts Erich Fromm and Karen Horney, the philosopher and art critic Arthur Danto, the poet Allen Ginsberg, the Trappist scholar Thomas Merton, and, some say, the writer J. D. Salinger, attended. Cage was profoundly moved by what he heard. Suzuki touched on the personal, the psychological, the spiritual, and the universal in his lectures. He did not teach meditation but he taught the Buddhist way of approaching life, a philosophy that had a real impact on many of the participants. Some years later, Erich Fromm hosted a conference in Mexico City about the confluence of Zen and therapy and published an influential book on the subject. Suzuki's contribution gives a hint of what his lectures might have been like.

> But let a man once look within in all sincerity and he will then realize that he is not lonely, forlorn, and deserted; there is within him a certain feeling of a royally magnificent aloneness, standing all by himself and yet not separated from the rest of existence. This unique situation, apparently or objectively contradicting, is brought about when he approaches reality in the Zen way. What makes him feel that way comes from his personally experiencing creativity or originality which is his when he transcends the realm of intellection and abstraction.

Suzuki, in his own way, was talking about going beyond the ego and making contact with the soul: a royally magnificent aloneness, all by itself yet not separated from the rest of existence. Cage determined to set this experience to music.

In the interview I read, Cage's debt to Suzuki was palpable. Cage reported that he had never engaged in sitting meditation practice, having already promised his teacher Arnold Schoenberg that he would devote his life to music, and that any extra sitting, on top of what it took to create music, would be too much. But, in lieu of sitting meditation, Cage decided to bring what Suzuki had taught him into his music, much as I have tried to bring what I have learned from insight meditation into the practice of therapy. The interview was studded with pithy quotes from Cage about how he did this. I found Cage's language to be a perfect description of mindfulness.

"If you develop an ear for sounds that are musical it is like developing an ego," he said. "You begin to refuse sounds that are not musical and that way cut yourself off from a good deal of experience." And "If I liked Muzak, which I don't, the world would be more open to me. I intend to work on it." And "I think that life is marvelously complex and that no matter what we do there's room to be irritated. I don't think we ever arrive at the stillness that we imagine. I love the story of the Zen monk who said, 'Now that I'm enlightened, I'm just as miserable as ever.'" And, in a beautiful description of his version of inner peace, he said, "I began to understand that a sober and quiet mind is one in which the ego does not obstruct the fluency of the things that come in through our senses and up through our dreams. Our business in life is to become fluent with the life we are living, and art can help this."

Cage set an important agenda for himself after his introduction to Buddhism. He wanted to erase the differences between musical and ordinary sounds, between silence and music, and between music and meditation. He wanted to bring mindfulness to life. In light of what I had learned from meditation, his intention made perfect sense to me. If I had gathered anything from studying mindfulness, it was this: don't push away the unpleasant and don't cling to the pleasant, but give impartial attention to everything there is to observe. This is no easy task but it is one that I found continually compelling, as well as challenging. When I first became familiar with meditation, while working with Dr. Benson, the approach was almost exactly the opposite: Shut out all disturbances and focus the mind on a single object. Let relaxation be your goal. When I met Joseph Goldstein, Jack Kornfield, and Ram Dass and learned about mindfulness, they completely rearranged my orientation. Be open to everything, they counseled. Learn how to give loving attention to your whole experience. Open yourself, even to those aspects you would rather do away with. Cultivate equanimity rather than searching for the next peak experience.

This stance was one that fit right in with my understanding of therapy. It seemed like a natural thing to deploy mindful attention in the office, to listen to my patients the way I had learned to listen to my own mind. "Suspend judgment . . . and give impartial attention to everything there is to observe," advised Freud to budding psychoanalysts early in his career, sounding every bit like a Zen master of old. Therapists have a hard time with this and often end up thinking too much about what they are hearing rather than staying with the listening process and trusting their minds to show them what they need to see, and what they need to say. I wanted to let listening guide me. I mean this in a meditative way and also in a psychotherapeutic way because I do not really think there is any difference.

Just as Cage wanted to erase the difference between music and ordinary sound, I set out to erase the difference between meditative stillness and the stuff of therapy and ordinary life. I used Cage's approach to sound as a metaphor for being with emotional experience. "Don't latch on to specific feelings and get stuck in clinging to them," I thought. "And don't try to shut everything out so as to attain an imagined stillness. Don't cling and don't condemn, don't hold on and don't push away. Stay with emotion as process, as flow, and find where it takes you. Be as open to emotion as Cage was to sound." Rather than directing his attention inwardly, Cage used external sound as his primary meditation object, but a close reading of his work made clear that he, like the Zen poets of old, directed the same kind of openness to his internal life as well. I found his example clarifying. There are thoughts or feelings that catch us, make us feel embarrassed or ashamed or squeamish or, alternatively, that are captivating and entrancing. Some seem musical and some do not but they are all opportunities to cultivate our minds.

As I continued to accumulate sessions for this book, I began to look for examples of how mindfulness has informed my therapy practice. While at times I give explicit instruction, more often than not, I discovered, I look for ways of making mindfulness relevant in the midst of conversations with my patients. While it can be practiced on the meditation cushion, mindfulness can also be applied in life. Cage was often in the back of my mind in these discussions. His method of finding stillness in sound and music in silence helped me to bridge the gap between therapy and meditation. In the examples that follow, I hope that some of what I found so stirring in Cage seeps through. For Cage understood that music, like mindfulness and like therapy, was not something that could be dispensed like a medicine but was an inner experience that had to be discovered by the listener. Learn to be mindful, he seemed to say, by applying it to whatever you are already doing. As he said in a 1962 interview, "We must arrange our music, we must arrange our Art, we must arrange everything, I believe, so that people realize that they themselves are doing it, and not that something is being done to them." Something similar is true in psychotherapy as well. Therapy is not something that a psychiatrist does to a patient, nor is it solely a place to complain about indignities one has suffered; it is a space in which a person can learn to listen to their own voice. Mindfulness can be a big help in this endeavor.

MINDFULNESS

A monk asked, "By what means is 'hearing without hearing' accomplished?"

The Master said, "Setting aside not hearing, what do you hear?"

CHAO-CHOU, Recorded Sayings, #148

Fred · 3/21/19: 11:00 a.m.

Fred, a twenty-nine-year-old software engineer, has been drawn to meditation for some time. He is busy, successful, and stressed by both work and family issues. "I haven't been meditating at all," he complains. "There are so many choices, so many kinds of meditation, I don't know what to do." I am puzzled at first, until he explains. "It's the apps," he tells me. "The meditation apps. People my age are used to the phone solving any problem," he continues. "You reach for it, it's one second away, and it will do it for you." Now I understand what he is getting at. "Of course. The apps. They can't do it for you; you have to do it for yourself!" I am energized by the conversation. "Doing it for yourself is the whole thing," I tell him. "It's all about that. You have to find the way that works for you. Trial and error."

I tell Fred how simple meditation can be. "You really don't need the apps. Meditation is doing nothing. Just sit there and watch your mind. It's purposeless," I say. "As soon as someone tells you how to do it, you will have expectations for what is supposed to happen. Meditation is about opening a window into yourself with no expectations of what you will find. That's how it can be surprising. You just sit there. Try not to complicate it."

We talk about *how* to meditate, and then, rather quickly, we talk about *when*. Fred has had trouble finding a time that works. He has periods blocked out on his phone calendar, but even though it is written down and there are no obvious conflicts at the office, he has not done it. "I think it might be too hard at work," I say. "There are too many competing demands; there's always something else to do instead that will seem more important." I sweep my hand around my office room. "I don't even meditate down here," I tell him. "It doesn't feel right." We talk about when the right time might be.

"I used to meditate first thing in the morning, just sitting up in bed, when I was younger," I say. "Before I had to be at work and before we had children. Then I switched to doing it before I went to bed. That works sometimes if I am not going to sleep at the same time as my wife. If I wake up in the night and don't fall back asleep, I will get out of bed and sit. That's a good time. Very quiet. And then if I start to get tired, I know there's a good chance I can fall back asleep. I remember when my kids were young, there was always a nice time after they went to sleep at night when the house would get very still, around seven thirty or eight or nine. Before reading the paper or having dinner or watching TV, I would sometimes sit. And often, after reading stories, my children would want me to stay in the room with them, so I brought in my cushion and I would sit and meditate while they went to sleep. I still remember my daughter calling out to me, when she was having trouble falling asleep, 'Would you come meditate, Daddy?' That worked well for a while."

Fred got the point. Meditation has to fit into real life.

• • •

With the recent popularity of mindfulness and the proliferation of apps and blogs and podcasts about it, people like Fred tend to look to it as a kind of mental gymnastics, good for one's health and beneficial if practiced on a regular basis. This is not necessarily mistaken, but it can make meditation feel like just another thing one is doing wrong. While some of my patients have been able to prioritize the regular sitting practice of mindfulness, many others, in the midst of busy work and family life, cannot. This does not mean that there are no opportunities to practice! Sitting is not the only posture. As John Cage repeated, there is music to be found everywhere. Our minds are always with us. We always have the capacity to pay attention to them. We always have a choice about how we are going to relate to a given situation. Mindfulness affords us that opportunity.

What I liked about this conversation was talking about mindfulness as doing nothing. So many people get into trouble with it because of their desire to always be in control. The line between helpful discipline and rigidifying control is not always so clear, and when there is a tendency toward perfectionistic striving, meditation can be recruited into serving that master. I didn't want Fred to fall into that trap. His superego did not need a boost from meditation.

Craig · 3/28/19: 10:30 a.m.

Craig asks for a special session because he is becoming desta-bilized after a series of attacking emails and texts from his ex-girlfriend, from whom he has been separated for years but with whom he is still collaborating in a business they founded together. Craig agreed, for both of their sakes, to stay involved with the business, but his ex's attacks have worn him down. He reads me one of the emails. It is familiar. There have been lots of these over the past several months. She accuses him of abandon-ing her and ruining her life. "You expect me to treat you with a measure of civility after what you did to me," she writes.

Craig is endlessly arguing with her in his head, defending him-self against her criticisms, and it is driving him crazy. I jump in. "You *do* expect her to treat you with civility," I say. "Of course you expect that." I have recently returned from a weeklong silent retreat, and the power of mindfulness is very much in my head. I can sense how Craig is defending himself against his ex's accu-sations, and I am aware of how skillful she is at getting under his skin. She knows she is not treating him with civility, and she is excusing herself by blaming him for her own bad behavior.

Craig has a self-destructive loop playing. His ex's attacks touch on his guilt about leaving her. He hates that guilt and wants it to go away. Instead of acknowledging it mindfully (or, in psy-chological language, nondefensively), he argues, in his mind, with the superficial details of her latest accusations. He is trying to win a battle he can never win. He wants to show his ex that he is a responsible person, committed to their joint welfare, but he can never assuage the hurt he caused by leaving her in the first place. She will never forgive him for that. I make this point. He agrees.

. . .

My effort in this session was to help Craig stay balanced in the face of his ex's anger. This is one of the great gifts of mindfulness. Ordinarily, we are programmed to meet anger with anger. But mindfulness teaches us to treat strong emotion as just another musical sound. I have rarely found this to be completely possible—our nervous systems are wired to respond emotionally on pathways that move faster than thought, so I will usually feel my own anger arising before I have had a chance to think anything through—but I have been successful, at times, at relating to my own anger as a curiosity rather than as a force that takes me over. This gives me room to choose a response. "I can't be the person you need me to be when you are attacking me like this," I proposed that Craig say. "You are pushing me away at the same time as you are reaching out to me for help."

Craig liked my suggestion. He is trying to do a difficult thing. When things calm down between them and they collaborate in their work, things go well for a while but then his ex's feelings of betrayal become rekindled. This brings renewed anger from her and despair in him. I think the best he can do is meet her anger with his truth rather than spinning into an endless series of self-justifications and denials. Being mindful of his guilt, rather than defensive about it, will help. And being mindful of his anger when her accusations get the better of him will also be of service.

Beth · 4/16/19: 1:30 p.m.

Beth is a fifty-year-old anesthesiologist with a history, when much younger, of anorexia. Today she starts the session by saying, "I think probably I should eat a little lunch these days— just not too much, so I don't feel too full." I focus on her hesitations: "I think" and "probably." In my world, we call these retroflections, when someone puts out an intention but then partially takes it back. My therapist used to call me out on this whenever I said the word "really." "I really like her," I might say. "Oh, what don't you like about her?" he would ask. Until he pointed it out, I was not aware of saying the word "really" when I said it, but the therapy's function was to make me more aware. In this way, it was very much of a piece with mindfulness, shedding light on those dark spaces that allow us to hide from ourselves.

Beth's hesitations suggest that she doesn't actually want to eat lunch; I suspect she would sometimes rather do without her customary dinner as well. She likes the empty powerful feeling that not eating gives her, and routinely goes for days eating very little. After some time of this she eats a plate of cooked vegetables, but then she feels "fat" or "bloated" and vows not to eat again for a while. She does not like the discomfort of feeling too full. We talk about how she is being run by a pleasure/unpleasure duality. Unlike most people, Beth gets pleasure from *not* eating and feels discomfort when she does. "Men go to prostitutes because they like how it feels," I say, somewhat tastelessly. "It doesn't mean it's good for them. Heroin too," I add. Just going by what feels good or bad is a rather primitive way to live, I am trying to say. I suggest she impose a treatment plan on herself, as if she were another person, a patient. Take personal choice out of it for a while. Like a Buddhist monk or nun after alms rounds in the local village, eating only what is placed in the begging bowl. Or like John Cage throwing the I *Ching* to determine his musical compositions, taking his own ego out of the process. Beth gives a nod to my suggestion but I do not feel I have convinced her. The subject is likely to come up again.

. . .

In this session I am thinking not only about John Cage but also about a concept derived from Winnicott called "the mind object." They are related, I think. Winnicott, a pediatrician by training, was one of the first psychoanalysts to focus on children's actual developmental challenges. He was especially attuned to those children who precociously center themselves in their thinking minds—he called this an "overgrowth of the mental function"— and who come to rely on thinking as their major safeguard in a difficult and unpredictable world.

As Adam Phillips describes it, "In Winnicott's view, the mind is that part of the self invented to cover for, to manage, any felt unreliability in the caregiving environment. It is, as it were, a necessary fiction, born of expedience, and therefore potentially tainted by (unconscious) resentment. Whenever the world is not good enough one has a mind instead."

Like my previous patient Craig, Beth is struggling with her version of the mind object, just as I have done on many previous meditation retreats. The struggle is, perhaps, most obvious in Craig's repetitive internal arguments with his ex, in which he is trying to reason his way out of her blame and his guilt. But it is also operating in Beth's repetitive thoughts about food. She is not accustomed to knowing her body's needs from the inside and is more comfortable approaching them from her mind's eye. Her unconscious resentment is visible in her hesitations, in the way she tells herself one thing but simultaneously undermines it in language she is not fully aware of.

In his reliance on "chance operations" like the *I Ching*, John Cage was explicitly circumventing his own thinking process, preferring, like the Zen poets he so admired, to let nature be his guide. I could not emulate Cage directly, but I was nonetheless trying to nudge both Craig and Beth out of their oppressive mental loops, using whatever advice I could think of. That I was resorting to my own discursive thinking was an irony not lost on me. My advice to Beth, however well intentioned, was not able to conclusively penetrate the mental walls she had erected. I did not feel that I was living up to John Cage's injunction to arrange my Art so that my patient could realize that she herself was doing it. I was still working a little too hard. The sound of one hand is not always so easy to invoke, even in the relative silence of a therapist's office.

Sunday. Mother's Day. Not therapy.

• 5/12/19: 1:00 p.m.

A good friend of mine from high school has just died after a three-year battle with cancer, and we are visiting his wife several days later to bring her some food. Her son and daughter-in-law and their two-and-a-half-year-old son are also there. We bring them bread from a bakery near us, chopped liver, an eggplant dip my wife has prepared, and a polenta-and-spinach casserole. After sitting and talking and eating, I get up to wash the dishes. The son and daughter-in-law are in the kitchen with me and, to my surprise, ask if they can ask a professional question. "What should we say to our son?" they want to know. It has not occurred to me that their son would not yet know about his grandfather's death; I feel for their predicament. How are they to introduce death to their open, trusting, and loving child? "He keeps asking, 'Where's Grandpa?'" they say. "We told him he was away for a while."

"You didn't tell him anything yet?" I inquire, stalling a bit, not yet knowing how to best say what I am thinking. "How come?"

"I didn't see the point of ruining his perfect life," the father responds.

"It's up to you how you want to deal with it," I begin, knowing in my heart that the boy's perfect life has already been disrupted, "but I think you should just tell him the truth. How you phrase it depends on what you think, but I might say something like, 'Grandpa died. His body couldn't go on any longer so he's had to let it go and get ready for the next one.' I actually believe that," I continue, gathering steam. "So it would be natural for me to phrase it that way, but what you say is less important than acknowledging the fact. He's going to sense that something has happened, he will hear conversation about it and there's a funeral coming, and if you don't explain it, he will make something up about it that will be all the more confusing because you won't know what he is thinking. The worst thing would be that he feels your tension around it or your sadness at the loss and thinks that it's because of something he did. Kids feel what's going on around them but they can't understand, and they make it be about them if you don't help to explain it. Death is very hard for any of us to understand; it certainly will be difficult for him, but he will grow into it and you can help him over the years."

I tell them how our son, at an early age, got very anxious when we did not explain to him what was going on when his grandmother was diagnosed with cancer. It finally emerged that he had heard the word "cancer" and not known what it meant. He understood that it was bad but he wrongly assumed that his mother, not his grandmother, had it. His anxiety settled down after we did our best to explain what was going on.

. . .

I remember the children's book we read to my son in those days when the threat of death first made an appearance in his life. Called *The Mountains of Tibet*, by Mordicai Gerstein, it became one of my favorite books of all time. An old woodcutter dies at the start of the book and his spirit goes to the bardo, the between place, where he gets to choose what world he wants to come back to. He picks the earth, attracted by its blue color, and then has a series of additional choices to make. Which continent, which landscape, which climate, which culture, which parents does he find appealing? The woodcutter settles on Tibet once again. Something, some vestige of memory, keeps pulling him there. I remember the picture of all the parents with their arms in the air reaching out for a new baby. In a Tibetan version of Freud's Oedipus complex, he feels attracted to his new parents and then is given one more choice. Boy or girl this time? He chooses a new gender identity and opts, biologically, to be a she.

There was something immensely comforting about this story, comforting to me anyway, as we tried to navigate the mystery of my mother-in-law's cancer. Life as a process without beginning or end. We read that story scores of times. My son (now approaching age thirty) claims not to remember it at all. But in reading it over and over we learned one of the great lessons of mindfulness: trying to avoid that which makes us uncomfortable only makes us more tense, irritable, anxious, and afraid.

It was very natural that my friends did not want to tell their son about his grandfather's death. Who wants death in their children's lives? But avoiding its reality is not a good solution. A lot of anxiety has its roots in this kind of avoidance. The Buddha noted this in his first noble truth when he used the word "dukkha" to describe the unsatisfactoriness that shadows our lives. The word "dukkha," generally translated as "suffering," actually means "hard to face." "Kha" is "face" and "duk" means "difficult to." Death is one of those things that are hard to face. But mindfulness, like John Cage's music, encourages us to pay attention to the noxious sounds as well as to the melodic ones. As the Buddha never tired of reminding us, "Everything that arises must also pass away," and we are more capable than we think of looking this in the face.

Zach · 5/15/19: 8:30 a.m.

Zach is a gifted poet who has been able to write without having to compete in the marketplace because he inherited a good deal of money. As a result, he shows his poems only to a few close artist friends who both envy him his privilege and look down on him for it. They are competitive in a way that seems obvious to me but is not at all clear to Zach. He takes their not-quite-disguised critiques personally and this feeds his insecurity. Talking about it brings up his relationship with his now-deceased father, an intellectual who recognized and supported his son's literary talents but whose academic accomplishments seemed intimidating to Zach, whose talents lay elsewhere. Zach sees a pattern in his male friendships: he sets himself up to feel ashamed in comparison. Rather than letting his work into the wider world, he shows it only to those few who are, perhaps, not the best judges of its worth. He is about to visit with one of these old friends, a professor who is strong on the kind of cultural theory Zach is not conversant with. "I can see him seeing me," Zach tells me, "and I just feel shame."

"Conceit is one of the last fetters," I say in response. Zach, obviously, does not at first understand what I am talking about, but I am intent on explaining. From the point of view of Buddhist psychology, the tendency to compare oneself with others is a deeply ingrained, almost instinctive, ego habit. This is what is meant by conceit. It does not mean positive self-regard; in a way it is just the opposite. The word used in Buddhism actually means "measuring." Most people are continually comparing themselves—their looks, their intelligence, their wealth, their achievements—with others; Zach is no different in that regard, he is just oriented in a particular way. Even very realized spiritual adepts are still prone to comparing their meditative accomplishments with others'; their egos are still operational. One of the things Buddhist psychology is best at is itemizing which emotional tendencies are the most ingrained. They are listed as the "ten fetters," and this tendency to measure oneself is said to be one of the most subtle and difficult to uproot. Even lust and anger are easier to deal with than conceit.

Zach finds this only vaguely reassuring. He is apprehensive about his upcoming visit with his friend and looks to me for concrete advice rather than philosophical speculation. He has studied meditation for a long time and wants to try to use it to shake up the dynamic with his friend. I do not think he has to rush to show him his new poems, and I tell him so. Why set himself up for feeling bad? "What should I do instead?" he asks. "Send him metta?" "Metta" is the word for loving-kindness in the Pali language of the Buddha's time. There are classical meditation exercises in which one deliberately sends loving thoughts to other people, first to those one is close to, then to those one feels neutral toward, and finally to those one perceives as enemies. I am not so sure that sending metta to his friend during their visit is going to do the trick. It seems too artificial to interject a meditation in the midst of their time together.

"Just be his friend," I suggest. "Keep it simple." Zach is taken aback by my comment, but I can feel I am onto something. With all of his measuring and comparing, Zach is getting lost in his own mind. He is seeing his friend seeing him and then fighting with this perception of himself and losing the battle, ending up in the all-too-familiar territory of not measuring up. When I advise him to just be his friend, I am encouraging something simpler and different. They are going to spend a spring week together in San Francisco. Zach knows San Francisco and can show his friend around. "Be generous," I say. Putting out for his friend is a much better use of his energy than turning the friendship into an opportunity to feel bad about himself. But doing this requires a clear and persistent intent. It will be easy for Zach to fall back into the old pattern if he is not mindful.

. . .

There is something in this session that reminds me of Ram Dass's pivotal conversation with Lakshman, when he told him to "love the thoughts" and see himself as a soul. And there is something of the mind object and the Freudian superego as well. Self-judgment is such a prominent part of Zach's identity. It has been present for a very long time. Zach objectifies himself and feels insufficient. He compares himself with his father, with his friends, and with an imagined ideal, and he always comes up short. His negative thoughts about himself are compounded by the shame he feels whenever he sees himself through the eyes of another. While I did not suggest that he love his negative thoughts (although the thought did cross my mind), I did try to encourage some distance from them by telling him about the ten fetters.

While many therapists would explain persistent negativity like Zach's as the result of deficient parenting, Buddhist psychology sees it more as an inevitable outgrowth of the built-in difficulties of a human birth. We cannot help treating ourselves as objects and comparing ourselves with others. Our ego-driven conceptual minds cling to certainty, and when we look for it inside ourselves, it is not there, at least not in the form we have learned to expect. We are constantly calibrating ourselves, and there is always someone doing better than we are. If Zach could see his negative thoughts not as a reflection of his inherent inadequacy but as the understandable misperceptions of an unenlightened mind, he might not feel so much shame.

I am reminded of the four qualities of the Zen Buddhist aesthetic (simplicity, naturalness, directness, and profundity) and the four dominant moods of Zen poetry (isolation, poverty, impermanence, and mystery). Can Zach find within himself the royally magnificent aloneness that Suzuki helped John Cage to know? Can he simply be a friend to his friend? Can he show him San Francisco without feeling like a failure, without his ego or superego getting in the way? Could he echo, at the close of his week's vacation, the eighteenth-century Zen poet Bakusui's haiku in which he wrote sparingly but utterly succinctly of the surprise of coming home to himself one fine spring day?

Returning
by an unused path—
violets.

The unused path, in Zach's situation, is the path of simple friendship. When not compounding it with his usual judgments, comparisons, inadequacies, and shame, he might notice something surprising springing up. Violets.

I think I came closer in this session than in many of the previous ones to encouraging the kind of shift I am after for my patients. It did not come through my explanation of the concept of conceit but from the surprise of suggesting that Zach simply be a friend to his friend. The element of surprise was important. Startled by my comment, Zach had a glimpse of another way of relating. It made sense to him in the moment, not just conceptually but personally. The Zen poem connotes a similar feeling, returning by an unused path. Could that also be mindfulness, coming back via an intrinsic but unfamiliar resource to find the unexpected? But when I read the poem to Zach at a later date, instead of hearing "violets," he heard the final word as "violence." A Freudian slip, we might conclude.

Sarah · 5/15/19: 4:00 p.m.

Sarah has two small children and a full-time job. She is separated from her husband but on good terms with him and is trying to raise their children together with him while living apart. Her mother is visiting from the Midwest and staying with her, sleeping on the couch in Sarah's small Brooklyn apartment. While grateful for her mother's babysitting help, Sarah is frustrated by her mother's passivity. When she comes home from a long day at work, she finds her mother sitting with the children waiting for Sarah to make dinner. There is extra work to do as a result of her visit, not less. In addition, her mom shows no interest in any of the cultural activities of the city. She helps bring the children to and from childcare and reads to them when they are home, but that's about it. Sarah has a hard time feeling close to her mom. "She doesn't really know me," she says. "I always kind of freeze up when I'm around her. What can I do to break through?"

I am curious about the food thing. "She doesn't cook?" I ask. I find this somewhat unusual. "No," Sarah replies. "When I visit her house, there's just a huge pile of Trader Joe's microwave meal containers in her kitchen." "Do you have a microwave?" I ask, feeling pretty sure that Sarah does not. She does not. "Well, that's my first suggestion," I say. "Get your mom to buy you a microwave. One you can hide in the closet when she's not here, if you don't want it around. Could she do that for you?" "Yes." Sarah smiles. "I can send her to Target. It's close." Once she has the microwave, I think, maybe her mom can make food for dinner. "That would be a huge help if I didn't have to always cook," Sarah says. Sarah's daughter might even like the microwave meals from Trader Joe's for a while.

Then I try to talk about the other thing, the trouble of not feeling close. I ask Sarah if I've ever told her about my breakthrough with my father. It's a story I sometimes tell to my patients, and I'm not sure if I've already mentioned it. My father was a professor of medicine, a kidney doctor back when nephrologists were the elite physicians of internal medicine, sort of like the neuroscientists of today. He loved the profession of medicine and always wanted me to be a doctor. The only problem was, I had no interest in kidneys, nor any driving wish to be a doctor. Throughout my college days, my father would ask me repeatedly if I was considering going to medical school. Once I found Buddhism and decided, for lack of a better plan, that becoming a psychiatrist made sense, he would ask me repeatedly how medical school was going. I didn't really like medical school and always recoiled at his questions.

In a similar way to Sarah, I felt that my father did not really know me. He never asked about my friends or about stuff I was actually interested in. After medical school, he always wanted to talk about my private practice but rarely about my children. Finally, somewhere in my late thirties, I had an epiphany. It dawned on me that all the questions about being a doctor were just my father's way of trying to make contact. He didn't know any other way. When I stopped resenting his questions and judging him for them and just answered, without truculence, things got much better between us. We could actually talk! I thought this might be helpful for Sarah to hear. We can benefit from meeting our parents where they are, instead of resenting them for where they are not. In her judgments of her mother's timidity, Sarah was distancing herself unnecessarily. If she could accept her mom on her mother's own terms, while encouraging her to microwave some dinners, I was sure she could break through with her too.

. . .

In talking to Sarah about my own struggles with my father, I was once again thinking about the Buddhist concept of injured innocence, which I had broached in the winter with my patient Sally on her return from the Caribbean. I love this concept for the way it links Buddhist thought and the work of psychoanalysts who focus on emotional neglect and the (at best) righteous indignation or (at worst) crippling psychological emptiness that follows such inattention. Buddhist thought has been helpful for me with this because the Buddha's first noble truth—that life is tinged with a sense of pervasive unsatisfactoriness (or suffering)—takes it as a given that there is always some way that we feel unseen, unknown, or unrecognized. Psychoanalysis has explored many of the most obvious parental failings that contribute to such feelings but, in trying to find the source, or the cause, of personal uncertainty, it has encouraged people to overly blame their families of origin rather than taking on the responsibility of reaching out to establish whatever kinds of connections are actually possible in life.

No matter how intimate people are, there is always room for disharmony. John Cage knew this and tried to bring noxious, nonmusical sounds into his compositions. Buddhist teachers know this too. The self that they suggest is illusory finds its basis in feelings of being unseen. As the Dalai Lama repeatedly points out, the self-cherishing instinct, the feeling of "me, me, me," arises most distinctly when one feels unjustly accused or ignored. The mind object, in which one overly solidifies one's own sense of identity by thinking about it all the time, is the unfortunate result. Buddhist therapy, of whatever ilk, seeks to undermine this false identity by making it the target of inquiry. My efforts with Sarah were inclined in this direction. She could stay feeling hurt or help her mother feed the family. Target was close by and, not for the first time, could be of service to one of my patients. The true target, of course, from a Buddhist perspective at least, is the overly inflated sense of self that is nourished by one's personal grievances. Once one identifies *that* target, it becomes possible to free oneself from an exclusive identification with it. In that direction lies freedom.

Jean · 5/31/19: 9:00 a.m.

Jean is a forty-five-year-old orthopedist who, in my view, is being unjustly penalized by the Feds for prescribing an opioid to a longtime patient with chronic pain. She has had her board certification rescinded, lost a consulting job at a local hospital, had her prescription license suspended, has to have her medical records audited for three years, and has to take a mandated remedial course in proper prescription practices. In addition, she has just found out that she has to pay a $250,000 fine. This is about a third of all the money she has earmarked for retirement. In contrast to the way she is feeling, I am relieved to hear about the penalty. "The money is a concept," I say. "Everyone says, 'It's only money,'" she replies with a tone of exasperation. "I'm not saying that," I tell her. "It's a lot of money, but at the moment it's still just a number on your bank statement. Once it's gone, are you really going to miss it? It's not like you are going to stop working anytime soon." I have been through similar things with patients who are getting divorced. They have to give up half of their net worth and it feels agonizing until it's over, and then it hardly matters. Life goes on. I was worried they would try to make more of an example of Jean and take away her medical license or even threaten her with prison. She will be fine.

In her session she alternates between self-pity and humiliation. "Which is worse," I ask her, "being a victim or feeling the shame?" I am trying to loosen her identification with both. "You have to tune in to your Christian heritage," I say. Jean looks at me askance. She comes from a secular family, she reminds me. "Do you know what Jesus meant when he said 'turn the other cheek'?" I persevere. "I just found out myself. I always thought that he meant 'turn away,' but he meant 'offer up the other cheek if you have already been struck once before.'" It is not clear that Jean is following my reasoning.

"Why does Jesus take on the suffering of others?" I continue. I am out on a limb here, but I can tell I have piqued her curiosity, and at times I can be relentless. "So they can be free?" she says hesitantly. That seems right to me. Could Jean be doing something similar here? I wonder. She can handle this amount of suffering. "Jesus knew his body wasn't real," I suggest. "That's why he could be resurrected. It's the same with your retirement account." Jean is a good sport and puts up with my logic. She gets ready to leave and I have the feeling she is a bit disoriented. All this talk about Jesus has slightly turned her around. I want her to be willing to suffer, even if her suffering is unjust, rather than rushing to feel persecution or shame. "Forgive them, Father, for they know not what they do," I say as she hands me a check for the session. The fine is one thing but the self-concepts resulting from it are another.

· · ·

It would, of course, have been tempting to focus exclusively on the range of feelings Jean might have been having in addition to the shame she expressed. She was bound to be angry as well as humiliated, and, in another session, or with another patient, I might have felt it to be therapeutic to help bring her anger into awareness. Left unacknowledged, anger could continue to feed Jean's self-loathing, turning, as it tends to do, from its object back onto the self. But something pushed me to take a different approach in this session. It was uncharacteristic of me to talk about Jesus, but I took a chance. The "turn the other cheek" phrase had been in my head recently; I remember I looked it up on my computer when I realized I did not truly understand the reference. And my patient who had been in Calcutta working with Mother Teresa's nuns had made a big impression on me too. The way she had described seeing each and every person who came for help as Jesus, cleaning their wounds and looking in their eyes and seeing them as Christ, had touched me in a deep way.

Jean was an enormously giving person. The punishments inflicted on her seemed way out of proportion, and yet I knew that she could emerge from this unscathed, if not untouched. Like Zach, Jean did not have to be exclusively identified with her shame. Nor did she have to compound her suffering with added feelings of unworthiness. At another time I might have quoted from the fifteenth-century Zen poet Ikkyū, who understood that lurking behind one's everyday worries and concerns lies another, more authentic, reality, one that mindfulness reveals as the everyday judgments of good and bad are peeled away:

self other right wrong wasting your life arguing
you're happy really you are *happy*

or even the seventeenth-century haiku of Masahide, who found unexpected illumination after losing his home (or after deconstructing his falsely conceived self?) to a fire:

Barn's burnt down—
now
I can see the moon.

But Jesus was enough for one day.

Rebecca · 5/31/19: 11:00 a.m.

Rebecca has come to see me twice before. I am still getting to know her. Today she tells me she has a frozen shoulder and has recently seen a bodyworker who, in the process of treating her discomfort, did something unexpected. "When I am massaging this frozen area, you need to make a sound," he told her. She felt clueless when he said this, and was hard pressed to comply. He tried to lead her by saying, "It's a sound you hate; one you would rather die than make," but she still drew a blank. Finally, he modeled a whimpering sound for her and had her repeat it over and over. He was right, she did hate that sound, it was a far cry from her usual self-confident demeanor, but as she forced herself, she began to feel it working its magic on her shoulder.

This whimpering is interesting to me, reminding me of the ever-evasive sound of one hand. "What feeling goes with that sound?" I ask her. Rebecca's first answers do not strike me as real. "Fear? Shame?" she wonders, but I do not sense that she is connected to these words. I am surprised at her difficulty, but only a little. The bodyworker's move suggested that he felt her frozen shoulder to be a manifestation of, or at least associated with, a forbidden emotion, one that Rebecca had pushed out of her consciousness. In calling for her to make a sound, he was trying to get her to reconnect to something she has pushed away. I wait quite a long time for Rebecca to find another explanation for her whimpering, but she is stymied.

"What about sadness?" I finally ask. Boom. "My parents got divorced when I was nine," Rebecca suddenly tells me. The story pours out of her. "My mother took my sister, our dog, and me into the city to a small apartment where the neighbors complained about the dog barking all the time. My mother took the dog to the vet and he cut the nerve to its vocal cords so he wouldn't make a sound but it didn't totally work and he still barked and barked all the time. The sound he made was like mine." I am startled by the suddenness of Rebecca's association. It is almost like a textbook therapy thing, something that rarely happens, a crystalline memory that explains so much. We are back to when she was nine and her parents split up, but there is still something missing. As traumatic as this memory is, Rebecca still seems curiously unfazed.

"That's when I mobilized myself," she says. "There was no choice; I had to succeed." And she did. Rebecca has an outgoing and extroverted personality. She took care of her mother, pushed to the top of her profession, married, and had children. What is the missing piece? My mind scans the landscape. "Your father," I say. "What about your father?" At first Rebecca denies much of a relationship with him. "He got remarried right away and said he'd never been happier. He had no time for us and we just had to go forward," she says. But I push.

"Only the dog got to have feelings?" I ask. I talk to Rebecca about mindfulness somewhere along the way, about how the original word in the language of the Buddha meant remembering. Re-membering, as in reattaching her frozen shoulder and reintegrating her forbidden sadness. Because the loss of her father has to have mattered. A child naturally loves her parents, and the inevitable sadness at losing one of them is a manifestation of that love. Loyalty to her mother has made Rebecca distance herself from her need for her father. Her sadness has become a secret even to herself.

Rebecca is interested in what I have to say and, I think, is a little bit moved. It is early in the therapy and we will have to see whether my intervention bears any fruit, whether the loss of her father is something that continues to peek out from her unconscious. For the moment, I am thrilled with the session. I hope it will prove useful for her.

· · ·

John Cage often told an intriguing story about a visit he once had with the Japanese sculptor Isamu Noguchi that reminds me of Rebecca's session. He used it as part of a "musical" accompaniment to one of Merce Cunningham's dances, called *How to Pass, Kick, Fall, and Run*. When it was first produced, in 1965, Cage would sit to the side of the stage at a table with a microphone, ashtray, texts, and a bottle of wine and intermittently tell his stories, in a sequence determined by chance, while the dancers performed. The dances were not choreographed to the stories; they merely took place at the same time. Whatever coordination occurred happened by chance. His Noguchi narrative went as follows:

> *One evening when I was*
> *still living at Grand Street and*
> *Monroe, Isamu Noguchi came*
> *to visit me. There was nothing*
> *in the room (no furniture, no*
> *paintings). The floor was cov-*
> *ered, wall to wall, with cocoa*
> *matting. The windows had no*
> *curtains, no drapes. Isamu No-*
> *guchi said, "An old shoe would*
> *look beautiful in this room."*

Rebecca's father was like the old shoe in Cage's story, the missing element in the unadorned bleakness of her memory, summoned out of the icy expanse of her frozen shoulder. I have heard similar things over the years from other children of divorce. The narrative is always something like this: One parent, often out of well-meaning concern for the welfare of their children but sometimes out of spite, prevents contact with the other parent. The children have to adapt, and the love for (and need for) the spurned parent has to go underground. While classical Buddhist psychology never addresses these kinds of problems specifically, the "remembering" aspect of mindfulness, like the bodywork Rebecca underwent, tends to bring forth people's lost, hidden, or forbidden emotions. By adopting a neutral stance in the face of one's entire mental and physical experience, mindfulness gives space for such repressed feelings to declare themselves.

Cage's empty room covered in cocoa matting is another version of my psychotherapy office, unadorned but lying in wait for whatever old shoe might complete the picture. As the hidden material begins to peek out of the darkness, it is not often clear what it represents. But sometimes, as in Rebecca's case, it bursts onto the scene only thinly disguised. Psychotherapy can be an important spiritual tool in such situations. This is further demonstrated in the following session.

David · 5/31/19: 12:00 p.m.

David is a sixty-five-year-old musician who is learning to be a mindfulness coach. He has to present to his class about mindfulness of emotions, and he wants to know whether I have any tips. Of course I do. Most people who are drawn to mindfulness are somewhat disdainful of emotional life, I tell him. They tend to see it as indulgent at best and as an impediment at worst. The Dalai Lama often talks about "destructive emotions," and there is a trope in Buddhism that describes greed, hatred, and delusion as "the three poisons." Mindfulness has proven very useful for people who tend to act out their feelings rather than experience them internally by encouraging them to reflect rather than react, but therapists like Marsha Linehan, the founder of dialectical behavioral therapy, have discovered that these very people, who seem so "emotional," actually have very little idea what they are feeling. Linehan, a behaviorist, had the insight that such people are actually phobic toward their own emotions, that when they get an inkling of a disturbing feeling, they go into a kind of panic and, in running away from the experience, express it, or act it out, rather than experience it.

For therapists, I tell David, emotion is the key. "Follow the affect" is the most helpful advice beginning therapists can receive. I reach for an example for David, knowing that he has been in recovery for many years, thinking, in the back of my mind, of

Rebecca's whimpering and the longing for her missing father that it signified. "Yearning," I say. "It often comes up in meditation. It's like the yearning of a young child for comfort, for closeness, for the mother's breast. Longing. Most people can relate to longing. There's a longing in meditation for relief, for transcendence, for a merger with something greater than oneself, or even to disappear. We have to make space for that longing in meditation and explore it without indulging it or looking for a quick fix. Turn it into an object of contemplation rather than allowing it to unconsciously run things."

David listens carefully. I can see that he connects to what I am saying. He has his own version of this yearning, stemming, as it does, from his lonely childhood with a depressed and alcoholic mother. "One of my earliest memories," he says, "is of coming into the darkened living room and seeing the glow of my mother's Chesterfield as she was lying on her BarcaLounger. She was fuming." He laughs at his pun. She was angry and depressed and drinking and smoking. Fuming, as he said. "'You're different than usual,' I said to her." (Perhaps she had been better at hiding her depression before this memorable encounter.) "'No, I'm not,' she told me. That's when I learned to doubt myself. I had to believe her and not myself."

My theory is that most people get locked into feeling small or insufficient or unworthy because of their early experiences of dependency. David's experience is an intense version, compounded by the self-doubt and confusion that his mother's defensive reaction encouraged in him. I explain my theory to David. People identify with being in need instead of in love. Love was there in him from the beginning, but his mother's blocking of it left him askew, left him feeling most himself when he was thirsty and in need and doubting himself. But by making yearning into an object of mindfulness, as we are starting to do in our discussion, the love that exists behind it can start to surface. I think again of

Hakuin's sound of one hand. The cuckoo flying in the background while the monkey covers his ears is symbolic of that original love. "Staying with the feeling is key," I declare. "Most people go straight to what is wrong with them rather than staying with the feeling." David's eyes fill with tears. I can see that he is following my logic. "I'd like to believe it," he says quietly.

David's tears are important. His emotions are starting to flow. I tell him about Mara, the key figure in the story of the Buddha's awakening who tempts and obstructs him as he is closing in on his enlightenment. Mara is often thought of as the devil, but he is actually a demigod, and as such he is a good stand-in for the superego. He is always whispering in the Buddha's ear that he is foolish to pursue the spiritual life, that he should do what he was brought up to do, become a king or a ruler and take his place in society. Mara's nickname is the "drought demon." He is the force—in the agricultural terrain of the Buddha's time—that stops the flow necessary for the harvest. As the superego, Mara also stops the flow of emotion. This session is unexpectedly loosening Mara's grip. For what might be the first time in a long time, David is allowing his love for his mother to surface, the very natural inclination that propelled him toward her as a young boy. David gathers his coat, scarf, and bag and reaches for the door, leaving with one tender backward glance.

· · ·

I was pleased with this session because I managed to get David to feel behind all of his accrued self-doubt and into his heart. For an instant, when his tears began to flow, I knew he was connecting to a neglected but super-important part of himself. We had gotten to this place through a discussion of mindfulness, but our conversation did not stop at the intellectual level. David's memory had led us deeper into his personal history and straight to the defenses he had built around his mother's unavailability. By allowing himself to follow his affect rather than dwelling in his story, David was able to discover something true: the love he had always doubted was alive inside him.

So many of these recent sessions involve mindfully confronting a crudely oppressive superego whose aim is to restrict the flow of vital emotional energy. Mara! As a split-off aspect of the ego, devoted to maintaining order and obedience, the superego is easily invested with the mantle of truth, even when it has no idea what it is talking about. David's replacement of his own intuition with his mother's words is a concrete example of how this comes to pass. The superego operates with a strict "right or wrong" vocabulary. In David's situation, the message was clear. His mother was right and he was wrong. A similar pattern occurred with Rebecca (my patient with the frozen shoulder) when her parents split up. Her mother's shunning of her father encouraged Rebecca to shun him as well. Her superego aligned with her mother's, and any residual feeling she had for her father was therefore "wrong." Loyalty to her mother was more important than her feelings for her father, and paralysis was the result. Jean, the orthopedist penalized by the Feds, was also vulnerable in this way. She was all too ready to substitute the view of the authorities for her own version of the truth, sacrificing her self-regard on the altar of professional misconduct. Even though she had acted out of legitimate concern for her suffering patient, she still felt "wrong."

An overly primitive superego is one of the primary obstacles to spiritual understanding. Its punitive voice slips into our thoughts and colonizes our identities. One of mindfulness's great gifts is to help us notice the way this oppressive voice sneaks itself into every conversation. Even the Buddha was vulnerable to it. Until the childhood memory of his joy under the rose-apple tree, he was driven by a self-loathing every bit as harsh as any of my patients'. His revelatory thought in the aftermath of that memory—that he was afraid of the happiness contained in it—is worth paying attention to. When we are run by the superego, the natural joy that underlies our very being feels scary. Were we to let it in, it would upend our whole conception of ourselves.

It was Freud who developed the whole notion of id, ego, and superego. According to Adam Phillips, one of Freud's main inspirations for his theory came from his teenage fascination with Cervantes's famous novel *Don Quixote*. Freud and his best friend at the time, Eduard Silberstein, taught themselves Spanish in order to read the book they had become jointly obsessed with in its original language. Phillips found evidence of their obsession in a famous passage from the *New Introductory Lectures* (1933) in which Freud described the relationship between the ego and the id—"between the person's conscious sense of themselves and their more unconscious desires"—as like a man riding a somewhat unruly horse. The passage in question is as follows:

> *The horse supplies the locomotive energy, while the rider has the privilege of deciding on the goal, and of guiding the powerful animal's movement. But only too often there arises between the ego and the id the not precisely ideal solution of the rider being obliged to guide the horse along the path by which it itself wants to go.*

Freud's point is that the ego, despite its best attempts, is not always in charge in the way it thinks it is. Unconscious desires often take us where *they* want to go, even as we convince ourselves that we are the ones actually making the decision. Things would be difficult enough if there were only the ego and the id to worry about, but Freud inserted another character into the mix. The superego, as we have seen in some of these sessions, often superimposes its own brutal commentary on whatever it observes.

Phillips locates the origin of Freud's superego in Don Quixote's sidekick Sancho Panza. "What does the Freudian superego look like if you take away its endemic cruelty, its unrelenting sadism?" Phillips asks. He quotes a famous literary critic on this. Because "panza" means "belly," Sancho Panza, "lazy, greedy, cheeky, loquacious, cowardly, ignorant, and above all, nitwitted," is like a sixteenth-century paunchy Spanish clown. This is the superego's true nature? The great Oz revealed behind a screen as a cowardly little fat-bellied fellow?

Upon reading Phillips's piece, I began to imagine my patients replacing their overwrought superegos with someone like Sancho Panza. I realized that many of my efforts to poke gentle fun at their self-loathing were in line with this vision. It comforted me to imagine that Freud might have approved, that he had a similar agenda for his patients a century ago, and that he, too, was struck by the way ordinary people can't help but think the worst about themselves, privileging the voice of what amounts to not much more than a Spanish clown.

But of course, the superego has its place, even for those engaged in meditation. Without it, there is no spur, no prod, no whip, and no rope, no motivation to tame the unruly mind. This is evident in the next session, where my patient, despite my protestations, demanded that I leave her superego alone.

Margaret · 6/3/19: 6:00 p.m.

Margaret has a question about mindfulness. Most of the time, she says, nothing is happening when she meditates. I know what she means, although, of course, there is no such thing as nothing. Something is always happening, but, for Margaret, whatever is happening is not that edifying. I agree with her though. "Nothing happens most of the time," I say. "It's like in Zen where they sit all day facing the wall." "Well, what's the point then?" she asks. "It's pointless," I say. "That's one of the things about it that's different. You just sit there. Once in a while, something breaks through and you touch something that is otherwise inaccessible, but there's no making it happen." Margaret knows this but when it doesn't happen on a regular basis, she is convinced she is doing it wrong.

"You don't have to do it, you know," I remind her, but she reprimands me. "I am the queen of procrastination," she says. "I won't do it if there is no point." "It's not about touching the highs," I say. "It's about learning to relate to whatever is happening in a different way, not identifying so much with the thoughts, even the thoughts of nothing happening. Sometimes there are bits of grace but they can't be predicted; that's why they are grace. They come or they don't come, it's not up to you." "What about those retreats you go on?" she wants to know. Every year I try to go away for a week to the Forest Refuge, where I practice on my own, more or less continuously, for the days I am there.

"Even there," I tell her, "it takes at least three days for my mind to settle down at all. My joke to myself is that even on the retreat there is no time to meditate. By the time you go to the meals, wash up, go for a walk, take a nap, stretch, and so on, there's hardly any time left in the day to meditate." I am being coy, of course, but my point is serious. The advantage of the retreat is that, even in all those times of officially "not meditating," one can actually be mindful. The division between meditation and real life is artificial. Doing each thing with full attention turns everything into a meditation.

"It takes a while but eventually the light comes in," I tell her. "But it's important not to get attached to that either. One can get addicted to anything." Margaret says that her experience is far from blissful. "I sit, my phone is there in front of me, and I reach for it when it gets frustrating," she tells me. "Then I hate myself." "The self-loathing is separate from the frustration," I say. It's natural to be frustrated in meditation; what is interesting is how each person deals with this frustration. Margaret's way is to hate herself for it.

If I am successful with Margaret, I will get her to mindfully observe her self-hatred rather than remaining a victim of it. It is patterned in very deeply; she reflexively moves in that direction when given the opportunity, but she has the chance to pull away from a complete identification with the self that is doing the hating. I am trying to get her to see that even when nothing is happening in her meditation, something important is going on. But she resists me. "If there's not a reason, like stress reduction or lowering blood pressure, I won't do it," she says. "Then don't do it if you don't want to," I say. "Unless you're the kind of person who needs to be told what to do." "No, don't say that to me," she exclaims. "I am that kind of person." "Okay." I give in. "Then sit every day!" I command, every bit as harsh as the superego of old.

. . .

Margaret's session reminds me of a story I have heard Joseph Goldstein tell on several occasions about what I would designate as his own superego. Joseph is a seventy-five-year-old Buddhist teacher of mindfulness and insight meditation who has done an awful lot of solitary meditation over the years. I met him more than forty-five years ago and have considered him my friend and teacher ever since. The clarity and power of his instruction comes directly out of his fierce intelligence and his love for this practice. Once, on retreat, when he was doing walking meditation outside of the main building of the Insight Meditation Society, he glanced at an upstairs window and saw his teacher standing there watching him while he was walking. This teacher was someone Joseph had long admired, a strict, severe visiting Burmese meditation master, an expert in mindfulness. Upon seeing his teacher, Joseph straightened his posture and started walking much more slowly, trying to look as mindful as possible, knowing that he was being observed. The sight of the teacher kicked Joseph's superego into gear, activating the whip, the rope, the spur, and the prod, and Joseph, rather self-consciously, strode deliberately back and forth for the next half hour or so, doing his best to be, and to look, mindful. Eventually, he dared to glance up at the window again. His teacher was still there. He hadn't moved an inch. Joseph looked closer and realized that the shape in the window was not his teacher at all; it was a lampshade. Joseph laughed to himself and relaxed. He had been doing his practice for the approval of a lampshade. His conclusion: "We create all kinds of suffering for ourselves!"

I would put a slightly different gloss on the story. Seeing his superego, not as a strict and severe Burmese authority figure but as an innocuous lampshade, was like seeing it, as per Adam Phillips and Don Quixote, as a Spanish clown. Cowardly, ignorant, and nitwitted! Something that makes you smile rather than something to live by. Seeing the joke of it relaxed something in Joseph and relaxed something in his approach to mindfulness. It was as if he took the shade off his own light and let it shine a little brighter.

Five

Summer

The heart of the Buddha's message is that there is no self. What he meant by that is open to interpretation, and there has been no end to debate about it over the centuries, but however we choose to understand it, there is no question that he was getting at something profound, difficult to comprehend, and central to his teaching. Rather than digging too deeply into the endless academic debates about this core doctrine, where the language of philosophy threatens to overwhelm the felt truth of this bold statement, let's stay close to the actual words. There is no self. How strange. I don't know whether you react the same way as I do, but I actually find this relieving.

Deep down, I have never been sure that I had a self, or enough of a self, or the right kind of self, or that my self was okay, or that it was even there. What self? I looked at my parents and they had selves, I looked at my friends and siblings and they had selves, I looked at the other boys in my class and they seemed to have selves, and the girls, no question, definitely had selves. But my own self was hard to pin down. There were swirls of thoughts and feelings for sure and certainly a recurrent sense of inadequacy coupled with a wish to please and happiness when I was praised or pride when I was successful at something, but from an early age I had a nagging kind of doubt when I compared myself with those around me. Not self-doubt as much as doubts about my own completeness. How I seemed from the inside did not match up with how other people appeared from the outside. Was I who I was supposed to be, or was I somehow wanting? There wasn't much I could do with this question; I pretty much had to bury it and just pretend.

Now that I am a psychiatrist and have been treating people for forty years, I know that these kinds of feelings are far from unique. In one form or another, they might even be the norm. Psychotherapists have come up with different explanations for their ubiquity and given the feelings different names, but beneath all of the various theories, the felt insecurity seems remarkably similar. Freud, who uncovered the fact that sexual feelings are present in childhood and often directed at one's parents, saw it mostly in terms of eros. As he explained in his theory of the Oedipus complex, young children are cognizant of their genital inferiority vis-à-vis their grown parents. As consciousness dawns in a four-to-six-year-old child, he proposed, so does a feeling of inadequacy.

The next generation of psychoanalysts was not content to look solely through a libidinal lens. They focused on the same felt sense of insufficiency but tied it to even earlier developmental struggles. Some thought that relentless self-criticism, self-loathing, and low self-esteem were the result of aggression turned back on oneself. This theory focused on the unbridled anger of an infant or young child whose caregivers were somehow deficient. Murderous rage for the very people who are most necessary for one's survival creates a problem. Were it to be successful, even in fantasy, the result would be devastating. Who would be left to take care of us? So the solution is to split off the anger and turn it back on oneself. There must be something wrong with me, the argument goes, or I would not be treated so callously. Rage against the self is an attempt to solve a frustrating problem. It protects loved ones who are not only loved but also hated. Therapists who work within this paradigm look to the transference relationship to help a person heal. Encouraging a patient to articulate angry feelings toward the therapist is often a useful way of unpacking some of that stored energy that has heretofore only been able to express itself against the self. From this perspective, it is an achievement to be ambivalent, to hate those who are also loved without turning the hatred back on oneself.

Other therapists were not satisfied to see either desire or destruction as primary. They focused on the underlying feelings of emptiness instead. They saw these feelings as internalized remnants of deficiencies in adequate attention, signs of an absence in early life where there should have been a presence. A "good-enough" parent is able to "hold" a child empathically, helping them to be comfortable with themselves and with their feelings and to trust in a nurturing relationship that is there to back the child up. This is the heart of what has become known in the field as "attachment theory." When parents are too intrusive, too abandoning, or too chaotic, the theory goes, a child is forced to compensate to the best of the child's ability. This often means the creation of a "false" or "caretaker" self, precociously created by the immature mind to manage an otherwise impossible situation. Beneath this mind object—superficially constructed and often held together by obsessive and overly rigid rituals—lies an emptiness that reflects care that was not given, a void that stands in for a trust that was never really established.

All of these theories, so cogent and persuasive, treat underlying feelings of doubts about the self as pathological and seek to explain them by not so obliquely finding someone or something to blame. As you can see from the various examples recounted in this book, I have found each of these models helpful in individual cases. But I do not think it necessary to pathologize the entire phenomenon of doubts about the self. Who gets out of their childhood intact? When we presume that a core self exists, we are forced to consider intimations of "no self" as signs of emotional illness or developmental lapses. An industry has been made out of blaming one's mother for such feelings, as if their very existence is proof of a parent's deficiency. The Buddha's teachings run counter to this tendency to find fault. He normalized feelings of inadequacy and threw responsibility back onto the individual to sort them out. He taught mindfulness as a method of probing the self and found that impartial attention to moment-to-moment experience yields surprising but predictable insights into the self's contingent and relational nature. These insights, which precipitate spontaneously out of concentrated attention and mindful reflection, make abundantly clear that our habitual efforts to defend ourselves against our intrinsic groundlessness make things even worse. As Samuel Beckett once put it, the ego, minister of dullness, is also an agent of security.

If we can assume that the Buddha knew what he was talking about, his insights upend much of the conventional logic that our current models of psychological health are based upon. If inklings of no self are not necessarily signs and symptoms of developmental deficits but perhaps windows into an underlying truth, how are we to proceed? I have found, far from rejecting the various psychoanalytic theories outlined above, that there is much to recommend them. They chart the perils and pitfalls of what might be called the psychological birth of the individual person and describe the psychic compromises, and creative adjustments, that our need to individuate entails. In detailing what can go wrong, they describe one end of a spectrum we are all part of, whether we suffer from early relational failures or not.

But the Buddhist view is that "good-enough" can never be

good enough, that there is always a leftover feeling of something missing, something wrong, something hard to face, or something out of reach, and that this can be beneficial, as it prompts a search for the real. Even with good-enough upbringing and the consolidation of what might be called a good-enough self, according to the Buddha's logic, there will still be disquiet, confusion, and insecurity because we are all instinctively struggling to be something (independent, solid, coherent, and self-sufficient) we can never be. Even in healthy personality development, we emerge from childhood defending against the underlying truth of how contingent, provisional, and dependent we actually are. The persistence of such feelings, far from being a symptom of parental failures (even if there have been such failures), is actually the seed of wisdom. Fighting against them only rigidifies our defenses and isolates us further. Acknowledging the emptiness that frightens us, whatever its source may be, is the key to a deeper, and truer, understanding. The emptiness that we fear is not really empty. When it is successfully turned into an object of awareness, it reveals itself to be vast, luminous, and reassuringly, albeit mysteriously, alive.

In many of the sessions that follow, you will see me continue to wrestle with my patients' inadequacies from a number of different angles. At certain points I sound like a traditional psychodynamic therapist, unpacking the childhood origins of a patient's persistent negativity. At other times, I continue to offer explicit meditation instruction, hoping to guide someone away from their mind object with its recurrent loops of shame and blame. In still others I am reaching for something else, something my years of meditative practice have inched into my consciousness, the sense that there is an accessible vitality, present from birth, underlying our accrued personalities. In these more unconventional sessions, I use whatever I can to break through a patient's defenses or to shine a light on a patient's unexplored natural intelligence. There is no "one size fits all" in therapy. And yet, despite the infinite variation that exists in individual scenarios, running through each conversation is my conviction that the sound of one hand is available to all, even when they are not listening.

INSIGHT

A monk asked, "What is Buddha?"
The Master said, "Who are you?"

CHAO-CHOU, *Recorded Sayings*, #429

Tom and Willa · 7/10/19: 10:30 a.m. and 4:00 p.m.

have intense conversations today with two longtime patients who both tell me about incidents of sexual abuse when they were thirteen years old, pivotal events in their lives that had heretofore gone undiscussed. My morning patient is a forty-year-old man with thirteen-year-old twin daughters. Tom grew up overseas, the fourth child of a large extended family. He came to this country after university to work in the tech industry. He had a dream while on vacation that was actually a dream within a dream. Somewhere in my past I was told that dreams within dreams are especially noteworthy, that they often convey truth directly. I don't know whether this is really true, but it is in my mind as I listen to Tom's story. Tom begins the session by telling me that this was a dream he was unable to tell his wife about, that it was too shameful to reveal. In the dream within the dream he was masturbating. When he woke from that dream, still asleep, he found himself in another dream molesting his daughter. He woke from this dream with a start with his heart pounding. Telling me the dream leads him, in short order, to tell me about his uncle who would often share a room with him on family excursions when he was growing up. This uncle also sometimes hosted him and his cousin for sleepovers.

On one occasion, Tom and his cousin were sleeping on the floor on either side of his uncle. "We could all masturbate together," his uncle suggested out of the blue. "I mean, everyone does it; it's not a big deal." Tom and his cousin politely declined. The man continued. "Do you guys know about blow jobs?" he inquired. "I mean, I'm not gay or anything, but I could show you how they feel so you would have some experience." Again, uncomfortably, they said no. Another time, when camping in the countryside, Tom came upon his uncle masturbating. "Come see," he said. "We all do it. Don't be a prude." Tom kept these encounters to himself. As far as I know, they went no further, but they upset and confused him in a way he has never talked about.

Thinking of my patient Willa, I told him about women who were abused as girls, about how those experiences robbed them of the natural unfolding of their sexuality, of the sense of discovery, excitement, and agency that optimally accompanies the blossoming of one's erotic life. Early traumatic sexual experiences soil the whole thing. They are confusing because they can be arousing even while they are disturbing and they often lead, as in Tom's case, to a prolonged shame-filled silence about the actual events. Tom is a bright and attractive man who had meaningful relationships before marrying. He worries in the session that, somehow, some of his reluctance to commit himself wholeheartedly might be rooted in this time.

I wonder out loud whether, as he gets close to someone, his need to keep these early uncomfortable experiences private might lead him to pull away. There is a need to be vulnerable when one becomes intimate, to disclose one's secrets to a trusted partner in order to be close and to be real. Perhaps, I suggest, it has been difficult for him, sitting on these shame-inducing memories, to open up. I remind him that he began the session by saying that he could never tell these dreams to his wife. He nods and mentions that his daughters are now the same age he was at the time of his uncle's advances.

Later that day, Willa tells me about how she went with her

family to Buenos Aires for six months when she was thirteen and was sent to Catholic school there. She got her period on the day they arrived and remembers coming into her parents' room with blood dripping down her legs. In Catholic school they had to sit up straight at wooden desks and fold their hands in a certain way and wear white gloves to mass. But on the day John F. Kennedy was killed she forgot her gloves and was not allowed into the special service for him. While the school was strict, her travel to and from the school was anything but. "That's where the trouble with men began," she tells me. Men were all over her on the bus and the street, touching her, groping her, feeling her body, making crude comments. "Argentinian men are different," her mother told her when she tried to describe things to her. The following year, Willa's father began to secretly fondle her in her bed at night. She has told me about this previously but has never talked about the earlier time in Argentina before today.

· · ·

That evening, I had dinner with my former therapist and current friend, Michael Vincent Miller. I told him about the two sessions, about how it can take so many years for certain things to come out. I have enormous respect for Michael's therapeutic acumen. He helped me a lot as my therapist and has guided me for years while becoming a real friend, and I have referred many patients to him. In the past fifteen years, he has begun to meditate, and we now share an interest in how seamlessly the two disciplines of Buddhism and psychotherapy can fit together. "You know what makes Buddhism and therapy similar?" he asked me. I waited for him to tell me. "They both aim for the restoration of innocence after experience."

I could never have formulated it like that, I told him, but it struck me as absolutely true. Completely counterintuitive, yet absolutely true. We are educated to think that experience is what matters, that we must learn from experience, that experience is what makes us mature. But I want my patients not to be weighed down by their experience. Can they be open to what happened to them without feeling that they are somehow to blame? Can they own their attractiveness, their beauty, and their erotic potential without being perpetually tarnished by early abusive encounters? In one way or another, we are all broken by experience and could easily spend our lives trying to come to terms with it. But there is something more important for us to do, and Michael had his finger on the pulse of it. The restoration of innocence after experience. I realized some time after our dinner that he had been pointing at the moon.

Jean · 7/12/19: 9:00 a.m.

J ean returns for another session. It is a hot summer day. "You know what you said that really helped me?" she asks midway through the visit. "When you talked about Jesus. I really thought about that. What it means to sacrifice, to be a sacrifice. Not to make it all about me." Her mood is notably lighter.

. . .

Upon reading this over a year later, Jean sent me an email that read, in part, as follows:

> The one thing I remember from the session in which we talked about Jesus that stuck with me is when you said, "You ARE Jesus." That truly dislodged my identification with shame and humiliation. As you point out, I didn't really get it, but I trust you and just let it in. Dislodged, disoriented me to self, and freed me up.

I can't quite believe that I was *that* bold, but she is probably right. Her memory is likely better than mine.

Beth · 7/16/19: 1:30 p.m.

Beth admits she is pushing it with her food refusal. She never eats breakfast and rarely has lunch, unless she is meeting someone. She is vegan and allergic to dairy and wheat; she cooks other foods for her family but her diet is mostly vegetables. She has just given herself a B_{12} shot, obtained from her physician, and her folic acid level is low, so she is taking replenishments. Otherwise, her health is good but she knows she is entering dangerous territory. She likes the empty feeling that comes when she hasn't eaten in a while; she knows this feeling is addictive, that it gives her some kind of power. Indeed, she is a strong and capable woman, busy with work and family most of the time.

This is familiar territory in our discussions. I know her patterns. She has an idea that I should encourage her to broaden her food choices at dinner, maybe add a little quinoa or lentils to the vegetables. I focus on lunch instead. I know that many people have a formula for when and how and what they eat. I eat variations of the same breakfast every morning, for instance, yogurt with fruit and raisins and a few nuts or some granola. Beth has her dinner routine down. It centers on roasted beets and can include other vegetables as the season permits. I tell her that many people live this way: in Africa people center their diet on cassava, in Egypt on pita bread, etc. She admits that for many years she imposed a lunch of yogurt and an apple on herself and that when her children were young she ate a bagel and cottage cheese every night for dinner. This worked to keep her healthy but now those foods, except for the apple, seem disgusting to her.

What could she eat for lunch? I want to know. "Salad?" she ventures, but I can tell she is going to fight me on this. Usually she is willing to take my advice, but the food thing is especially charged. I point this out to her. I remember having had this conversation with her before. Therapy goes round and round but here we are again. I make my case. The only way to make a change is to impose a schedule on yourself, I say, as if you were somebody else. "There's no time for lunch," she tells me. She's in meetings all day. "Don't you go to the bathroom?" I ask. "Hardly," she replies with a wry smile. "How long would it take to eat a little food you bring with you?" I ask. "Soup," she says. "I like soup." I tell her that we are going to continue to talk about this. She is gracious when she leaves, gathering her bags, sort of thanking me, I think, but I am not sure what we have accomplished.

. . .

Reflecting on this session, I am reminded once again of the concept of the mind object, both Beth's and my own. By focusing too much on the particulars of Beth's food issues and trying too hard to make a change in her behavior, I was getting drawn back in to her closed world instead of helping her break out of it. I had lost track of Michael Vincent Miller's essential point and was therefore, not surprisingly, sacrificing innocence for experience.

Over the course of our treatment, I have gotten to know Beth very well. Her food issues began in early adolescence when she found herself increasingly alone and unable to connect with her mother as reliably as she wished. The only way to find maternal approval was to give the impression of having everything together: to play sports, be thin, and look good. Not needing her mother was the closest she could come to connecting with her.

This was a setup for the perfectionism that was still bothering her.

In his piece on the mind object, Adam Phillips writes of the scenario Beth's upbringing was missing.

> *With good-enough maternal care, in Winnicott's particular sense of these terms, the mind would be, as it were, an ordinary participant in one's psychic life rather than an excessive preoccupation, a continuation of the mother one can take for granted rather than a substitute that one is continually rigging up.*

By dwelling exclusively on Beth's diet, I was unconsciously supporting the substitute she was rigging up rather than helping her find another way into herself. In Winnicott's way of thinking, the missing piece had to do with her mother's attention, with being held. Not necessarily being physically held (although that would have been nice) but the kind of holding one feels when one's internal life is taken seriously by another.

> *In this state mothers become able to put themselves into the infant's shoes, so to speak. That is to say, they develop an amazing capacity for identification with the baby, and this makes them able to meet the basic needs of the infant in a way that no machine can imitate, and no teaching can reach. May I take this for granted when I go on to state that the prototype of all infant care is holding? And I mean human holding. I am aware that I am stretching the meaning of the word "holding" to its limits, but I suggest that this is an economical statement, and true enough.*

Beth had turned food, or lack of food, into a maternal substitute that she could legislate from her mind. But the holding function was still lacking. Beth managed her anxieties by exerting control over what she ate, but this sometimes left her feeling tense, empty, or bloated. Over time, I realized that she needed me to serve as the holding environment rather than colluding too actively with her issues around food. I learned this gradually, and it took a fair amount of restraint on my part to pull it off. My desire to help and to fix was an ever-present obstacle to the holding environment Beth really needed.

This was a lesson I had also learned from meditation, and it was something I needed to bring more actively into my work as a therapist. When mindfulness is applied too rigidly, it can reinforce the mind object rather than help it let go. When it is applied gently, however, it serves a holding function, allowing one's inner life to be taken seriously, but not too seriously, much as a mother treats a fussing baby. It is this kind of holding that allows one to see how dominant the overgrowth of the mental function has become, and this is one of the first important insights that mindfulness can yield. When Ram Dass reminded me that I was not who I thought I was, this is what he was suggesting. Thoughts occur without a thinker; we come to identify with them but the identification is extra. Our innocence comes from a place that has nothing to do with how we think about ourselves.

April · 7/18/19: 11:30 a.m.

April is a successful advertising executive who suffers from terrible shyness and anxiety. She comes for a session after having had lunch with a company chairman who wants to hire her. She is upset with herself for how nervous she was during their conversation, and she is berating herself for dressing inappropriately for the meeting. He was perfectly attired in a tailored T-shirt and trim dark European-style jacket that he kept on despite the summer heat. She wore a jumper that her assistant had rolled her eyes at as she went out the door. "I just can't get it right," she complains. The lunch went fine but April was aware of her anxiety throughout and fears that she never really broke through with the chairman, that he will have found her to be fake, uptight, defensive, or shy.

"I have such a hard time relaxing," she says. "With men especially, and if I'm attracted to them it's worse." There is a longing in April to be known, to be reached, and to be seen, but she is frightened of it at the same time and cannot help but throw up obstacles seemingly in spite of herself. She might spill something in such a situation, for instance. When immersed in her work, April is the opposite. She can be funny, irreverent, spontaneous, innovative, and free. We talk about the paradox. When she loses herself, she is being herself. "It's very Buddhist," I say. "The self you think you are is not really you. The real you comes out when you are being someone you're not." April is lucky to have such experiences through her work. Many shy people never find a way of surrendering their false selves. April reflects back to her teenage years. "I had a high voice in high school because of how nervous I was," she tells me. "I remember one of the girls saying to me, 'You're very pretty but your voice is weird.' I stopped talking after that." She means what she says. She actually did stop talking for the better part of her senior year. I am aware of that aspect of her history but have never heard what led up to it.

Later in the session, I tell April that her anxiety, while severe, is not off the charts. "Lots of people are anxious in those kinds of situations," I say. "You tend to think you are the only one." "Not like this, Mark!" she exclaims. "And you're not anxious like this," she adds.

I tell April that when I was young I used to stammer. It was especially bad when we had to go around the room in class and introduce ourselves. I would become intensely anxious, rehearsing my name to myself in anticipation of my turn to speak, and then have to push against some invisible force in order to get my well-rehearsed words out. When I was nine years old, I was mercifully helped by a speech therapist my parents found for me who distracted me with board games while telling me stories of grown-ups who stuttered worse than I did.

Mrs. Stanton, the speech therapist, taught me to distract myself with secret movements nobody could see or with tiny adjustments in the words I used. If I lifted my foot and placed it down hard on the floor just before I had to say something, I was often able to speak more easily. Or if I said, "*My name is* Mark," instead of simply saying, "Mark," my words would somehow flow more gracefully. I learned to anticipate the approach of a difficult word and adjust myself at the last minute. By the time I was in seventh grade, I could successfully hide the internal battle that had long bedeviled me. I don't think anyone ever suspected that

I was still afflicted, in a silent way, long after. While my stammering became invisible to the outside world, I continued to be aware of it. The trauma of saying my name in the classroom never entirely left me. April has a hard time believing me when I tell her I still am very conscious of it in social situations. But I am.

In some way, this is what I want to convey to April. We all wish we could just eliminate the dysfunctional parts of us. In pushing against what we do not like in ourselves, we get more knotted up. The shame, discomfort, embarrassment, and pain just reinforce the hold the whole thing has over us, and, in the process, we over-identify with an aspect of ourselves that does not need to define us so completely. Seeing this over-identification clearly is what I think of as insight.

April's success in work has given her a way of getting in touch with a more spontaneous version of herself, but it is still split off from who she thinks she is. Who she truly is encompasses both aspects, the shy anxious one and the funny free one. A bit more humor and compassion is what I want April to grow into. Insights in meditation have shown me that it is possible.

. . .

This is yet another session with the specter of a punitive superego hanging over it. April's shyness is probably built in, a function of her temperament. But her self-criticism was learned. How she learned it, and who she learned it from, we do not know. Therapy could take a good deal of time trying to get answers to these questions, and the answers might be interesting and even potentially helpful, but it is much more important, I think, that April understand that she could learn to pull back from a complete identification with the self-critical voices in her head. My speech therapist did give me tricks that helped me deal with my stammer, but she did something even more useful. She let me see that I was not alone with the problem, that other people had it, too, and that it was not a sign of something terribly flawed in my personality. It might be an affliction, but it did not need to cast a shadow over my entire sense of myself.

I wanted something similar for April. It was time for her Freudian superego, "a censor, a judge, a dominating and frustrating father," to take off its mask and reveal itself as the clown it truly was. Mrs. Stanton taught me not to get bogged down in my self-critical thoughts but to focus on meeting the everyday challenges of speaking in public. In a certain way, by distracting me with board games and showing me that I was not broken, she accomplished a version of what Michael Vincent Miller had suggested was the most important thing: she returned me, at least temporarily, to a state of innocence after experience. Insight meditation, when it came along, reinforced this for me. It showed me how to make my experience into an object of awareness rather than letting it program me from the recesses of my mind. I have found this endlessly uplifting and hope that April might too.

Ricki · 7/23/19: 4:00 p.m.

guess I'm really grieving," Ricki tells me as she begins to weep. The session has just begun. Ricki's lover of fifteen years died after a short and unexpected illness several years ago and she has been distraught ever since. They called each other their soul mates although neither of them was particularly prone to new age language. By all accounts, their relationship was a solid, loving, and very fulfilling one, coming as it did in middle age after each of them had children with previous partners. I am not so sure Ricki is grieving, however. Her language suggests otherwise.

One of the things my own therapist taught me was to pay careful attention to the words people use as they describe their experience. "How in touch are they?" he would always want to know. When a patient begins a declarative sentence with "I guess," my ears go on alert. Often, these phrases are used out of habit, and if I stop and ask people to repeat or reflect on what they have just said, they will have no memory of using the given language. "I guess" is deployed unawares, but it telegraphs an unconscious meaning that an attuned therapist can often pick up on. What does she mean by "I guess"? Is she guessing? Does she know? Or is there something else going on that is harder to talk about, something that might fit more acceptably under the rubric of grief but not be grief at all?

Much of this is running through my mind as Ricki settles into her chair. "I don't want to live anymore—I know I'm not supposed to say that—but if it's going to be like this forever, I don't," she announces. I go on alert; Ricki is not a suicidal patient, I have never had an ounce of concern about that, but this sounds serious. I make some gentle inquiries and let my suspicions of her grief pass for the moment. A slew of difficulties flow from Ricki's mouth. She was out at the ocean for a month alone, something she had never actually done before, and it was lonely and difficult. The best thing about it was picking clams with her bare toes on the beach and then cooking and eating them. There was some joy there but it was bittersweet, as there was no one to enjoy it with. Plus, she wasn't sure she was going to have enough money to retire on, she had only X amount saved, and how was that ever going to be enough? She and her boyfriend had not married, and he had left all his money to his grown children. What kind of help was that? Things were rough in her business, she was working full time but not making the kind of money she was used to. And there were issues with her aging mother as well as with her bipolar father. "I'm wishing for a miracle," she cries, and she begins to sob.

"A miracle," I say. "Okay, I have just the thing." A patient of mine had brought back some prasad from her guru's ashram in India that had been blessed by a holy person. Prasad is food, bits of sugary candy in this case, that has been consecrated, or offered to the gods, and then returned to the disciples to eat. My patient brought me some as a gift, and I keep it on my bookshelf in a ceramic jar that my wife made long ago that also has a load of pennies inside. On rare occasions when a patient is asking for a miracle, I will take out the little plastic bag and count out a couple of sacred morsels. Sometimes people take the offering seriously and sometimes they see it as a joke, but, when I give it to them—and I don't do this often—I do it with the hope that it might actually help someone open their heart. Ricki looks at me as if I am crazy. "What are these?" she asks suspiciously before placing them in her mouth. But she takes them and it provides a pause. She gives a little smile as she sucks and toys at them with her tongue.

I take the opportunity to question Ricki in a way that feels out of character, but I have to do something to get inside the wall she is putting up. There is a barrage of emotion coming from her: sadness, tears, anger, fear, threats of suicide, feelings of despair, but I feel neither much of an actual back-and-forth nor much rapport. The gift of the prasad has made an opening though.

"*Are* you grieving?" I ask her. "I'm not so sure," I continue. "My instinct is that you're not. You're doing something, but what? Searching for security, it seems like. You're alone, not enough wealth, your industry is failing, and your partner didn't leave you any money. You must be angry with him for that. I hear a lot of pain but not so much grief." Ricki looks at me with a puzzled expression, much as she had when I pulled out the magic medicine. "There is some grieving in the clam story though," I add. "Nobody to share the thrill of it with."

"What do you mean?" says Ricki. "I'm not supposed to be in pain?"

"My sense is you can feel the grief when something unexpected, pleasant, and new happens, and you think, 'Oh, he would have liked this so much.' At moments like that you re-member him, in all the senses of that word, you take him back into you, you miss him because he would have loved it too. That can be painful, but it's a different kind of pain. It's certainly not joyful but there's something sweet in it, a fondness in memory that allows grief to come." I don't say much more but I have the sense that Ricki hears me. She is putting on a show of grief, I think to myself, but isn't allowing herself to miss her partner, to still love her partner, in all the little ways she could. I am gratified that Ricki seems to hear what I am saying without taking offense. She makes eye contact with me as she gets up to leave. There are no parting words, but I feel more of a connection than at the beginning of the hour.

. . .

The next evening I got an email from Ricki with the heading "Your magic placebo pill." It was sent at 10:45 p.m. In its entirety it read:

> Hi—Just wanted you to know that about 10 minutes ago, for no apparent reason, my headspace and heart space totally shifted and I felt normal in the sense of just feeling good/normal for the first time and I don't know how long. I doubt it will stay steadily, but you really should be sure to get as many of your magic pills as possible for your patience! And patients lol.

Ricki's email made me smile and think of a favorite Japanese haiku. This one dates from the beginning of the eighteenth century and was written by a painter and poet named Nakagawa Otsuyu:

Cry of the deer—
where at its depths
are antlers?

I have no idea what Otsuyu was thinking when he wrote this haiku, but the spirit of it, at least in my mind, applied equally to our session. Ricki, like the deer, had much to cry about, but there was still something missing, something more to be discovered in the depths of her emotional body. Where were her antlers?

Grief is a strange animal. We have lots of ideas of what it is supposed to look like, but when we are actually faced with acute loss, the way we grieve is rarely the way we imagine we should. In this respect, grief is a lot like the self. It is never as clear and distinct as we think it should be.

Will and Linnéa · 8/1/19: 11:30 a.m. in Bar Harbor, Maine (early in my two-week August vacation)

I am in Maine with my son Will and his girlfriend Linnéa, a visual artist from Stockholm, who are both twenty-nine years of age. To my surprise, they have asked me to give them some meditation instruction. We sit in the screened-in porch adjacent to the kitchen, looking out at the water. There are distant ocean sounds of lobster boats coming and going, seagull screeches, and the occasional noisy crow. I'm a little nervous, taken out of my father role, and wanting to give them something they will find useful. I have given basic meditation instruction many times, and I fall back on what I have done previously.

Close your eyes. Sit still in a comfortable position with your back relatively straight. Settle into your posture, into your body, letting your attention open up to whatever you find. Try not to try too hard, that just makes it more difficult, there's an element of surrender to mindfulness, allowing things to unfold by themselves as you put your usual self to one side. Pay attention to the sensation of the breath as it enters and leaves the nostrils or to the rising and falling of the abdomen as you breathe in and out. Notice the sensations, or the lack of sensations, no matter what you have the sense of, when you are inhaling and when you are exhaling. And notice that after you exhale, before you inhale again, there is often a pause. In that pause, it's helpful to have something specific to pay attention to, the sensation of your two lips touching or your seat against the chair. You can use a mental note or label to help keep you on point. "In" when you breathe in, "out" when you breathe out, and "touching, touching" when you are in between. The bulk of your attention stays on the direct physical sensations, but you can use the label in the back of your mind. And the meditation is not about how long you can stay with the breath, it's about recognizing when your mind wanders (which it will do) and bringing the awareness back to the breath when you notice it has wandered, even if it strays again a minute later.

I say all this in about five minutes and then sit silently with them for a bit. Once or twice I peek and they seem to be into it.

This is part one, I say. In part two, you let in the rest of your experience. Rather than focusing on the breath as the central object, pay attention in the same way to whatever is most obvious, most dominant, in your field of awareness. It might be outer sensations like the sounds of the water, the wind, or the birds, or it might be inner sensations in the body or thoughts or feelings. But let them stream through you, noticing when you attach or hold on or start to get caught up and then releasing yourself from whatever it is that has held you. You can toggle back and forth, foreground and background, between the breath and the rest of your experience. When it gets too complex or difficult to follow, come back to the breath. Let yourself play around. But first and foremost, notice how things are always shifting, always changing. Allow yourself to feel the flow of your own experience.

We sit like that for about fifteen or twenty minutes. They like it and ask if we can do it again sometime. Will says that it is much easier to feel the rising and falling of the abdomen when lying down, that when he sits up, the breath at the nostrils is better for him. Linnéa says it was relaxing. I caution her that it needn't always be relaxing, that sometimes it can be emotionally difficult or uncomfortable and that this isn't a sign of doing it wrong. The point is to relate to everything in an even manner, not trying to make it be one thing or another.

. . .

When the Buddha talked about insight, he framed it around recognition of what he called "the three marks of existence": dukkha, anicca, and anatta. Dukkha, as we have already seen, is the suffering that is hard to face. At its most extreme it refers to death, old age, and illness but it encompasses any kind of loneliness, frustration, or dissatisfaction. "Anatta" means "no self," and refers to the insubstantial nature of that which we wish could be concrete, permanent, and unchanging, like ourselves. "Anicca" means "impermanence." Everything is in flux, the wheel of fortune is always turning, or, as the late poet Gregory Corso was fond of saying, deliberately mangling a famous gnomic statement of Heraclitus, "You can't step in the same river once." Insight meditation is designed to counter resistance to these three marks of existence. In its focus on clinging as the source of suffering, it counts this resistance (called "ignorance" or "delusion" in Buddhist parlance) as the principal object of investigation. "Insight" means seeing resistance to the three marks up close. The Buddha's first promise is that seeing it clearly lets the resistance dissolve. His second promise is that the three marks of existence are not as frightening as they seem. They actually point to a freedom that our minds have a hard time understanding, a freedom in which we are not separate and suffering individuals locked into our own little realities but instead are inextricably and interdependently bound to a greater, and ever-evolving, whole.

In teaching meditation to Will and Linnéa, I tried to subtly introduce them to the three marks. Dukkha was implicit. Why else would they even be interested in meditation? Anicca is the easiest of the three to understand. We know that things are always changing. But it is important when learning mindfulness to, from the beginning, attend to how everything really is always in process. It is tempting to fasten onto whatever comes up: the sound, the thought, the memory, the plan, rather than allowing it to come and go as it will do if left alone. Anatta is the most obscure of the three. But mindful awareness does reveal how insubstantial things are. Once the mind object begins to lose its dominion, experience becomes much more porous.

Linnéa · 8/6/19: 4:30 p.m. High tide,
Great Spruce Head Island, Maine

We are now on an island off the coast of Maine for a week, an island with no electricity or cars where we have to bring our own food for the entire seven days. There are six of us, my wife and me, Will and Linnéa, and my daughter Sonia and her boyfriend Aron. There is a lagoon that cuts into this island where, at high tide, we can swim. The cold ocean water flows in over mudflats that are warmed by the sun, and when high tide hits on a sunny day it is wonderful. Linnéa and I run to catch a late afternoon swim, and when we get there it is empty, quiet, and beautiful. The sunlight is already slanting and the water is glowing green.

"We can meditate for a bit," I suggest, "at least until other people come." Since that morning in Bar Harbor there has been no time, even though we are all on vacation. We find spots that support us, Linnéa on a flat rock close to the water and me on a grassy knoll leaning against a young birch tree. I say very little, we just sit, allowing inner and outer experience to mix with the breath. There are birds, a breeze, the lapping of the water, and, soon enough, ants crawling across my lower limbs. After about five minutes, the sounds of people traipsing up the nearby path come, but they seem distant and we do not move. The people sounds rise and fall and then fade away. It is very pleasant. Then other people come and stay and lower themselves into the water. Linnéa and I open our eyes and talk for a moment before swimming.

This meditation is easier for Linnéa, the sounds of nature settle her mind, and I can tell she has had a pleasant experience. "You want to treat the inner and the outer the same," I remind her. "I do have these critical voices in my mind," she replies. "Repetitive and familiar. Sometimes I wonder if maybe I need them, though, to motivate me for my work." "Maybe," I say. "You get to examine them in meditation, though, seeing them from a different angle rather than just buying into them thoughtlessly. You might find other, less self-critical, motivations for your work, coming from deeper places inside of yourself."

A few minutes later, after I make it into the water, one of the other people on the island, also in the water, apologizes for disturbing us. "Sorry to intrude on your meditations," she says thoughtfully. "You didn't intrude," I reply. "You came into them. You were part of them," I add. She smiles and swims off.

· · ·

Meditating outside like this with the ants crawling over me, the sounds of the air and water all around, and the neighbors walking into "our" space put me in touch with another wonderful Japanese haiku. Kobayashi Issa (Issa means "cup of tea") was born in 1763 and is known as one of the most accomplished haiku masters in Japanese history. He led anything but an easy life, losing his mother when he was a baby and watching his three children die in infancy. Yet despite his many hardships he developed an extraordinary empathy for the natural world and all of its creatures, including even the lowliest insects. Walking away from the lagoon, I remembered the following poem of his:

I'm leaving—
now you can make love,
my flies.

Dukkha, anicca, and anatta did not stop Issa from reveling in nature's mystery. And even though *he* was leaving, he saw the insects as *his* flies. He was still a part of things even after (or maybe because of) realizing his own insubstantiality.

Menla Mountain House Retreat Center,
· **8/16/19: 9:00 p.m.** *Phoenicia, New York*

am teaching a weekend retreat with Professor Robert Thurman of Columbia University called "Getting Over Yourself: The Best of Buddhism and Psychotherapy," a version of which we have taught together (under various titles) for many years.

After my overview of the weekend and an introductory meditation in which Professor Thurman leads us (about seventy-five people) in an elaborate series of visualizations, there is time for questions before heading off to bed. One of the first questions is from a woman who says she is reading a book called *Autobiography of a Yogi* by Paramahansa Yogananda. Thurman has trouble hearing what she is saying (his hearing aids are not the best), and I repeat the name of the book for him. We are both familiar with it; it was first published in the 1940s but became very popular in the 1960s and 1970s; it depicts the spiritual adventures of a seeker named Yogananda and is credited with introducing many Westerners to the practice of yoga. The questioner wants to know about the role of the guru. It is a big part of Yogananda's story, and she wonders how important it is for her to find her own guru. A good friend, the person who gave her the book, in fact, has been telling her she needs to find her guru, that she can't proceed on her quest without one.

I tell her that Professor Thurman always says that the Tibetans say the best guru lives three valleys over. You don't want them living too close because then you begin to see all of their flaws. The guru is meant to reflect your own capacity for enlightenment. For those who have trouble believing they are already free, it is easier to imagine that someone else is. As Westerners, however, we have a rather naive view of the guru idea; we tend to think that self-proclaimed gurus are actually perfected beings (rather than imagined perfected beings), and we have the inclination to give ourselves over to them without making an accurate assessment of their strengths and weaknesses.

Professor Thurman goes in another direction in answer to her question. "The word 'guru,'" he says, "in the original Sanskrit, actually means 'heavy.' It has a paternalistic history and connotation. The heaviness sits on your forehead; it's the authority you submit to in the family and in the caste and in the culture. In Tibet, they changed the word to 'lama,' which has more of the meaning of 'chief' or 'teacher.' The real guru," Thurman continues, suddenly becoming very intense, "is your own intelligence." He looks at the woman in the audience and repeats the phrase. "Your own intelligence. In some forms of Buddhism," he explains, "they made a new concept, called a 'kalyana mitra' in Sanskrit, which means something like 'spiritual friend,' someone who cares about you enough to guide you in a good direction, someone who is motivated by love. The good guru," Thurman emphasizes, "puts the responsibility back on you. If you find one who says, 'Oh, you've finally returned, now you are home, I have it all, this is one-stop shopping, give me everything you have,' make sure to leave *that* guru behind. Run for the hills! Their agenda is not your agenda."

• • •

I was glad to have the concept of the spiritual friend raised in this context. Teaching these kinds of workshops is often an invitation for precisely the kind of idealization I was warning my questioner about. Therapists are trained to not take their patients' idealization of them too personally—this is where the concept of transference is so very helpful—but even well-trained therapists can find the pressure challenging. Most spiritual teachers have very little understanding of transference, and there have been endless stories during my lifetime of self-proclaimed gurus taking advantage of their credulous Western followers. I found Professor Thurman's comments very clarifying. That we could inspire people to shake off the paternalistic heaviness of the guru concept, while encouraging them to believe in their own intelligence, seemed like a real contribution.

Brad · 8/20/19: 1:30 p.m.

Brad is upset with his husband for yelling at him for every little thing. They have a nice life, grown children, cats and dogs, and a big house to take care of. The other day his husband yelled at him for throwing out a plastic bottle he had been drinking out of that still had some water left in it. Brad is right, his husband does criticize him a lot, and he has a hard time with it, but not for the reasons one might expect. His husband's criticisms affect him deeply; they play into ways he has felt bad about himself for a long time. When he is yelled at like this, he doesn't just get irritated; he takes it in as if there is really something wrong with him. I am just on the other side of teaching at Menla with Professor Thurman, and the weekend is still big in my head. I tell Brad something of what we talked about on the retreat, not about the guru thing but about the tendency people have to "absolutize" their emotional experiences. By "absolutizing" I mean turning it into a fixed object, relating to it as an "absolute" truth, and seeing it in isolation instead of in context. We were talking about anatta, about the relevance of "no self" in everyday life. Anatta challenges fixed notions of the self that limit or constrain us, as in "I am *this* kind of person or *that* kind of person," as if we could ever know ourselves "absolutely."

Brad internalizes his husband's criticisms and uses them to reinforce an "absolute" idea about what is wrong with him. He makes the criticism into a defect in his own character rather than seeing how prickly his husband can be. I point this out. It's not that he is unaware of being angry back. He is. But he is doing something in addition. It strikes me that Brad is protecting his husband. If Brad is the bad one, then his husband cannot be. This good/bad way of thinking is a problem. If the husband is bad, if Brad is not at least partially responsible, he might have to seek a divorce. Brad vowed long ago to stay married and he loves his husband, despite how difficult he can be. I think the way he internalizes criticism goes way back to his childhood. There were difficulties in his parents' marriage and he suffered as a child. If he could make himself the problem, if he were the bad one, his parents would be spared. I wonder about this and tell him of my therapist Isadore From's definition of family: "The worst invention of a god that doesn't exist." "What if you could see your husband's criticisms as empty?" I ask. "Instead of giving them so much authority." "I never thought of that," he replies. "Poor guy," I say. "Creating so much bad energy around him."

. . .

In fifteenth-century Japan there lived a famous Zen master named Ikkyū Sōjun who spent much of his monastic life in a hermitage in Kyoto. He was known for his irascible nature and his refusal to play by the rules of the Zen Buddhist orthodoxy. At the age of seventy-seven he fell in love with a blind woman many years his junior and wrote a plethora of verses about their love. "Harsh, delicate, brilliant, reckless, precise, intimate, ignorant, arrogant, aloof—Ikkyū comes across as a man of simultaneously miserable self-doubt and infinite self-confidence." In addition to integrating his passion with a lifetime's accrual of spiritual understanding, Ikkyū understood emptiness, that most elusive Buddhist concept, as well as anyone ever has. Emptiness is not one of the three original marks of existence, but, as Buddhism evolved, it rose to a place of prominence. It offered another slant on anatta by emphasizing the lack of independent and concrete substantiality in persons and things. Ikkyū's poems convey his understanding in a way I was hoping Brad might appreciate. Here is one example that speaks to the notion of absolutizing that Brad and I were talking about in our session.

> oh green green willow wonderfully red flower
> but I know the colors are not there

Remember the nonaffirming negative, the Dalai Lama's description of the person wearing sunglasses, from chapter 1? Such a person grasps emptiness, seeing the colors but simultaneously knowing they are not real. Could Brad do something similar with his husband's anger? Experience it fully but not give it absolute authority? Consider it, but then let it pass through him without swallowing it, without turning it into a judgment of his character? This is the ultimate Buddhist therapeutic maneuver. The trick is not to ignore the emotion but to leave it alone, allowing it to appear in its own way, appreciating it for what it seems to be without getting taken in by it. In Ikkyū's cryptic words:

> I didn't see one thing on my trip
> but I breathed and whatever I breathed was time

When Ikkyū writes of breathing time, he is showing us the depth of his insight. His understanding of emptiness does not mean that he has disappeared. But breath and time have become one.

Lukas · 8/27/19: 12:30 p.m.

ukas, who was married shortly after gay marriage was legalized, is struggling in married life. "I love my husband but lately I've been hating him so much," he tells me with tears welling up. He remembers how happy he was on his wedding day ("the happiest day of my life") and wishes he could feel that way now. "He's always in a rush," he says. "And always looking at his phone." He tells me about a recent visit to New Orleans for a friend's wedding when he finally said something to his husband after sitting in a park on a Sunday morning watching him scroll through his device. They had one talk. He told him that he was feeling ignored, and his partner explained what was going on at work that he had to check on. After that, things changed a little. He would warn Lukas when he had to do business rather than just reaching for his phone, and that felt better.

But this little episode was telling. Lukas often equates marriage with submission. He resists speaking up when whatever he might say has the potential for creating conflict. Sex has become an issue. "I have a sense of relief when it's over." He smiles. "Like I've done my job." He pauses for a moment. "And I like the closeness," he adds. "But often it hurts, he's always in a rush." I express wonder that he has not said anything to his husband; the idea of sex hurting him gives me pain. "I don't want him to feel inadequate," he replies.

I am surprised at this response; perhaps I shouldn't be, but I am. "You're not giving him a chance," I exclaim. "He needs to learn and you are the one to teach him." The session ends with Lukas trudging out of the office. I hope we will talk about this again.

. . .

This is an example of a situation demanding more self and not less. In showing deference to his husband past the point of his own comfort, Lukas was squelching his own vital energy. His talk with his husband about his preoccupation with his phone was a good start but there was more to be done, as his continuing distress made clear.

In our culture, we often have trouble distinguishing selflessness from submission, but they are very different things. Lukas was inclined to keep his feelings bottled up, but this scenario could not go on forever. His feelings were coming out in spite of himself, and his marriage needed more contribution from his side if it was to thrive. I think Lukas wanted his husband to understand what he needed without having to articulate it. There is a risk involved in speaking up, the age-old risk of loss of love. I didn't think Lukas gave himself enough credit in his relationship; I didn't think he valued himself enough. I meant it when I told him it was up to him to educate his partner. Sex was one important theater for this kind of exchange; I doubted that it was the only one.

Sandy · 9/4/19: 10:30 a.m.

Sandy comes with a dream. She does not often come with one, but she had this dream the night before therapy and it seems important. Sandy has been having a terribly hard time since her adolescent daughter died in a fire three years ago. Her friends have been urging her, not so discreetly, to get over it and move on. She is part of an evangelical circle that accepts the notion of an afterlife, and many of the people around her have been hoping she could connect to the ongoing presence of her daughter, albeit in her new heavenly form. This has put an added pressure on Sandy and she has been struggling. If her daughter is present in an afterlife, it is a poor consolation. In her dream, a mother is shot and killed, offstage, as it were. Sandy is aware of the mother having been shot but she does not witness it directly; the dream begins with the knowledge of the mother's death. Then she is in a room with her daughter, who is alive, along with a friend of her daughter's from junior high school who is transitioning from male to female. Sandy and her daughter are counseling the friend and are of one mind. This seems an important element. They are of one mind and there is a feeling of closeness at the end of the dream.

The dream comes as a surprise to Sandy. The past week has been terrible. A good friend told her over the weekend that her daughter was getting married. She didn't just *tell* her, she went on and on about it, and Sandy grew more and more upset as her friend talked to her relentlessly on the phone. It was so unfair, she thought. She was never going to see her own daughter get married. And why did she have to hear every detail? After the phone call she was so upset that she jumped in her car and drove away with no plan. It was Labor Day weekend and the traffic was impossible. She went from one location to another and back again, weeping, and it took at least three hours for her to stop crying. Even as she was telling me, Sandy's pain became vividly alive.

It so happened that the week before, I had seen Joseph Goldstein on one of his rare visits to New York City. Joseph, as I have already mentioned, has been my teacher and friend for many years, and I prize his insights very highly. Joseph knew I was working with a number of people who had recently lost loved ones, and, without mentioning it directly, he wondered whether I was familiar with his own take on the Buddhist approach to loss. He likes to tell the story of how the Buddha reacted when his two closest disciples, Sariputta and Moggallana, died within weeks of each other. In Joseph's memory, the Buddha said it was like the moon was taken out of the sky. This is no small thing, Joseph always reminds people. The moon! At the same time, in the same discourse, the Buddha affirmed that despite the gravity of his loss, he did not find a trace of grief, lamentation, or woe in his mind or heart. All conditioned things (including us) are destined to fall apart, the Buddha reminded his audience. How could it be otherwise?

For Joseph, this potential for loss uncontaminated by grief was very important. I had heard him speak of it on several occasions, and, while I understood the point, it always felt too cold to me. I said as much to Joseph. "None of us are that enlightened," I said, "but can't grief, if held mindfully, self-liberate? We can't expect not to feel it. The problem that I often see is that people can't hold their intense feelings mindfully. Either they deny or suppress them or they act them out without really feeling what is going on." I took the Buddha's story in a slightly different way than Joseph did. To me, the grief, lamentation, and woe that the Buddha referenced describe the extra layers of resistance we throw up to protect us from the intensity of loss. The Buddha could experience it purely; most of us are unable to, at least for a good long while. We have to find a way of letting those feelings settle, which they will do, over time, if we let them.

Over the weekend, I tried to find the citation in the sutras that Joseph was referring to, but I could not locate any reference to the moon. I found the Buddha speaking of his disciples' deaths as being both like a large branch breaking off a mighty hardwood tree and like a vast emptiness. I wrote to Joseph after our conversation, and he said that someone had told him the story of the moon but that he, too, had been unable to locate it in the scriptures to verify it. But a great emptiness was close enough.

After hearing about Sandy's weekend, with Joseph's conversation in mind, I return to her dream. It began with that mysterious murder of an unspecified mother. "Hearing about your friend's daughter getting married is like you getting murdered," I propose. "You're never going to have that experience. Seeing her grow up, fall in love, get married, have children. It's terrible." Sandy looks startled. I know that people don't usually talk to her like this; everyone is always trying to make her feel better. She is left with these thoughts, and she can't easily share them with anyone. I think her dream let her say it in a disguised manner. An anonymous mother had been shot. "I experience you as more angry than sad," I tell her. I am taking a chance, but I think Sandy can deal with it. While I don't totally agree with Joseph about being able to experience loss without any add-ons, I have the sense that Sandy is protecting herself from grief by being angry. She can handle being angry; I am not so sure she can be sad. "You're definitely being deprived of what you assumed was your right as a mother, but you act like it was an assault on you personally, like you're the one who was killed."

I remark to Sandy that the thing she and her daughter agree about in the dream, the thing they are of one mind about, is helping the friend transition. Maybe Sandy is the one transitioning? And maybe this is the way to feel close to her daughter again. Not by trying to feel her as still alive but by agreeing with her on the fact of her death.

. . .

Two hundred years ago, in 1819, the Japanese poet Issa (he of the lovemaking flies) composed a remarkable document chronicling what, in many ways, was his happiest year. He was fifty-seven. Entitled *The Year of My Life*, the work is part autobiography, part poetry, part Zen diary, part observation of nature, and, often, a combination of all the above. In recounting his experience, Issa did not shy away from its painful aspects: he had a terrible relationship with his stepmother, for example, with whom he had a prolonged and bitter struggle for much of his life.

> *I was the first-born—the first flower to blossom—in our family, and yet I have been relegated to a place beside the late-born weeds. I have been nippled by the chill wind that blows from the slopes of the "stepmother mountain," and I have not known a single day in which I might rejoice in freedom, beneath the open sky. It is a wonder to me that the thin thread of my life has endured these fifty-seven long years— Ah, dear chestnut tree, forgive me! I had not thought of passing on to you the pattern of my own ill-fated life when I planted you inside my garden.*

No stranger to grief, Issa took refuge both in the Buddha's teachings about suffering and in the fulsomeness of the natural world, impervious as it was to his personal struggles. As an adult, he wandered throughout Japan: poet, philosopher, and Zen priest rolled into one. In 1813, at the age of fifty-one, he finally made peace with his stepmother, settled in his home village, and married a twenty-seven-year-old woman who bore him three children, all of whom perished within a year of their births. The first two babies, both boys, died within a month of being born, but the third, a girl named Sato, lived for a full year, bringing Issa and his wife tremendous joy before dying just past her first birthday. Her year of life was the year that Issa documented in his book *The Year of My Life*. His most famous haiku is one he claimed to have written in the aftermath of his daughter's passing, although it is now known that he actually composed an initial version of it after the death of his firstborn son. I remembered the final iteration of this poem sometime after my session with Sandy:

The world of dew
Is the world of dew,
And yet . . .
And yet . . .

Issa's poem resolved my quibble with Joseph. Yes, this world is impermanent. Yes, that which we take to be so substantial cannot deliver all that we demand of it. Yes, emptiness is the best counterweight to our inclination to cling to people and things that cannot last. But the love that binds us to each other has its own reality. Issa's "And yet . . ." makes clear how profound loss feels, even when one has a firm grasp of emptiness. The Tibetan Buddhist tradition makes a similar point in one of its best known teaching stories. After the death of the child of a revered lama, his students saw him weeping inconsolably. "Why are you crying?" they asked him. "You told us that this world is illusion!" "Ah, yes," the lama replied. "And the loss of a child is the greatest illusion."

This was something Sandy and I could agree upon.

Willa · 9/11/19: 4:00 p.m.

Willa begins her session by explaining how difficult it was for her to attend her good friend's seventy-fifth birthday party. She had gone to high school with him and had remained friends with him and his wife all this time. But she hates parties and had to force herself to go. "I feel like a nothingburger at those things," she says, "so much of nothing." I am not sure I hear her correctly. A nothingburger? But I get the point. I push on it a little. "So much of nothing?" I smile. "Kind of a contradiction. What does it feel like to be so much of nothing?" There is obviously an exaggeration happening in Willa's mind; she is a wonderful friend who is very dear to many people. "So many accomplished people and what have I done?" she explains. Willa is a talented photographer who has rarely shown her work publicly and has had to work as an administrator in a Wall Street firm for many years to support herself. Her shyness at parties extends to shyness in the professional world. "I understand you haven't accomplished what you might have, but that makes you feel like nothing?" I ask. Willa is blanking herself out for some reason and I want to know why. She begins to tell me about another friend, whose husband has died recently, and who always invites her to her Christmas parties but whom Willa has lost touch with. She hasn't shown up at the last few parties, and now her friend's husband has died. A nothingburger again. "Look at that feeling a little more closely," I suggest. "What do you find?" "Shame," she says after a brief pause.

I know that when Willa was a teenager her father molested her and that this has been a pivotal and traumatic experience in her life. We have talked about it a lot, but its effects are deeply buried and she still does not always make the connections that seem relevant. As soon as she says the word "shame" I know we are in that territory again. "I think it's displaced from somewhere else," I suggest. "Any thoughts?" The molestation left her with a profound loneliness in her teenage years. While her father came into her bed in the night, he ignored her during the day. Her mother, who maybe knew and maybe did not know, was distant and critical, and Willa had to pretend that nothing was happening while at the same time she did not entirely understand what *was* happening. She remembers the cold fall and winter evenings when she was outside walking after school and would not, or could not, come home. "It was so cold," she says. She was in what we would now call a dissociated state and at the time there were no words for the feelings of confusion that clouded her mind. "What's wrong with you, Willa, that you can't go home?" she remembers asking herself. She really didn't know; things did not make sense.

Some time ago, Willa described the feeling of coming downstairs for breakfast after her father had been in her bed. Her siblings were there, her mother was doing her depressed best to feed everyone, and her father was at the head of the table and would not look up. "He wouldn't look at me," she said. "I didn't belong in my own family." We tie this not belonging to her present-day discomfort at parties, that feeling of being out in the cold, of something being wrong with her, of something shameful that she does not really understand. "If I were my sister, I would have screamed at my father," she says, one more bit of self-criticism surfacing all these years later. "But I tried to do what he asked me to do. I loved him."

Willa is cheerful on her way out and thanks me for a good session.

. . .

For me, it felt like a big deal for Willa to speak so easily at the end of the session about her love for her father. It's not like this was the most obvious sentiment she had for him. But there it was. Behind her anger, her shame, her confusion, and her feelings of something being wrong with her was this quiet but unrelenting love. I might have supposed that her father's behavior would have eliminated any trace of such affection, and I was very surprised when the words came out of her mouth, but I knew at once how important they were. I do not think Willa could have felt herself as a whole person without acknowledging the original innocent feelings that bound her to her dad. His abuse had threatened her very core—made her into a nothingburger—but in following her shame back to its source and retrieving her original love, she was putting a crucial limit on the damage he had caused. This was insight at its most insightful, Willa's fixed and traumatized idea of herself giving way to a more nuanced appreciation of her original relational nature.

Donald · 9/20/19: 5:15 p.m.

Donald, a fifty-year-old well-intentioned hedge fund manager who bears a striking resemblance to the young Antonio Banderas, has a temper that can be scary for his wife and daughters. The other day, as he was getting ready to leave work, he decided to stop at the Hale and Hearty across the street from his office to pick up some soup and sandwiches for dinner. He texted with his girls and his wife, got their orders, and stood in line to collect everything. He had to decide whether to get a whole avocado sandwich for one daughter for ten dollars or settle for half a sandwich, and, thinking that she never finished her food anyway, he opted for the half.

When Donald got everything home, the first thing his wife said to him was "Half a sandwich?" She had asked for a medium soup, and he had gotten a large one for himself and a medium one for her, but when she saw the difference she said, "I asked for a *medium* soup." "That *is* a medium soup," he had replied, his irritation plainly visible. He was angry and hurt, he tells me, and the rest of the evening had been marred by this brief, yet pointed, exchange. Working all day, making money, stopping for food, bringing it all home, he had been met with nothing but criticism. I tell him, from a Buddhist perspective, this was a golden opportunity to hear the cry of the self that doesn't exist, the clear voice of the false self, the central target of insight meditation. Donald is new to Buddhism but he read one of my books and came to see me because the desire for inner peace had been kindled in him. He is a quick learner but is struggling with all of the demands that work and family place upon him. He has no idea what I am talking about—the cry of the self that doesn't exist. I try to explain.

Self is an elusive concept. We all know what it means—sort of—but if we try to actually find "the self," we have difficulty. The pressures we are under to perform, to survive as individuals in a challenging environment, to be a single little person in a competitive world where most people are out for themselves, lead us to create a false front, a false entity, that is established at the expense of the ability to relax and have faith in the support of the surround. To some degree, we all suffer from this. Buddhism tries to undercut this false self. Its meditations are designed to evoke a place of inner stillness that is beyond—or behind—conceptual thought. This encourages openness where there was once conviction, and relationship where there was primarily separation, especially in terms of the self.

One of my favorite descriptions comes from Professor Thurman's Mongolian Buddhist teacher who disputed the notion of there being no self at all. It's not that the self is not real, he told Thurman, but most people take it to be "really real." The Dalai Lama had said much the same thing to me when he explained that the self is never as real as we think it is. We invest the notion of self with more substance than it needs and then react defensively when the self's primacy is challenged. In a Tibetan version of insight meditation, people are encouraged to find the self as it actually appears in their experience and to recognize that it is primarily a mental construction, not a real thing. This, as mentioned above, is difficult, and it is said that the best time to find this false construction is when we are unjustly accused by someone we love. The reaction of righteous indignation—of "*I* didn't do that"—is said to be the best opportunity of zeroing in on the felt sense of self, on the "I" that we take to be more real than it really is.

I do my best to explain this to Donald and he listens carefully, stopping me on occasion to type some words into his phone. I assure him that I am not counseling him to become submissive or masochistic but am offering an alternative to a habitual reaction that is conditioned by his own insecurity and self-importance, two contradictory qualities that tend nevertheless to go hand in hand. Donald follows everything I say but still seems unsure of how to apply any of it in the middle of something like the other evening. "What would you say to me if you were there in the room and were invisible and could whisper to me?" he asks. It is a good question, and for a long moment I am stumped. I have just explained what I can explain, and I would want him to put it to use himself in that situation. But I know that what I explained is a bit abstract. If I were there as he asked, what *would* I say, what might I say, that would make a difference?

"Have a sense of humor at your own predicament," I reply, surprising myself a bit.

Donald smiles and shakes his head approvingly. He likes it. I am relieved.

• • •

A sense of humor is one of the things that help most in these kinds of situations. Winnicott knew this when he wrote a famous paper, "Hate in the Counter-Transference," in which he outlined the myriad reasons why a mother hates her baby on his way to explaining how important it is to make room for these uncomfortable feelings. Only by making room for hatred (in herself and in her offspring) can her child learn that its mother is a separate person worthy of sympathy and respect:

He is suspicious, refuses her good food, and makes her doubt herself, but eats well with his aunt.

After an awful morning with him she goes out, and he smiles at a stranger, who says: "Isn't he sweet?"

Winnicott's lightness—his ability to find humor in the midst of painful emotional experience—is something that he shares with John Cage. Cage's stories, the soundtracks for Merce Cunningham's dances, seem to come from a very similar place:

An old rabbi in Poland or some place thereabouts was walking in a thunderstorm from one village to another. His health was poor. He was blind, covered with sores. All the afflictions of Job were his. Stumbling over something he fell in the mud. Pulling himself up with difficulty, he raised his hands towards heaven and cried out, "Praise God! The Devil is on Earth and doing his work beautifully!"

Even Issa, the Zen poet, at the end of his most wonderful and devastating year, turned to humor to help guide him through his travails. On December 27 he woke to what he wrote was a fine day. His wife prepared a hot breakfast and they waited for their neighbor to bring over the freshly baked rice cakes he had promised to drop off. They were looking forward to having the warm cakes with their usual modest breakfast. "We waited and waited," Issa recounted, "but alas—the cakes did not come. When we finally decided to eat—our breakfast had grown cold." Issa closed his remembrance with the following verse:

The rice cakes
Only appeared

To come
To my gate.

Each of these vignettes would have shed light on, or given context to, Donald's Hale and Hearty debacle. In all of them the feeling of injured innocence, or righteous indignation, bears the brunt of the joke. In order to find the peace he was seeking, Donald needed not to take himself, or his reactions, so seriously. In this regard, the crucible of family life was functioning like a long meditation retreat, slowly whittling away at his pride. Of course Donald deserved appreciation from his wife for bringing home their supper, just as the mother in Winnicott's paper deserved gratitude from her baby boy for all she did for him. But when it was not forthcoming, Donald did not have to turn its absence into a catastrophe. Like the rabbi in Cage's story, he could learn to find humor in the situation, praising God while remembering that the devil was in the details.

When I sent Donald these pages to review, he wrote me back right away to give his permission. He added that he had recently been listening to an audiobook about couples entitled *Fierce Intimacy* and that he had been thinking of me and of this very session. In the narrative, a middle-aged husband goes to the supermarket with a giant list his wife has given him. Upon the husband's return home, as Donald remembered it, they unload the groceries together and she asks him pointedly, "Where are the asparagus?" Instead of taking his usual offense at her query, he replies, "I forgot." His wife becomes emotional. "I've been waiting for twenty years for you to say that," she cries with relief.

Donald knew I would like this story. The only change he wanted me to make in my account was to describe him as bearing a striking resemblance to the young Antonio Banderas. He does look a lot like him, in fact.

Six

Fall

As a therapist, I have been taught to pay close attention to the intimate details of people's lives in order to help them decipher the mystery of who and what they have become. But as a meditator, I have learned that experience isn't everything. It can just as easily obscure one's truth as reveal it. This is the paradox I have faced in bringing these two worlds together. Traditional therapy unpacks in order to make sense. Meditation asks us to stop making sense so that we can find where happiness truly abides. Therapy examines the accumulated self, the one that is shaped by all the defenses we have used to get through life. Meditation asks us to divest ourselves of those very defenses so that we can recapture the original and intrinsic vitality we were born with.

We are all wounded in some way. Nobody gets out of here alive. We were all messed with by society, by scarcity, by peer pressure, by some unfeeling aspect of family, friends, boyfriends, girlfriends, schools, classmates, teammates, teachers, coaches, doctors, policemen, or priests. We all have minds that seek to apportion blame. But, as important as it is to understand the sources and details of one's pain, understanding is rarely enough. My patients come to therapy wanting the burden of their accumulated experience lifted. Yes, they want to make sense of their lives, but that is not usually their fundamental or exclusive aim. First and foremost, they are trying to get over their accumulated trauma in order to feel less fearful, isolated, forlorn, helpless, alone, anxious, or depressed. They might not be able to say it so clearly, but they are reaching for things beyond thought, trying to make contact with essential capacities that have been sacrificed in their efforts to adapt, adjust, comply, cope, or conform.

As the warm days of summer gave way to the cool nights of autumn, one thing became increasingly clear to me. Anger was the underlying emotion holding many of my patients in its sway. While I had begun to think about it in the aftermath of my December session with Anne and my February meeting with Violette, it had now moved to center stage. Sometimes anger manifested in my patients' self-punishing thoughts or actions, sometimes it was apparent to me in our conversations but not obvious to them, and sometimes it was on full display in their reports about their intimate relationships. No matter how mindful or insightful they could be, however, no matter how much of their childhood traumas they managed to excavate, if I could not help them in their relationship to anger, their therapy would fall short.

Anger is a tricky issue though. Some people deny their angry feelings altogether, while others try to reflexively counter them with loving thoughts. Still others, as my patients with punitive superegos amply demonstrate, turn their aggression on themselves rather than expressing it outwardly. And many people, as we know, allow themselves to be taken over by their critical thoughts or their internal rage, self-righteously justifying their most destructive words or actions. In therapy, as in meditation, it is all too tempting to fall into the trap that D. H. Lawrence outlined in his snake poem, seeing anger as the enemy and beating it with a stick. But attacking violence with violence, no matter how wholesome the motivation, does not often solve the problem. Lawrence demonstrated this in his poem while suggesting that there was, in fact, an alternative, one that was there in his initial fascination before his rationalized judgments got in his way. How much there is to learn from the uncrowned kings of the underworld! In this vision, Lawrence was very much in line with both the Buddha and Winnicott, who each believed that aggression, if beheld correctly, could become a force for good.

In examining my work as a therapist, I can see that I agree. The synergy of Buddhism and therapy has taught me that it is so. The wiring for change is built in, but some sort of benevolent attention has to activate it. Winnicott called this the "facilitating environment" and linked it to a mother's natural, and "good-enough," devotion. He believed that aggression is intrinsic to a baby's psyche, that it shows up as an aspect of an infant's inherent self-centeredness, and that a good-enough parent coaxes a child—over time—from total demandingness into a recognition of the parent as a person in their own right. He called this a "maturational process" but recognized that it does not always go easily and that many an adult still has therapeutic work to do. The Buddha, who did not use the word "meditation," spoke instead of "mental development" in a similar manner. His version of good-enough attention (i.e., mindfulness) came in the aftermath of his interaction with Sujata. Rather than beating himself into submission as he had been doing in his years of asceticism, he changed his relationship to his inner turmoil, adopting a more compassionate stance. The effect was startling. His mind, as if it were a lotus long starved of nourishment, flourished into full flower.

In the following series of sessions, you can see me improvising off the many ways that aggression manifests in my patients' lives. In the back of my mind, as is evident in many of my added reflections, were Winnicott's efforts to paint aggression as a force that can be harnessed for one's own development. Reconfiguring anger is a mysterious process, not one that can be easily described, but it is something that a therapist, as spiritual friend, can help to enable. As these sessions confirm, when enough trust is built up in the therapeutic relationship, there is a chance to release, and be released from, grudges that no longer serve a reasonable purpose. The path I have outlined—confronting clinging, being mindful, and acknowledging the insights that self-reflection enables—eventually leads to a reckoning with one's own inner violence.

This takes me back to the Buddha's memory of sitting under the rose-apple tree, to the remembered joy that was the foundation of his self-analysis. Over many years, historically speaking, the story of his memory gradually morphed. It became embellished, as mythic tales often are, with new and intriguing elements. In many ways, these new elements were reflective of ongoing developments in Buddhist thought. Early Buddhism was vulnerable to the dualism that is common to the way most of us still think. Disturbing emotions like anger and lust were described as unwholesome, and benign ones like compassion and empathy were venerated as healthy. Enlightenment came when the dark forces were eliminated, and nirvana was seen as an ultimate release from this contaminated world. Dark/light, good/bad, wholesome/unwholesome, worldly/unworldly, loving/hating, healthy/unhealthy: the world was split into diametrically opposing forces.

In later Buddhism, the emphasis on individual deliverance from toxic existence gave way to a drive for universal freedom. Awakened beings, rather than escaping to a nirvana that was out of this world, were said to remain in this world to work selflessly for the benefit of others. Nirvana was no longer thought to exist apart from the realm of everyday suffering; it is right here, right now, invisible to most of us but always peeking out of the shadows, ready to reveal itself when conditions are right. While the keystone practice of early Buddhism was the elimination of troubling emotions to allow a penetrating insight into the constructed nature of self and other, later Buddhism gave more and more credence to the possibilities of transformation—rather than elimination— of emotional life. This latter approach was taken up, centuries later, by John Cage, whose orientation was all about opening to all the sounds of the world, those we find harmonious as well as those we do not. His method, like that of the later Buddhists, was a direct challenge to the dualistic view, freeing aggression and other disturbing emotions to become allies in the quest for awakening.

In later versions of the Buddha's memory, a reckoning with violence is as much a part of the story as his remembered joy. Rather than sitting alone in the cool shade of the rose-apple tree while his father tilled the fields in the distance, the young Buddha, seven years old, was said to be left by his nurses to witness the royal court's yearly plowing festival in which his father, now portrayed as a king, was a central participant. The festival was, to most eyes, an enjoyable affair, meant to reassert the king's authority over the land and its inhabitants. The young Buddha's attendants were excited by it and stole away to get closer to the festivities, temporarily abandoning him under the rose-apple tree.

But the young boy was not moved by the celebrations before him. He focused instead on the destruction of bugs and worms turned up by the plows and on the torn-up grass and mutilated insect eggs they engendered. A "strange sorrow" welled up in him at the sight of the carnage, and the young boy, rapt as he was at the suffering before him, was swept away by the feeling. For several hours, while the festival continued, the Buddha-to-be was lost in reverie, his sympathy for the suffering creatures so strong that he was completely taken over by it. It was this confrontation with destruction that propelled him into the absorption that he later remembered as "joyful."

In this iteration of the story, it was said that even the natural world recognized the strength of his heart and vowed to keep him safe. As the sun moved across the sky, the shadow of the rose-apple tree remained stationary over the young boy's head, the earth holding him in her cool and soothing embrace. In this version, his childhood memory serves as a direct precursor to the adult Buddha's reconfiguration of his aggression. Seeing his self-hatred as another version of the plow's desecration of the earth's creatures, the Buddha turned toward compassion. He unhooked his aggression from its usual object and allowed it to energize his self-analysis.

How wonderful to be able to reach for this in therapy!

In an intriguing book called *Bring Me the Rhinoceros: And Other Zen Koans That Will Save Your Life*, John Tarrant, a Western Zen teacher and psychotherapist, outlines seven qualities that explain how Zen Buddhism uses koans to achieve this kind of breakthrough. Koans are riddles for which there are no rational answers. Dating from the origins of Zen Buddhism in China a thousand years after the time of the Buddha and ensconced in the Zen tradition of Japan, these questions—like Hakuin's famous "What is the sound of one hand?"—have been used for centuries as vehicles of mental and emotional transformation. Tarrant describes their special healing properties as follows:

> *Koans show you that you can depend on creative moves.*
> *Koans encourage doubt and curiosity.*
> *Koans rely on uncertainty as a path to happiness.*
> *Koans will undermine your reasons and your explanations.*
> *Koans lead you to see life as funny rather than tragic.*
> *Koans will change your idea of who you are, and this will require courage.*
> *Koans reveal a hidden kindness in life.*

It is no accident that Tarrant's seven principles could just as well describe what Buddhism brings to the practice of psychotherapy. A good therapy, like an inspired koan, finds ways to get us around ourselves, not to fall into an abyss of self-doubt, but to uncover and sustain an intelligence and creativity that feeds who we each are uniquely capable of being. Tarrant paints a vivid picture of how challenging this can be. In one of my favorite passages, he puts it like this:

> If you are used to living in a small room and suddenly discover a wide meadow, you might feel unsafe. Everyone thinks that they want happiness, but they might not. They might rather keep their stories about who they are and about what is impossible. Happiness is not an add-on to what you already are; it requires you to become a different person from the one who set off seeking it.

People do not change easily. How often does someone emerge from therapy a different person from the one who came in? The Zen tradition is very sober about this. The word "koan" originally meant "public case," and famous compendiums of these "public cases" chronicled generations of practitioners struggling to get over themselves enough to change their perceptions of who they were. In this way, koans are similar to the "public cases" that are documented in this book. Therapy itself is like a koan. It changes minds by bringing forth unfamiliar qualities that are nevertheless intrinsic to our natures.

The following sessions come from the final season of my project, ending, unbeknownst to me, just before the advent of COVID-19. While they, like the others in this book, were chosen week by week, they reflect my increasing confidence in therapy's capacity to function like the koans of old. My patients both yearned for change and resisted it tenaciously, often bringing their unworked-through aggression into our sessions. And I needed to be provocative without being obnoxious, playful without being insensitive, and helpful without becoming intrusive. Like the Zen poets of old, who did their best to communicate a Buddhist sensibility through their evocative verses, therapy can help us live more fully in the world as creatures in touch with our humanity. One haiku that guided me through this time comes from Bashō, the most famous Japanese poet of the seventeenth-century Edo period.

Autumn moon,
tide foams
to the very gate.

I doubt I have the deepest understanding of Bashō's imagery (I think perhaps he is actually speaking of death approaching) but, to me, the autumn moon represents the mind that has succeeded in tapping its wellspring of aggression, moving away from self-centeredness and toward illumination. The tide foaming to the gate is like this unleashed potential lapping at the very edges of our personalities. Pointing to this potential, while watching someone come to their own understanding of it, is a joy in itself.

AGGRESSION

A monk asked, "The Second Patriarch cut off his arm, what sort of act is that?"

The Master said, "He was throwing his whole self into it."

The monk said, "To whom was the offering made?"

The Master said, "The offering was made to whoever came."

CHAO-CHOU, *Recorded Sayings*, #296

Shirley · 9/25/19: 9:00 a.m.

Shirley is a fifty-three-year-old entrepreneur with grown children who has been divorced for four years. I have seen her for a couple of sessions and have just been getting to know her. She is earnest, sincere, and likable, a college soccer player from an unassuming background who has made good and who has found meditation to be helpful in managing her stress. I know already, from our earlier sessions, that her divorce has been painful. She initiated it out of a growing disappointment in her marriage, but it is clear to me that her husband was blindsided by her decision to leave him. She has tried to be fair to him in the divorce negotiations—she was the major breadwinner in the family—and has been hoping, naively in my beginning assessment, for some kind of peace to descend upon them.

This morning, Shirley expresses disappointment with herself. During the past week, her ex has reopened their financial agreement, asking for a large increase in spousal support. Until she spoke with her lawyer later in the day, Shirley could not control the turmoil this news created in her. Her thoughts had spun out of control and her nervous system had seized up. "I shouldn't have been so rattled," she says. "I should have been able to calm myself down." Shirley is puzzled over two things. Why should she have been so distressed, and why did it take her lawyer's reassurance for her to calm down? Shouldn't she have more self-control by now? Her attorney has told her that it is rare for something like this to go anywhere, that her ex will have to show financial hardship to reopen the case. Is she really just concerned about the money? she wonders. It doesn't seem in character. What is going on?

My contribution is to point out, not for the first time, that her ex hates her now. Shirley's decision to leave him was a cool and rational one. She wasn't particularly happy in the marriage, and when she extrapolated twenty years into the future, she could see that it was only going to get worse. She had decided to cut her losses. But her ex, naturally enough, had, as I imagined it at least, felt betrayed. What recourse was there to make his feelings known other than fighting in court? Shirley is uncomfortable with, even intolerant of, her response to his fury. She longs for understanding, or at least acceptance. I suspect she even wants forgiveness. And she does not like to think that her ex's feelings could still affect her. "He is the father of your children," I remind her. She looks a little shocked. "He was the most important person in your life for twenty-five years," I say. "Of course it matters to you what he thinks of you."

In the back of my mind is Winnicott's "Hate in the Counter-Transference," the paper about anger in therapy and childcare. In order to deal with another person's hatred, Winnicott says, we must be able to deal with our own. He talks of the ruthless love that infants have for their mothers, the way they seek after them without regard for their mothers' feelings, and the difficulties parents have if they are always trying to be nice. A mother's love will naturally overcome her reactive hatred, Winnicott proposes, but not if she is in denial about the range of feelings her child's demands provoke. Winnicott extends this to the therapeutic couple. Patients can be demanding and frustrating and ask for more than even the best therapist can provide. A therapist who is unable to accept their own feelings will not be able to be helpful when such scenarios unfold.

There is something analogous happening with Shirley, I suppose. She does not want to be held responsible for betraying her ex, and she is not willing to consider his rage as justified. "He is going to hate you forever," I say. I try to explain something I have learned from meditation. "If you make room for your own anger, it will take care of itself," I suggest. Shirley does not immediately grasp what I am talking about, but we speak about it for a while. I want her to see a few things. She has hurt her ex more than she wants to acknowledge; that is the price of her freedom. She cares about his reactions more than she wants to, also. And, in the midst of his accusations, her own defensive, and ultimately impotent, anger makes her very uncomfortable. There is no way she is going to win her ex over to her way of seeing things, but she sees no good alternatives.

As we talk, Shirley begins to see what I am getting at. She makes reference to the way she is going about meditating. "I get very focused on watching my breath to the exclusion of all else," she says. "And when it's not going well, when there's emotional stuff going on, I feel I'm not doing it the way I should." She grasps that there is another approach, one not trying to blot everything else out, but where the meditation involves a wider lens, where even emotions like anger can become objects of meditative observation. Shirley is striving to be "indifferent," in her words, to her ex-husband's complaints, but I know there is an alternative to indifference that is closer to equanimity with a dose of compassion. Of course her ex is enraged and of course she feels unfairly attacked but, from an emotional perspective, he has a point. Just as a mother has to bear the hatred intrinsic to being a mother, Shirley will have to accept the consequences of her decision to divorce. Craving understanding from the person she has left is not going to get her anywhere.

. . .

When I began seeing patients as a psychiatrist, I did so with the belief that therapy worked best when it could provide a corrective emotional experience for a patient. This was not an uncommon notion in those days, and coming out of all of my spiritual pursuits, I took to it naturally. I had accessed a loving reservoir in myself in meditation, and I wanted to use this to help others. In many cases, this opened the door to a robust therapeutic relationship but in a few cases it was a disaster.

My training involved three years of working in a psychiatric hospital with both inpatients and outpatients. Some people suffered from intense mental illnesses and needed medication; others needed therapy without drugs for trauma, anxiety, or depression. Several of these patients responded well to therapy at first but grew increasingly demanding as time went on. My boundaries were not clear, and patients began calling in distress between sessions, threatening to harm themselves or lashing out at me for failing to help them sufficiently. I was chastened, frightened, and upset and turned to my supervisors for help and guidance. I got the most help from a prominent psychoanalyst named Otto Kernberg, who, at the time, was the senior psychiatrist at the hospital where I was in training. He supervised me for a year and taught me important things about anger.

Dr. Kernberg helped me to see a couple of things. First, simply being a loving presence was not going to do the trick, at least not in the way I was thinking about what a loving presence meant. Second, my patients who were acting so aggressively toward me were not necessarily aware of how angry they were. I got the first point, but the second point was more difficult. My patients thought of themselves as deprived and could also acknowledge feeling needy.

I thought of them that way, too, and figured that if I gave them the attention they had been denied earlier in life that they would feel better. Dr. Kernberg was kind to me and helped me to see that, while their deprivation may have been real, these patients had lots of internal conflict around anger that was holding them back. In showing me this, he also, without having to say it directly, made me see that I, too, was pushing anger away. He gave me language to use. "You might not be aware of how angry you are," he suggested I say. "But you are in danger of destroying the very support you need the most." By beginning my communication with "you might not be aware" rather than confronting my patients' anger directly, I could encourage them to reflect upon something they were otherwise just acting out unawares. My skills as a therapist improved dramatically as a result. Kindness without the proper intelligence to back it up was of little use, but the use of kindness in the service of therapy's insights was very helpful. This supervision laid the groundwork for my subsequent embrace of Winnicott. For Winnicott, like Kernberg, knew that anger is inevitable and that it cannot be wished away. Facing it, but not being intimidated by it, as most mothers are able to do with their infants, is the only path to peace.

In some way, Shirley's response to her ex-husband's demands reminded me of my own early attempts to soothe my angry patients with understanding. It was not going to work! He was going to stay angry with her no matter how conciliatory she was in her negotiations. Whenever she would contemplate making a new settlement offer, I would warn her that he would not agree, that he was going to torture her for as long as he possibly could. "That's not very Buddhist of you, Dr. Epstein," she would respond, but I disagreed. It took me a while, but I am now very clear eyed about how intractable anger can be, and that is a very Buddhist attitude. Parents have a hard enough time with anger when it arises with children whom they love with all their hearts.

Trying to make the anger of a spurned lover disappear is a recipe for disaster. Even the Buddha, it is said, upon returning to the wife he had abandoned when he left in search of enlightenment, shushed his followers when they tried to quiet her rage. "She has a right to be angry," he is said to have told them. "Let her speak."

At least that is one version of the story. The one I have chosen to believe.

thought a lot about our last session," Willa tells me as we begin again. It takes a moment for the details to float back down into my mind, but they come, like raindrops in a sudden storm: the nothingburger and the uncovering of her latent love for her father. "'What's wrong with me' was always the question bothering me," she continues. Willa tells me that in high school people were always telling her she could play Ophelia in *Hamlet*. "I was walking around looking slightly crazed," she reports. "Dazed and confused. But I didn't want to play Ophelia. I hated Ophelia." She speaks again of feeling her father's contempt for her at the breakfast table, of his refusal to make eye contact. I am struck by her repetition of "what's wrong with me" and seize upon it.

"What if we phrase the question simply as 'What's wrong?'" I suggest, "rather than 'What's wrong *with me*?' You knew but you didn't know. The reality of the situation was more than you could bear." Willa nods. Things are beginning to make sense for her. Her dazed and Ophelia-like confusion was emblematic of the dissociation common to victims of abuse. Rather than clearly seeing what was wrong, and laying the responsibility on her parents, she had remained vague, telegraphing her pain to those around her while simultaneously taking the burden upon herself. "You had to shut yourself off," I tell her. "To protect yourself, but also to protect your parents. You loved your father," I reminded her. "His behavior didn't make sense. You took it on yourself instead."

. . .

In talking about the influence of Zen Buddhism on his approach to art and music, John Cage had a very interesting point to make. I thought about it a lot when speaking with Willa because his point applies to therapy as much as to art and music. Cage spoke candidly about how confused he was when he was a young man both in his personal life and in his work. I don't know whether he had Willa's level of pain and distress but he was clearly not happy. Through the study of Buddhism, though, he became less confused, changing his approach to work and to himself.

> *I saw art not as something that consisted of a communication from the artist to an audience but rather as an activity of sounds in which the artist found a way to let the sounds be themselves. And in their being themselves to open the minds of the people who made them or listened to them to other possibilities than they had previously considered. To widen their experience, particularly to undermine the making of value judgments.*

I think it was this last phrase about undermining the making of value judgments that seemed so relevant at the time. Willa, in the aftermath of her confusing relationship with her father, was full of value judgments, and they were all self-directed. Something was wrong with her. She was a nothingburger. Her aggression was turned back on herself and manifested as bewilderment and shame. We had done a lot of good work in this past year to loosen these convictions, and therapy was now functioning in what I would consider a Cageian way. Encouraged by our conversations, Willa was finding it possible to let her recurrent thoughts—her sounds—be themselves without immediately grasping after them. There were other possibilities to consider, other dimensions to explore, a loosening of conviction—and aggression—that had unforeseen consequences. Willa could now reflect upon her thoughts rather than be taken over by them, and there were new and surprising feelings to make room for. The forsaken love that had first emerged in her unobjectionable positive transference toward me had subsequently come to include her severely flawed father. Innocence after experience, indeed.

Cage was often asked whether his revolutionary approach devalued the training of the virtuoso musician. If everyone is a musician, if every noise is musical, what about the whole tradition of acclaimed musical composition? This question could obviously apply to therapy, as well. If therapy works best as a koan, is a therapist trained in classical analysis of any use? But Cage had an answer for that too.

> It doesn't make the virtuoso not a musician. He remains a musician as he has been, but the other untrained people can become musicians also. I think it comes about through placing the center everywhere, in all the people whether they're composing or listening, and furthermore placing the center in the sounds themselves. So there is then an interpenetration of unlimited centers. This is a fundamental of Buddhism.

This interpenetration of unlimited centers is relevant in psychotherapy too. Rather than the therapist being the composer or authority figure, and the patient the dependent listener, therapy can be an environment in which the center is placed everywhere. In this manner, traumatic experiences, like those that Willa endured, can then reveal themselves in their own way. They can rise to the surface and be seen for what they are instead of lurking in the background while the shame they created takes center stage.

Rather than trapping and isolating the victim in a perpetual sense of separation and confusion, the interpenetration of relational centers—which trauma therapists often simply call a "relational home"—allows trauma to come out of its frozen state and back into the warmth of time. As Bashō said in his haiku about the autumn moon, "Tide foams to the very gate."

Steve · 10/3/19: 9:30 a.m.

Steve, fifty years old and twice divorced, has been thinking about why he has not dated in more than a decade. When he was younger he dated lots of women. It's not that he's not interested—he is regularly checking women out on the street, at social gatherings, and on the subway—but he has not gone out on a real date in a long time. He tells me about a woman who lives in his building whom he has been friendly with over the years. She is attractive, recently divorced, the mother of two grown children. He had dinner with her the other night, as a friend and neighbor. It wasn't a date but might have been a prelude to a date, but Steve was disconsolate and bitter in the dinner's aftermath. His neighbor had spoken about her son who was a talented musician in Providence. Steve had heard his work and it was very skilled. But the son was growing tired of life as a musician and wasn't sure what he might do next. His mother—Steve's neighbor—had never found meaningful work for herself. She had raised her children and devoted herself to her marriage but now found herself alone and unfocused. She was anxious for her son, but Steve was certain a good portion of her heightened concern was actually about her own situation. Her son's problems were mirroring her unresolved professional issues, and she was preoccupied. "I don't want to come home to it every night," he admits, and any thoughts of pursuing the relationship have evaporated.

At first, I challenge his conclusions. "Most people don't find meaningful work," I say. "She could be concerned for her son without it meaning there's something wrong with her." But this is not really the issue, and we soon get into a deeper discussion. In his relationship life, Steve was always looking for perfection, and whenever something was wrong with the person he was with, he would become fixated on it. His marriages had foundered as a result. Steve was very confident in his perceptions, and he assumed that, because he had zeroed in on a problem, his partner would want to fix it. That his partners did not necessarily agree with him was not something he had ever had much tolerance for. I try to talk with him about this, using his recent dinner as a jumping-off place. "Everyone is flawed, you know," I begin. "You see it and get critical right away. There are other possible responses. Confronting people with their flaws isn't exactly a route to success." Steve is indignant. If there is a problem, shouldn't it be dealt with? "People aren't so eager to change," I counter. "What about compassion as a response? Or forgiveness?"

Generally, I shy away from using the word "compassion." I feel that, in spiritual circles at least, the word is overused and has begun to lose its meaning. I prefer "empathy" or "sympathy" or "consideration" or "kindness," especially when talking about interpersonal relationships. "Compassion" can sometimes imply feeling sorry— from a safe distance—for those who are suffering in a manner that lets the compassionate person off the hook. Feeling compassionate, they can be reassured that they are a good person without having to do anything about it. But in this case, I use the word deliberately. Steve is so sure of himself that he has no patience for those who do not comply with his implicit demands for change.

Steve is genuinely puzzled by this turn in the conversation. "How is what I do any different from what you do?" he asks. He is talking about me as a therapist, complimenting me, in a way. Like him, I can see what is wrong with people. Like him, I can see their flaws. "I'm not trying to change anyone," I respond with a smile. Steve gets the joke, and the underlying truth. "That's why I'm still here," he says with a laugh. "Still with the same problems." It is a dig at me but said with affection. I think I detect a hint of surrender. He has been seeing me for years. "It's the key to sustaining long relationships," I say with a smile as I rise to signal the end of the session.

. . .

In one of his most important papers, "The Development of the Capacity for Concern," written in 1963, toward the end of his life, Winnicott explained how important it is to help patients explore the ways that anger has kept them under its spell. Concern for others, he made clear, depends on being able to see others as whole people in and of themselves rather than as being there only to serve one's needs. Like John Cage, Winnicott envisioned a time when the interpenetration of unlimited centers becomes a lived reality, but he made no bones about how difficult this is to achieve. An infant, for example, does not experience his or her mother as having her own center, at least for a while. He or she does not experience his or her own center yet either. The baby's instinctual needs are not yet separated out from the baby's emotional needs, and from the mother's point of view, the baby often seems a tightly packed explosive bundle of nonnegotiable demands.

Winnicott's favorite word was "ruthless." An infant experiences the raw material of erotic and aggressive drives simultaneously and directs them ruthlessly at the mother. A baby wants food and closeness and soothing and excitement and contact and stimulation, and he or she wants it without regard for a mother's feelings, and he or she wants it now. Winnicott said, for the purposes of his argument, that a mother in that situation has to be two different things: on the one hand she is the "object-mother" who has the wherewithal to satisfy the child's urgent needs with body, breast, or bottle, and on the other hand she is the "environment-mother" who is watching and handling and actively managing the emotional situation, in a manner we Buddhists might consider mindful.

In this language it is the environment-mother who receives all that can be called affection and sensuous co-existence; it is the object-mother who becomes the target for excited experience backed by crude instinct-tension. It is my thesis that concern turns up in the baby's life as a highly sophisticated experience in the coming-together in the infant's mind of the object-mother and the environment-mother.

Babies gradually learn that they cannot always get things exactly as they want, that their mothers are not perfect, that their mothers will make them wait, that their mothers will fail them, and that their mothers' frustrated or disappointed anger is justified and tolerable. But the good-enough mother in Winnicott's view, the environment-mother, will not disillusion her baby too precipitously; she will only very gradually say that enough is enough, she will let her child down slowly, she won't let them wait past the point of self-soothing so that the child begins to see that the person who inevitably disappoints her is the same one the child needs so much. This is the foundation, from the baby's side, of what Winnicott called the capacity for concern, of regard for the other. It's worth it to put up with some disappointment because the child knows that the parent will be there shortly and is deserving of some empathy. This cycle of rupture and repair is characteristic of intimate relationships of all types.

The patients that Dr. Kernberg supervised me on were often stuck in one of the places Winnicott excelled at describing. They were relentlessly in pursuit of an "object-mother," demanding that their needs be attended to above all else, even to the point of destruction of the therapeutic relationship. They had not integrated the "environment-mother" into their psyches and had not yet found the capacity for concern that might have helped them manage their own inner violence while sustaining the intimacy they so craved.

Superficially, Steve bore no resemblance to the young patients Dr. Kernberg once helped me with, but his issues resonated with theirs nonetheless. In subsequent conversations, we inevitably circled back to Steve's early life and, specifically, to his relationship with his mother, who might be best described as provocative. Steve's mother was a flirtatious and self-centered woman who insisted on being right all of the time. When Steve, as a boy, attempted to assert his own point of view, he was inevitably overruled. His mother was a compelling figure, the center of the household, who indulged Steve as long as he did not question her, but ignored him when he did. We might say she was there as an "object-mother" but erratic as an "environment-mother." This created a big problem for him. There was no room for integrating his anger in this relationship, no possibility of Steve's mom ever admitting a flaw, and no acknowledgment of Steve's independent point of view. The natural give-and-take of a mother-child relationship, in which both parent and child get disappointed with one another but learn to tolerate, and forgive, on the road to becoming interpenetrating centers never happened.

Steve, we began to see, was never given the chance to work productively with his own aggression. It was as if he had no guidance through the inevitable disappointments of early life. In all probability, Steve's mother had enjoyed him as an infant but shunned him when he became problematic. He was left dangling. His need for his mother compelled him to be complicit with her self-centeredness, but his need to safely move away from her was complicated by how alone he was with his anger. This seemed to be what he was playing out in his intimate relationships. Steve valued closeness but had real trouble handling disappointment. When things became imperfect, he would attack relentlessly, as if making up for lost time. Anger as a natural part of intimate relationships was not something that Steve had room for. He always had to win.

Winnicott suggested that therapy can make a difference in situations like Steve's, and in some way my comment to him at the end of the session about tolerance being the key to sustaining long relationships was in line with this view.

> *All we do in successful psychoanalysis is to unhitch developmental hold-ups, and to release developmental processes and the inherited tendencies of the individual patient. In a peculiar way we can actually alter the patient's past, so that a patient whose maternal development was not good enough can change into a person who has had a good-enough facilitating environment, and whose personal growth has therefore been able to take place, though late. When this happens the analyst gets a reward that is far removed from gratitude, and is very much like that which a parent gets when a child achieves autonomy. In the context of good-enough holding and handling the new individual now comes to realize some of his or her potential. Somehow we have silently communicated reliability and the patient has responded with the growth that might have taken place in the very early stages in the context of human care.*

Did any of this unhitching happen through Steve's years of therapy with me? Have we released any developmental processes or inherited tendencies? Steve has stayed with me for a long time. I know he appreciates my reliability, and while his capacity for concern may not be ready for prime time, it is growing some shoots and leaves.

Hunter · 10/10/19: 4:30 p.m.

Hunter, a fifty-year-old father of two, had a disappointing day at work this week or, rather, a disappointing series of days. Feeling down, he turned to his wife for "attention and comfort" but felt her pull away. This did not sit well with him and, feeling hurt, he began to simmer. His wife, sensitive to his anger, became even more withdrawn, provoking him further. This was a familiar cycle for this couple, and it did not take much probing on my part for Hunter to say directly that the attention and comfort he was seeking was actually sex.

While sympathetic to Hunter's plight, I can see how his wife might have felt his sexual desire as a demand rather than an overture. I describe to him how it appears to me.

"When she pulls away or doesn't respond the way you wish, you feel rejected and abandoned, as if it's all over, as if she is never going to give you what you want. You exaggerate the temporary feeling and make it absolute, and then it becomes a catastrophe." There are variations on this dynamic in lots of relationships, and sometimes I encourage the person in Hunter's wife's position to be more flexible and work on adapting to her partner's needs. But in this case I do not feel this to be the right move. There is something extra in Hunter's complaint, and there is a danger that his wife could turn it against herself and allow it to erode her desire for him.

Hunter can see this, too, and, while a bit defensive when I bring it up, he is willing to talk about it. I explain how the need for attention and comfort has its infantile roots in the first years of life, when the primary erotogenic zone is the mouth and a baby is completely dependent on its caretakers for holding, nourishment, soothing, reassurance, and instinctual gratification. As a child matures and discovers his or her genital sensations, the primary erotogenic zone shifts to the genitals, and masturbation is often discovered. This shift is important for emotional development, as it signals progress toward becoming an individual who is at least partially able to care for oneself. Most people, however, continue to have what are called "oral" needs for comfort and security, but these are sometimes disguised as sexual and expressed more as angry demands than respectful requests.

Hunter becomes very somber as I talk and finally says, with sadness, that this is at the core of his marital difficulties. But the only reasonable solution he can envision is that his wife could adapt more willingly to his needs. I agree with him that this is a core issue but float the possibility that this core is his responsibility, too, and not solely hers. He remembers that when his mother was dying when he was a teenager, he was forced to deal with losing her, and he did. "I just sucked it up," he says. "But this is different," I say. "In this situation, you have a choice. It's up to you how you respond. Your wife is not dead, she's just pulling away from your demand."

Sometimes, I suggest, when, as an adult, you find someone who steps in and tries to be the parent you never had and comforts you the way you had always hoped, it can feel too cloying. Gratifications that were appropriate for an infant are no longer really so satisfying when acted out in adult life. Hunter knows what I am talking about. He actually values his wife's independence, her refusal to orient herself completely around him. He remembers a previous girlfriend who made chocolate chip cookies as a surprise for him. That had been a turnoff, too maternal, not what he was looking for. There can be too much pressure on a marriage to be everything for each other, I say. We all fail.

But Hunter's story does not end there. "Did you make up?" I ask. Hunter gives me the rundown. "She said, 'You're angry with me?' I said yes. She said sorry. I said, 'It can't just go away so easily just because you said sorry.' We pulled away after that and it was distant between us but not terrible. Days later she came into my office at home while I was working. 'Want to have sex?' she said. 'Yes!' I replied." There is a nice light in Hunter's eyes as he looks up at me. A mixture of triumph and relief, I think.

. . .

Hunter's struggle around demandingness and clinging is close to many of the cases I described in the earlier part of this book. Sometimes this is expressed purely in sexual terms, as seemed to be the case here; sometimes as a need for closeness, comfort, attention, or connection; and sometimes as jealousy, envy, or an overwhelming need to control the behavior of the other. When the demands are extreme, things can easily become abusive, and when the clinging is extreme, these relationships can become claustrophobic. But such dynamics are often operating in more healthy relationships, too, without people understanding what is motivating them. In talking with Hunter about the oral stage, I wanted to give him a feel for something that has been very helpful in my own life. Many couples run into problems when one or both of the partners try to solve their unmet oral needs (for nurturance, holding, soothing, attention, or comfort) through what amounts to a kind of extortion. It is only through recognizing this tendency in oneself that one can take responsibility for it and not simply lay the problem on one's partner. This is one of those developmental holdups that therapy can unhitch us from, where a primitive form of unworked-through anger has survived into adulthood and threatens to destroy that which the person actually values.

Meditation is uniquely positioned to help people deal with their unmet oral needs because of the way in which it can serve as a transitional object. Transitional objects first become important when young children begin to have a sense of their own separateness. A special blanket or teddy bear or other stuffed animal becomes a vehicle for navigating the to-and-fro that is essential as a child emerges from utter dependency and begins to function as their own person. A transitional object has the peculiar quality of being both "me" and "not-me." It is a link to the parents and a link to the self, but it has its own unique and liminal status. It has a special role, recognized by "good-enough" parents, of helping children offset the inevitable aloneness that comes with burgeoning self-awareness.

There is a wide variation to be found in a sequence of events that starts with a newborn infant's fist-in-mouth activities, and leads eventually on to attachment to a teddy, a doll or soft toy, or to a hard toy. . . .

I have introduced the terms "transitional objects" and "transitional phenomena" for designation of the intermediate area of experience, between the thumb and the teddy bear, between the oral eroticism and the true object-relationship . . . between primary unawareness of indebtedness and the acknowledgement of indebtedness. . . .

. . . I am here staking a claim for an intermediate state between a baby's inability and his growing ability to recognize and accept reality.

When Dr. Benson first coined the phrase "relaxation response," he was flagging the soothing benefits of meditation, long known to its adherents. Looked at from the outside, using the tools of modern medicine to document it, the signs of relaxation came in the form of decreased heart rate, oxygen consumption, and blood pressure. But what might be happening inside the mind when a person settles into a contemplative state? Because Dr. Benson was a cardiologist, this was not part of his inquiry, but from the point of view of a therapist, or a meditator, it is very relevant.

Winnicott proposed that therapy has many of the qualities of a transitional object and that it uses them to help people recognize and accept reality in the service of unleashing the empathy they are capable of. To my mind, meditation also does. Using the breath as its primary focus (is the breath "me" or "not-me"?), meditation provides a refuge, a resting place, a holding environment, a container, or "an intermediate area" in which the usual need to "keep oneself together" can be temporarily relinquished. At the same time, an enhanced quality of self-observation is cultivated so that one can witness, under the protective canopy of mindfulness, all of the longings that would ordinarily be driving one's coercive demands.

For someone like Hunter, who might well have made sex his transitional object, this adjustment could be very useful. And it would probably lead to more intimate marital relations rather than less.

Jean · 10/11/19: 9:00 a.m.

Jean is back and she is putting a good face on but it is not so convincing. She is suffering, and I want to know what is going on. She is a year and a half into her three years of probation after being taken to task by the authorities for prescribing an opioid for a longtime patient who had moved away. An auditor from the state has been coming to inspect her medical records periodically, and she has to put a lot of time and effort into doing things right. "I should be doing more," she tells me right off the bat without being at all specific about what she should be doing more of. I imagine all kinds of things she should be doing more of before she fills in the blanks. "I'm resisting the electronic records," she says. I try to make a distinction between what she has to do and what she thinks she should be doing. Jean has not made peace with what she perceives as the unfairness of her predicament. "It's like you're on a three-year retreat," I propose. "You are seeing it only as a punishment. You know, those Zen retreats where you are in the kitchen or in the garden or sweeping the floors. That's what doing the electronic records could be like."

Jean confesses that many evenings after work—she doesn't get home till eight o'clock or so—she is watching multiple episodes of streaming TV. "Confesses" is the right word; she obviously feels a lot of judgment about it. I don't go directly at her shame but ask her whether she is eating dinner on those nights. She demurs.

"Olives," she says. Then I ask her what she is watching. I know she has good taste in television; she was the first to tell me about *Peaky Blinders*, which is now my favorite show. She mentions two programs I have never heard of, *Velvet* (a Spanish series about fashion in the 1950s) and *Good Omens* (a sci-fi miniseries about the battle between good and evil). "Sometimes I stay up till one thirty or two in the morning," she says guiltily. I know she is expecting me to join in her castigation, but I refuse. "How terrible!" I say with obvious sarcasm. She looks at me askance.

Jean is criticizing herself for doing something harmless while at the same time rebelling against doing the one thing she has to do to keep her medical license. She is proclaiming her innocence in regard to the opioid prescription but pleading guilty to watching too much TV. Things are all twisted, and I do my best to straighten them out. "There's a big difference between turning off the TV because you are tired and turning it off because you are supposed to," I say. Jean has every right to watch as much TV as she wants; it is her only pleasure these days, the only relief from the surveillance she is under. I continue to talk with her about changing the story she is telling herself, about treating this time as a retreat (with TV!) into which she can surrender. Surrender becomes a theme we can explore. Jean is a conscientious and experienced clinician. She is devoted to her patients, and she knows that clinical work is much more important, and meaningful, than the electronic medical records being demanded of her. But right now, for the next year and a half, the medical records have to have priority. Can she submit to that with patience? Can TV be her reward? Or will her sense of the injustice perpetrated upon her paralyze her even further?

. . .

This session with Jean reminds me of one of the core principles of Zen referred to at the beginning of this chapter: "Koans will undermine your reasons and your explanations." If I were to have simply concurred with Jean about the injustice done to her, I would not have offered her anything she could not think of herself. In my role as her therapist, I had other options. Jean had reason to rebel against her punishment, reason to feel shame about her predicament, and reason to judge herself for watching too much television. She had reason to be unhappy and reason to be angry with the authorities for the severity of her treatment. All of those reasons were boxing her in, turning her home, office, and mind into prisons she could not escape from. My task, as I saw it, was to turn her mind around, to free her from all of these perfectly plausible explanations that were obstructing her view, and, ultimately, to rescue her from the split-off anger that was paralyzing her. As John Tarrant describes it in *Bring Me the Rhinoceros*,

> *If you have a reason for happiness, then that happiness can be taken away. The person you love could leave, the job could stop being interesting. If you have a reason for loving life, what happens if that reason fails? With koans you may find that life and love are so strong and vivid that they can't be explained or justified. Koans open a happiness that comes for no good reason. That happiness exists before reasons have appeared in the universe.*

There was no good reason for Jean to be happy, that was for sure. And yet, and yet . . . she could be, I could sense it in her. How could I help her get there? The koan that Tarrant based his book on offered a clue. In its entirety it reads as follows:

> *One day, Yanguan called to his assistant, "Bring me the rhinoceros fan."*
> *The assistant said, "It is broken."*
> *Yanguan said, "In that case, bring me the rhinoceros."*

In this koan, Yanguan's assistant was being asked for something impossible. Where would he find a rhinoceros? Grappling with this impossibility, his thoughts stopped and his mind opened. Doubt and confusion gave way to empty space. "His rhinoceros," writes Tarrant, "was a doubt about everything he was." Jean had no doubts about who she was. Not only was she wrong to have written the forbidden prescriptions, she couldn't even focus on her medical records. Nothing was working out the way she hoped. The fan in her life was definitely broken. Were I to focus only on what was broken, I would be pulled into her suffering instead of pointing the way out. I wanted more uncertainty for Jean, more of that Zen doubt. Whatever conclusion she aggressively threw at me, I parried it back at her until we reached a truce. Surrender was Jean's rhinoceros. It went against everything she thought.

Violette · 10/15/19: 12:30 p.m.

Violette exudes joy today. She removed herself from the theater piece her friend had wanted her to perform in and has recently begun writing a script based on an idea that has been germinating since graduate school. "I'm feeling much better," she says at the beginning of our session, explaining how satisfying the writing is now. She is making something of her own rather than interpreting other people's words, and this feels like a good direction. But there is still something that does not feel quite right. "The feelings I have when immersed in the work are scary to me. So intense. But I'm giving it a chance." I ask her what she means by the scary feelings. Is she talking about the old performance anxiety? It doesn't sound that way but I need to be sure. If not, what is so frightening about what she is feeling? "It takes me away from my husband," Violette responds. "It's not actually *when* I'm writing," she reconsiders. "It's just when I'm finishing. I've been off somewhere by myself. It makes me feel guilty."

I am not expecting this, although once Violette says it, it begins to make sense. Her idea of what it means to be a good partner involves maintaining closeness. It isn't just that she feels guilty about entering territory alien to her husband, she also wishes that he could appreciate what it is doing for her, and that it could do it for him too. But her husband is not a writer, he has been working his way up in the medical establishment for a decade, and, while he is supportive of Violette's independence, he does not often participate in her world. As excited as Violette is to have found a new challenge, she is alone with it, and she worries that this aloneness affirms something inadequate in her marriage. "It's not my ideal," she says regretfully.

I try to talk to Violette about how this could be good, about how the concept of what is ideal might be getting in the way of what is true, and possibly good enough. In the back of my mind are earlier discussions we have had about how her desire to please might be getting in the way of her own enjoyment. "You are going deeper into your own space," I suggest. "Your husband can get the runoff. That will be nourishing for him. He can appreciate you as other and you will feel affirmed." Violette is not necessarily having it. "Still, it's not ideal," she replies. But then she reflects upon some earlier relationships with actors who had more embodied her sense of the ideal. She had tended to submerge herself in those relationships, privileging their talents over her own, and had ended up feeling used and unappreciated. "I might not be so happy in the ideal," she admits. "This is real," I repeat. "Grappling with the real is the way to go."

Somewhere in the midst of this conversation, Violette interrupts herself to ask me something. "Am I still interesting to you?" she wants to know. "I need to make sure." Her question is odd. I am loving this discussion; I am totally engaged by it. In checking with me, Violette is checking herself; she is interrupting her own flow in a manner that reminds me of her past reports of performance anxiety onstage. I point out the pattern. "You get self-conscious," I say, "and then pull away. Your self-doubt takes over and it becomes a self-fulfilling prophecy." The parallels to both sex and meditation are clear to me.

I reassure Violette that I am interested in the full catastrophe. She understands the reference. Her writing has brought her deeper into conversation with herself and I think her partner will be grateful despite the presumed distance her new pursuits may bring.

In a subsequent session with Violette, she told me that when she was little, she would often be given time-outs by her well-meaning parents whenever she exhibited any hint of anger. "I grew up in the time of time-outs," she said with a slight smile. She remembered one time when she was four years old—already an actor—marching around the house pretending to be a soldier, when her parents took her foot stomping as a sign of defiance rather than play and sent her to her room. "I was raised to be obedient," Violette said. "Even crying wasn't allowed." It had taken a year of therapy for her to reveal this, but once it emerged, Violette's issues made more sense. Anger, and the separation it entailed, was threatening. Her parents had made sure of that. But aggression is a fact of life and it is not always bad. In fact, it is often necessary.

Violette's parents had taught her about anger's dangerous side. "It should be regarded as like stale urine mixed with poison, or as a forest fire that burns up its own support," reads one ancient Buddhist commentary that they would have approved of, but they had not helped her integrate what we might term healthy aggression. By suppressing any manifestation of self-assertion, they had encouraged Violette to favor submission over her own agency. Her spontaneous worry that she was no longer "interesting" to me was evidence of this, as were her conflicts over maintaining an independent creative focus. This is territory that has been mapped by a number of feminist psychoanalysts, one of whom once reported visiting a friend who had just given birth in the hospital only to find that while the newborn boys were greeted with a blue sign reading I'M A BOY! the girls' bassinets were adorned with pink signs reading IT'S A GIRL! The lack of support for female agency was not unique to Violette's background.

Violette had a wonderful feeling for the joy of connection and

the benefits of generosity. She was a selfless person in many regards. But her upbringing had not made enough room for healthy
aggression, and this had made it difficult for her to balance the
inevitable give-and-take of separation and connection. Beneath
her compliant exterior lay an aggression that made her feel guilty
and removed from the people she loved. Surrender was not going
to be Violette's rhinoceros. She knew about surrender already.
Her rhinoceros was much more likely to look like a rhinoceros.

Margaret · 10/22/19: 6:00 p.m.

Margaret was on retreat in upstate New York for a week and had a dream while there of her mother, dead for many years, descending through the cracks in the ceiling onto her sleeping body and fighting with her. It was a physical altercation, she was hitting, biting, and scratching Margaret and eventually ripped Margaret's glasses off her face. I listen wide eyed. I have seen Margaret for several years but there are details of her growing up I am still ignorant of. This is the most in-depth description of her relationship with her mother I have ever heard. It turns out that this kind of fight was not unusual in Margaret's early home life. She was an only child and her mother was a single mother; Margaret's father left the family when she was a year old, and her thirty-five-year-old mother never recovered, remaining depressed and often suicidal for much of her life. They lived in a small, cramped apartment, and Margaret's main escape was in the local air-conditioned library, where she became a voracious reader. But her mother often lashed out, criticizing her, hitting her, and calling her names.

Margaret always felt that she didn't love her mother enough, there was just "nothing there," it was "so boring" at home, and she always felt bad about her negative feelings. In high school, Margaret discovered LSD and found that when she was mildly tripping, her mother didn't bother her so much. I am incredulous that she could trip while at home with her mother, but Margaret says that it worked for her. She was a teenager and didn't have an endless supply of the drug, but she used to break what she had into little pieces and use it in a manner that today would be called microdosing. The drug took her fury away while allowing her to remain physically present. Instead of being in her usual uncomfortable state with her mother, in her mind she would be marveling at the universe! As a result, she felt less responsible for her mother's pain and instead felt some compassion for her predicament.

In the dream, after her mother rips the glasses off her face, Margaret tries to get her to look her in the eye. The implication (in my mind) is that she can calm her mother by getting her to look at her and that this kind of looking is what is missing in their relationship. Her mother does look at her in the dream, there is some kind of meaningful exchange, and Margaret has a feeling of accomplishment. It is a positive outcome, a nightmare turned on its head, her mother descending through the crack in the ceiling to assault her but yielding to her daughter's plea for human contact. I congratulate Margaret and speak of the significance of the dream coming in the midst of her retreat. Something is seeking healing.

Margaret throws out a confession: her mother's violence was not always so unprovoked. At some point Margaret discovered that if she could get her mother to hit her, in her mother's subsequent remorse, Margaret was free. She could leave the claustrophobic apartment—her ultimate goal—without so much guilt. The dream seems to have brought all of this to the fore. Margaret blamed herself, as children often do, for her mother's unhappiness and zeroed in on what she took to be the ultimate problem. "If I liked her more, she would have had an easier time," she says.

I am not so sure that her diagnosis is correct. Making oneself the problem, as noble as it can be to take responsibility for one's bad behavior, is often the ego's solution to otherwise unsolvable situations. "Maybe your mother was just beleaguered and overwhelmed," I suggest. "Maybe it wasn't that you didn't love her enough but that you wanted her to be happier and took responsibility the way kids often do. What if it wasn't your fault and you were just fishing around for the reason for her unhappiness? As a child, you can't read the situation as it actually is; you can't help but put yourself at the center of things."

In Margaret's dream, she got her mother to look into her eyes. I wonder out loud whether that gaze might have gone in the other direction too. Could seeing her mother more clearly lessen some of the guilt Margaret is carrying? Did John Cage's vision of a world of unlimited interpenetrating centers apply here too?

. . .

This session was a striking example of how a dream can peel away the accumulated pain of experience to reveal a soft core of fundamental empathy. In previous work I have called this essential substrate one's "implicit memory," to indicate that it is available, not as an explicit recollection, but as an intrinsic capacity. Margaret's dream took her backward in time, from the abuse she fielded at the hand of her mother to the gaze that bound them as mother and daughter from the earliest moments of her life. That she had the dream while on retreat, and could talk about it while in therapy, shows how possible it is for therapy and meditation to work in harmony. Margaret's triumphal dream brought her back to something essential in herself. It let her see her mother once again with eyes untainted by all they had been through.

In Winnicott's article on the capacity for concern, he addresses precisely the scenario that Margaret rectified in her dream.

In the initial stages of development, if there is no reliable mother-figure to receive the reparation-gesture, the guilt becomes intolerable, and concern cannot be felt. Failure of reparation leads to a losing of the capacity for concern, and to its replacement by primitive forms of guilt and anxiety.

In establishing eye contact with her mother in the dream, Margaret was successfully making the reparative gesture she had been previously denied. Her mother was able, in the dream, to put aside her own ongoing rage and acknowledge Margaret's overture. If Winnicott is correct, we would expect to see a diminution in Margaret's guilt as a result, more enduring than that temporarily afforded her by LSD.

Carol · 10/30/19: 11:30 a.m.

Carol is a longtime patient, now in her early fifties, who moved to London seven or eight years ago to live with her boyfriend, a professor of economics at the Royal College. Carol's mother killed herself when Carol was four, and much of our early work together involved making sense of the emotional residue of this act. I learned a lot about what is called "developmental trauma" from working with Carol. Developmental trauma is trauma that occurs when we are children, from either bad things happening or good-enough things not happening. The classic example is of an infant crying for its mother past the point of self-soothing. The emotional consequences are too intense for the child to bear and, to protect himself or herself, dissociation takes place in which the unbearable feelings are closed off and put aside so that the child can go forward safely. A kind of armor is created, but the unmanageable feelings lurk and rise up unbidden at inopportune times as if out of nowhere. Winnicott described such feelings as like being "infinitely dropped," and eloquently wrote of how the afflicted person often fears a breakdown that has already happened. The person projects the thing from the past into the future because they were not able to be present with the breakdown when it was actually taking place. To be free, they have to be able to remember the trauma that was never fully experienced, and they have to be able to put it in its proper place in history.

Carol taught me a lot about this. Her mother died before Carol could process the loss. She grew up with an absence that no one in her extended family was ever willing to address, and she learned to pretend that everything was okay. But her inner life was suffused with an inexplicable (to her) longing that threatened her adult intimate relationships. No matter how close she was to someone, there was always a place within her that could not be touched. She experienced it as longing or depression or frustration, as a darkness that would periodically take her over and that she did not understand. Over time, in our work together, we were able to make sense of these feelings. They were the emotions of a young child who did not yet have the language to describe what she was feeling. I would often read, and reread, and then paraphrase to her a famous late paper of Winnicott's called "Fear of Breakdown," in which he described his vision of such a scenario.

Today's session is the only time I am likely to see Carol this year. She is visiting from London, and I detect a change in her prevailing mood. She seems settled into herself, comfortable, and she is exuding a confidence that has a faint sensuality about it. I have noticed this before but it is stronger now. "You know that dark, spiky thing we've talked so much about," she begins. "It comes into focus now and again but it doesn't have the same power it used to. What should I be doing with it now?" This dark and spiky thing used to frighten and threaten to overwhelm Carol. It has haunted her since she was young. Is it her mother? The absence of her mother? Her own anger or fear? "Me-in-her, her-as-me." Carol smiles. "It's like you're seeing it in the rearview mirror now," I say. "I've been sitting again a little bit," she replies. She means she is meditating again. "You told me not to do it before," she adds. Indeed, I told her not to meditate when she was in the midst of the darkness. Her mind did not have the collectedness to tolerate the feelings that leapt out at her. She needed understanding, verbal and conceptual framing, before she could use meditation in any profitable way. "Now when I sit I mostly have a transparent feeling; I feel sort of porous," she says. "Is this wrong?"

I don't think it is wrong at all; I think it is absolutely right. Carol is letting go of her former identity, centered as it was on an insatiable longing for a mother she barely knew. In its place is the mature woman she has become. "You know," she says, "I think I buried the lede. Bob and I got married last month. At a register office, just a couple of friends, we went out for lunch after, took a nap, and then went to dinner. It was wonderful." I get a few more details and then the conversation drifts back to previous territory. "This thought came into my head recently," she says. "She's more dead now . . . she would be seventy-nine." I think of Ram Dass's long-ago question to me: "Do you see them as already free?" Carol has become the person she was always meant to be. I felt it in her from the beginning of our relationship, but now she can feel it too. I sense an unparalleled satisfaction as Carol gets up to leave.

• • •

In Winnicott's "Fear of Breakdown" paper, he spent considerable time (for him) on the topic of emptiness, not Buddhist emptiness per se, but the psychological kind, the psychic remnant of nothing happening when something might have. Carol had experienced a lot of this kind of emptiness, and we had traced it to the death of her mother, the loss that she could never properly process when she was young.

> *Now, emptiness is a prerequisite for eagerness to gather in. Primary emptiness simply means: before starting to fill up. A considerable maturity is needed for this state to be meaningful.*

Emptiness occurring in a treatment is a state that the patient is trying to experience, a past state that cannot be remembered except by being experienced for the first time now.

In practice the difficulty is that the patient fears the awfulness of emptiness, and in defence will organise a controlled emptiness by not eating or not learning, or else will ruthlessly fill up by a greediness which is compulsive and which feels mad. When the patient can reach to emptiness itself and tolerate this state . . . then, taking in can start up as a pleasurable function . . . also it is in this way that some of our patients who cannot learn can begin to learn pleasurably.

Suffice it to say that Carol has reached the state of considerable maturity that Winnicott describes. She is starting to fill up, and her new husband is fortunate to be by her side. The tide, once again, is foaming at the very gate.

Corinne · 11/12/19: 11:00 a.m.

Corinne is back after a nine-month break. She was in Japan for six months with her husband and ten-year-old son and then in the country for the summer. October was too busy and November is shaping up as no easier. Her husband's birthday was last week and her son's is next week. Corinne is a human rights lawyer in her late forties who is taking care of her aging parents as well as her husband and son. I feel a great deal of sympathy for her. Today she describes herself as overwhelmed with a jangly, tired feeling behind her eyes. Not getting sufficient sleep, she understands for the first time what people mean when they say they cannot take the incessant input from the media. It's all rubbing her the wrong way: the phone, the computer, social media, and the radio talking at her in the kitchen with its endlessly cycling news. She feels barraged. She and her husband are recovering from a big fight with their son over his wish/demand for a smartphone for his eleventh birthday. They are not ready to capitulate but agreed to get him a portable gaming console he can play in the car instead. Now she has to decide where to host his birthday party. They did a paintball party last year but the sight of all those boys with their guns was too much for her. There is an arcade on Forty-Second Street he is interested in, or it's possible an escape room might be better. Corinne is tired of how precious all the birthday parties have become. Why can't they just have people over to the house for barbecue and birthday cake? Corinne wants to start taking better care of herself. She is busy, too busy, and is drinking more than one glass of wine at night. Her stomach has had a knot in it for a day or two, and she thinks that there must also be a hormonal aspect to her discomfort.

In an effort to take better care of herself, Corinne stopped at Whole Foods yesterday to pick up some fish for dinner before getting her son from school. She wants cleaner food and was planning to make a Japanese-inspired dinner that night of fresh fish and vegetables. She made an effort while preparing dinner to settle herself down. She turned off the radio and concentrated her mind on the simple act of chopping the vegetables. "That was the best I could do," she said. "There was no time to meditate or anything but I told myself I could just chop the vegetables carefully. I didn't try to look at any of the thousands of emails I hadn't had time to read. I just did the one thing." Her son paid attention. He could sometimes lose his temper in ways that frightened his parents, but he was sweet with her while she worked. "He was happy because he could have sushi for lunch the next day," Corinne says. I exclaim, "He gets sushi for lunch? Wow!" Corinne tells me about a plastic mold for easily making sushi and explains that she can use a bit of the leftover cooked fish with the rice. I make a mental note.

"I still ate too fast," Corinne tells me with a bit of a smile. "I couldn't maintain that deliberate attention I had while chopping vegetables. But it was something."

"That would make a good magazine piece," I say to her. "A good column." Corinne and I sometimes talk about writing ideas. She is good at it, and I enjoy showing her how the things she spontaneously talks to me about have lots of inherent wisdom in them. She agrees. "It wouldn't be the usual 'everything's perfect' kind of report," she says. "Those pieces are of no use: 'I chopped the vegetables and realized this was the way to perfect harmony.'

But I can see that this is where the struggle is. How to give myself some islands of sanity in the midst of everything I have to do."

The Japanese poet Issa, whose haiku about mating flies had so charmed me on the island in Maine and whose poem about the death of his child had so moved me later that summer, wrote another haiku that Corinne's session brought to mind.

Never forget:
we walk on hell,
gazing at flowers.

There she was making sushi for her son even while feeling totally stressed out. Winnicott, with his compassion for mothers everywhere, would have appreciated Corinne's resilience, her primary maternal preoccupation, and her heart. Despite all the reasons to be irritated, Corinne did not give in. She could find flowers even while walking on hell.

Zach is upset with himself for always being in a rush. He eats too fast, drinks too much, and is always onto the next thing before he has finished the last. He recently had a visit in which a colleague found much to praise in several of his recent poems and urged him to continue to develop them further. Zach was surprised. He had already dismissed these works as inferior, rushing through them much as he described hurrying his eating and drinking, and was back to feeling stuck and uninspired. Zach expresses a kind of resignation that is not unfamiliar in our conversations. Then, rather uncharacteristically, he tells me of a dream he had the night before.

In the dream, Zach is at a party. There are lots of people there. Someone points an attractive woman in his direction and tells her that Zach is interested in her. Off to the side a couple is having sex standing up. The man is forcefully fucking in what seems almost a parody of pornographic sex. Zach goes down on his newfound friend but cannot "find her vagina" due to a thicket of pubic hair in his way. He is aware of the fornicating couple in his periphery and feels inadequate in comparison.

I ask Zach if he would like to analyze the dream. He is surprised. "Do you do that?" he says. "We can," I reply. "Can you tell me the dream from the woman's perspective?" I inquire. Zach does not quite know what to do with the question. He retells me the dream, but it is still basically from the perspective of the dreamer; he continues to refer to the woman in the third person and can't get past describing his own experience as inadequate. I explain to him that since the dream is his creation, all of the characters in it quite possibly are aspects of himself. I compare the picture of the man in the periphery engaged in rhythmic but emotionless sex with that of the woman Zach is going down on. "Doing versus being," I say, thinking of the distinction between the male and female elements present in all of us. The masculine element *does* while the female one *is*. Winnicott describes nursing mothers who let their infants find the breast as embodying the female element while those who force their breast on their babies are acting out the male principle. Meditation, I often think, requires surrendering to, or empowering, one's female aspect, becoming more of the "environment-mother" he talked about in his paper on concern; even though the application of the technique when one is first learning is more of an active and intentional process.

I remind Zach of what he has already told me about rushing through things and about reflexively critiquing his own work. Both of these functions are dominated by the male element. "Your dream might suggest that you are in search of the female aspect of your personality," I say. "Didn't you say you couldn't find the vagina?" Zach is a bit embarrassed. "I meant the clitoris," he says. But he is also intrigued. He is not sure what I mean by the female element in himself and asks me to explain in other words. I know that Zach has taken a class or two in qigong, a Chinese martial art, and try to use language from Taoism to explain. "You know in the *I Ching* how one hexagram is six straight lines and represents the dynamic, creative, active yang principle, and another is six broken lines and represents the receptive, yielding, earth yin principle?" I begin. Zach does not know what I am talking about. He has never consulted the *I Ching*, except perhaps one time online.

I go over to my bookshelf and take down my well-thumbed copy of Richard Wilhelm's Bollingen version. I give Zach three pennies and instruct him to throw them six times. "Let's see what the *Ching* says about your dream," I say. Zach is happy to comply. The *I Ching* is an ancient oracle; it was a favorite of John Cage, who used it to bypass his ego when composing music. The pennies' heads count as three and their tails as two. Three heads is a nine, an unbroken straight yang line. Three tails is a six, a broken yin line. Two heads and a tail make an eight, a broken line that changes to a straight one, and two tails and a head yield a seven, a straight line that changes to a broken one. There are sixty-four possible hexagrams, and each one has a title with a specific message attached. In addition, each changing line (the sevens and the eights) has its own specific oracular pronouncement.

Zach throws hexagram twenty-one: *Biting Through.*

The first lines of the interpretation read as follows. Crouching by his side, I read it aloud to Zach:

This hexagram represents an open mouth . . . with an obstruction . . . between the teeth. As a result the lips cannot meet. To bring them together one must bite energetically through the obstacle.

We are both incredulous. The hexagram is describing Zach's dream, the thicket of pubic hair blocking his mouth from his partner's genitals. This allows us to talk at some length about how Zach gets in his own way, about how his image of who he is supposed to be (like the man on the periphery of his dream fucking mechanically) obscures who he actually is or could be.

It wasn't the first time that the *I Ching* has come to my rescue.

. . .

It is interesting that the article in which Winnicott most deeply explores the male/female dichotomy is ostensibly about creativity. Entitled "Creativity and Its Origins," his paper begins with a powerfully succinct statement that might have been directed exclusively at Zach.

> *It is creative apperception more than anything else that makes the individual feel that life is worth living. Contrasted with this is a relationship to external reality which is one of compliance, the world and its details being recognized but only as something to be fitted in with or demanding adaptation. Compliance carries with it a sense of futility for the individual and is associated with the idea that nothing matters and that life is not worth living. In a tantalizing way many individuals have experienced just enough of creative living to recognize that for most of their time they are living uncreatively, as if caught up in the creativity of someone else, or of a machine.*

Zach could relate to this formulation. He was dogged by a tenuous connection to his own creativity, undercutting it by presumptively comparing himself with others. He had often expressed the kind of futility that Winnicott so deftly described.

Winnicott tied "being" to the infant's earliest relationship with the mother. His formulation is a little bit difficult to understand at first, but when it clicks it definitely makes sense. The infant, in his view, does not have a self at the beginning of life, so the proverbial "infant at the breast" is not a "being-at-one-with" experience, it is not a "union" of two selves becoming one. A nursing infant finds himself or herself when he or she finds the breast. That is the key point for Winnicott: self-knowledge comes from connection. "Two separate persons can *feel* at one," he writes, "but here at the place that I am examining the baby and the object *are* one." Winnicott, and here the parallels to the Buddha are difficult to ignore, believed that "being" precedes "doing," and that its recovery is the route back to our original nature. He felt that "being" is everyone's birthright, but that it is something of a lost art, that compliance often robs people of it, that creativity depends on it, and that therapy can serve as a means of rediscovering it if a therapist is sensitive to the need and does not let their male element, in the form of intrusive interpretations, however erudite they may be, interfere. The Buddha, to my mind, thought along the same lines. He said that our original nature is obscured by our cravings and our frustrations, that the ego that emerges in healthy emotional development, while necessary for some things, also blocks us from our underlying and inherent freedom. "Be here now," my old friend Ram Dass used to proclaim, making it sound as if it were the easiest thing in the world.

While he never directly referenced Buddhism in his writings, Winnicott came close in his paper on creativity, referring instead to the heroic figures of Greek myth who sound, to my ears at least, suspiciously like the yogis and tantric monks of Tibet and the Indian subcontinent.

Psychoanalysts have perhaps . . . neglected the subject-object identity to which I am drawing attention here, which is at the basis of the capacity to be. The male element does while the female element (in males and females) is. Here would come in those males in Greek myth who tried to be at one with the supreme goddess. Here also is a way of stating a male person's very deep-seated envy of women whose female element men take for granted, sometimes in error.

We might take Zach's dream to be another example of this age-old yearning to be one with the beloved. Or, from a Buddhist perspective, we might take it one step further, into territory that Winnicott actually had in mind when he wrote about the fertile place that exists before subject and object make their first appearances. Buddhism uses words like "is-ness," "thusness," "nonduality," or "emptiness" to express what it feels like when this place is rediscovered later in life. Winnicott knew that it was there from the beginning.

Buddhism agrees that our fundamental reality is rooted in the experience of nonduality and that it remains accessible throughout life, a potential reservoir of inspiration and nourishment. The Buddha's own recovery of his childhood joy under the rose-apple tree was evidence of this. Our true nature, like the sound of one hand, is hiding in plain sight, the story reminds us, although most of us, like Zach in his dream and the Buddha before his awakening, are confused about how, and where, to find it. In needing to "bite through" his obstruction, Zach's dream reinforced an important Buddhist principle: aggression is a double-edged sword. It can be used destructively or it can be recruited to push past that which keeps us removed from our capacity to be.

Chloe · 12/5/19: 10:30 a.m.

Chloe is a new patient, relatively new. She is coming every other week, and I have met with her half a dozen times since the summer. She is thirty-nine years old, married, and the mother of a one-and-a-half-year-old son. A nutritionist who previously worked in fashion, Chloe has a good energy. She is smart and funny, and we have had some meaningful conversations about the pressures she feels in her competing roles of family and work. In something of an aside in the midst of today's conversation, Chloe looks at me quizzically and says, "What is your method, anyway? It's like 'friendly conversation' with occasional moments of illumination, is that it?" "That's about right," I reply, glad for the nod to illumination. Sometime later she adds the following: "I was thinking, with the baby and all, right now you're my only friend." I know she is exaggerating, but I am grateful for the compliment. "I'm happy to come to see you," she adds, "and then I'm happy to go back home again."

. . .

I never had to do much more than reflect Chloe's own energy back to her. She was open and spontaneous in her conversations with me, always able, even when struggling with something that bothered her, to see humor in the situation. The freedom that I knew was possible for many of my patients was very obvious in

Chloe. She took this freedom for granted, I think, and did not necessarily realize how special it was but I did my best to make room for it when she was with me. There was a lightness and ease to our discussions that was very affirming for both of us. I was happy for her when she told me several weeks later that she was once again pregnant.

PART THREE

THE GATE OF ONENESS

A monk asked, "What is one word?"

The Master said, "Two words."

CHAO-CHOU, *Recorded Sayings,* #257

Seven

Kindness

What did I learn this year about Buddhism's influence on my work? Chloe's offhand comment about my method being one of friendly conversation with moments of illumination was as good an answer as any. She was onto me, and I appreciated her insouciance as well as her affection. But I will try to say more. I learned a lot in this year. The act of retrieving, recording, and documenting the details of these sessions let me envision every one as a haiku. The minutiae of each ordinary conversation, like the tiny particulars of the natural world that inspired the Zen masters, hinted at larger truths. I knew when I chose to write down a session that something in it contained a clue about my approach. Some bit of spiritual friendship had unfurled, some nugget of Buddhism had guided my words and behavior, but it was not often clear to me what it actually was. I had the feeling but not the words to explain it. In exploring the session in each accompanying reflection, I tried to find my reasons for choosing it.

This process led me from a focus on clinging to an explication of mindfulness to an emphasis on insight to a reassessment of aggression. All of those things are of critical importance, and my efforts to illuminate them for my patients contributed to the spiritual dimension of our dialogue. But at the same time my self-reflection made me circle a more intangible quality of therapy, one that some might dismiss as placebo effect but that I have come to believe is at the core of what makes therapy therapeutic. In this book, I have called this quality the Zen of therapy but I might also have called it the art of therapy or simply called it kindness. This is what Chloe was remarking on, and it was what, in turn, I felt from her. Kindness is the thread that runs through the work of Winnicott, Cage, and the Buddha, each of whom discovered that noninterfering attentiveness—in a mother, an artist, a meditator, or a therapist—is, by its very nature, transformative. This attitude is redolent in the words of Ram Dass to my patient Lakshman—"love the thoughts" and "see yourself as a soul"—and in his early query to me, "Do you see them [my patients] as already free?" It is there in Michael Vincent Miller's praise of innocence after experience, in Adam Phillips's implicit critique of therapy as feeding our grievances, and in John Tarrant's explication of the koan as a vehicle for changing our views of ourselves. I hope it comes through in many of my sessions as well.

How has Buddhism used me in my role as therapist? How have I used Buddhism? As I think about this year's worth of work, I can see one thing very clearly. Let me put it in a nutshell: I introduce my patients to a meditative sensibility by the way in which I relate to them. Maybe this should have been obvious from the start! But in examining my method, I can see that while I am different with every patient, I am myself with all of them. I learned from meditation how to let myself be, and this is the quality that guides me. As is evident in my write-ups, I do not model this sensibility by resting calmly in a meditative state while my patients free-associate. I engage actively. But I am very quiet inside when I am working; all of my concentration, all of my attention, goes to the person I am with. And I want to know everything, from the television shows they are watching to the food they are eating to their most dreadful thoughts and reflections. I believe in the power of awareness to heal. I want my patients to see how and when and where their egos, or superegos, are getting the best of them, because I know that if and when they can see this clearly, something in them will release. And their best chance of seeing it comes when my mind is quiet. Somehow, my inner silence resonates in them and feeds their awareness. Each person is like a koan I cannot solve with my rational mind. I have to give myself over completely, while staying very much myself, to let their koan and my response to it become one thing. When this one thing fills the interpersonal field, the hidden kindness in life, present in each of us, gets revealed.

Winnicott, in his final major paper, came to a similar understanding about his therapeutic technique. He was by no means a Buddhist, but I believe he, too, healed by modeling being. He mostly used mother/infant vocabulary to describe his mode of relating, but this did not stop him from describing, in disarmingly frank terms, his own internal process:

> It is only in recent years that I have become able to wait and wait . . . and to avoid breaking up this natural process by making interpretations. . . . It appals me to think how much deep change I have prevented or delayed . . . by my personal need to interpret. If only we can wait, the patient arrives at understanding creatively and with immense joy, and I now enjoy this joy more than I used to enjoy the sense of having been clever. I think I interpret mainly to let the patient know the limits of my understanding. The principle is that it is the patient and only the patient who has the answers. We may or may not enable him or her to encompass what is known or become aware of it with acceptance.

The Zen of therapy rests on just this kind of attitude. People come with all kinds of strange sorrows. They want to understand their experiences and learn from them. They want to make sense of what happened to make them what they are. And while that is interesting to me, too, I know that learning from experience is not all that it is cracked up to be. There is more to a person than who they think they are. Sometimes therapy has to act like the unmoving shadow of the rose-apple tree, creating circumstances conducive for unlearning, creativity, and joy.

Learning by unlearning. How often in this book have I disoriented people to the systems and explanations they have created for themselves? Disorienting systems is something both Buddhism and therapy can agree on. Things that feel fixed, set, permanent, and unchanging, like one's self-righteous anger, are never as real as they seem. Problems are not hard and fast, selves are not static and motionless, even memory is nothing we can be certain about. The Zen of therapy wants to get things moving again. It wants to open things up, make people less sure of themselves, and in the process release some of the energy that has become stuck in the mud. Rational explanations have their place, but irrational breakthroughs, like those that come out of koan practice, are invigorating because they alert us to capacities we do not know we have.

As this year of sessions has confirmed for me, when enough trust is built up in the therapeutic relationship, there is a chance to release, and be released from, a self-preoccupation that is no longer serving a reasonable purpose. The path I have outlined eventually leads to the realization that simple kindness is the fuel of the peace of mind we all crave. When the mind object drops away, even for an instant, all kinds of latent interpersonal possibilities emerge—for connection, empathy, insight, joy, and, dare we say, love. How to make this happen remains the trickiest of questions. There is no formula to follow, no script that can be written that will ensure success. But this project has affirmed for me that therapy does indeed have the potential to catalyze such openings. Therapy can bring out the hidden intimacy that gives meaning to life. I have chronicled these sessions to explore what such openings look like when they occur and to describe what brings them forth. What risks I have sometimes taken with my patients! How brave and vulnerable they have been in response!

Maybe it is because many of my patients are now between the ages of forty and seventy, but more and more I have been hearing stories about reconciliation—of sorts—with aging parents who were parental disasters. Many of these parents were caught up in the societal upheavals of their youth and were unprepared for the sacrifice, discipline, and demands of having children. But have children they did. Some of my patients' parents were alcoholics or drug dealers; some were academics, revolutionaries, chefs, gamblers, actors, or self-proclaimed healers; others retreated to lesbian communes in Vermont or were on spiritual paths of one sort or another; some were just trying to survive. Certain of them were physically cruel; others were abusive in their neglect or in their physical and mental absence. A number of them divorced when my patients were in elementary school; more than a few of the departing husbands found their way back to their spurned wives decades later when their subsequent relationships foundered. My patients, only some of whom have made it into this volume, are survivors (I object to the overuse of that term but it is not inappropriate) one and all. They gravitated to New York City, prospered, and used therapy to, among other things, gain perspective on what they had been through. And, to my endless surprise and amazement, almost uniformly, as their parents have aged, these children (now adults themselves) have reached out with a care and consideration that my more cynical self would not have foretold.

I do not feel in any way that this behavior is unique to *my* patients, and I think, at best, it must be just a by-product of our therapy, but I am in the position, by virtue of being their doctor, to observe something that is much more universal, although not often remarked upon in our culture. It is not forgiveness necessarily ("forbearance" might be a better word) but something much more basic: an expression of the regard we all have for those who did or did not care for us before we had any idea of who or what we are. Why does that statement of Ram Dass's, "we are all walking each other home," have such resonance? What is the home we are all walking toward?

Babies come into life programmed to search out their mothers' faces. The simple trust and affection we are born with remains operational even when mishandled by those we depend on. What I see in my patients is that, while they have not necessarily absolved or condoned the behavior of their misbegotten parents, they have worked hard not to be destroyed by it. In their latter-day regard for those very same people, they are demonstrating their own resilience, declaring to their parents, themselves, their own children, and the world that the qualities that make us most human endure. This declaration is a natural outgrowth of a meditative sensibility. When I observe it in my patients, I know that the therapy is on the right track.

The movement from grievance to gratitude is the essence of what the confluence of Buddhism and psychotherapy engenders. Yes, it is important to make sense of one's personal experiences, to face all of the distressing aspects of one's history, to name the abuses and traumas and neglect, and to own the shame, anger, addictive cravings, and low self-esteem that one's identity has coalesced around as a result. But it is also important to know that one does not have to be defined by these things. To hold them all lightly, the way a mother holds a baby, is to let an underlying, fundamental, and interpersonally entangled benevolence shine through. Eventually, through the peeling away of overly elaborated, and often punitive, self-concepts, one discovers that this underlying truth is accessible, even in the midst of everyday difficulties. This is the gate of oneness, a doorway that is nothing but open space.

How to best describe this sensibility? I can give a few examples.

I gave a virtual interview for an online social university the other day (before COVID I had no idea that online social universities even existed, and I am still not sure exactly what they are) and had a surprising conversation with the host as we were setting up the Zoom connection that spoke to all this. We had a half hour to kill before the portal was open for the attendees, and we needed to pass the time. I was participating rather grudgingly as Zeki, my host, asked me what seemed like rather formulaic questions. About halfway through, as I was eyeing the clock on my computer, Zeki asked my thoughts about the current fascination with the therapeutic use of "plant medicines." I knew he was referring to psychedelic substances like psilocybin and ayahuasca, and I told him how, for me, this "new" interest was actually a "renewed" interest in something that I was already familiar with from my time around Ram Dass in the aftermath of his dismissal from Harvard in the 1960s. Many people I knew had had intense and revelatory experiences with these substances and had let their drug-assisted insights inspire them, often with the backing and support of therapy and meditation. But others failed to integrate their revelations and remained overly stuck in their pre-psychedelic selves or, even worse, used their insights to justify or rationalize continuing insensitive or abusive behavior. Zeki then opened up about his own recent experience with ayahuasca, and the tenor of our conversation changed. Worrying now that we had only fifteen minutes left to talk, I did my best to elicit his story from him.

"I'm Jewish," Zeki began. "I grew up in Turkey until we moved to Scotland when I was ten. My grandmother is the one who taught me about Judaism. She gave me this prayer, 'God is one.' I have it here, inscribed, around my neck." Zeki fingered a stone or an amulet under his T-shirt, the contours of which remained invisible to me as we spoke.

I knew the prayer he was referring to: "Hear, O Israel, the Lord our God, the Lord is One." It is a prayer from the Torah that is often recited in temple but not one that had ever meant much to me. When I was young, I always thought people were saying, "Here, O Israel," rather than "hear," and I would mostly tune out when it was recited. But Zeki was emphasizing the final phrase and simplifying it a little. "God is one" has a slightly different ring than "the Lord is One."

"This was my only psychedelic experience," Zeki continued, "and that prayer resounded all the way through. 'God is one.' My grandmother came to me at the beginning (she's been dead for many years but there she was) and I felt this incredible love she had for me. An outpouring of love, it was all around me. Then I felt the love of others in my family: my brother, my parents, and so on. And I realized how selfish I've been in return, how I haven't been able to love as freely and completely as they have. And then the prayer took off in my head, the prayer from my grandmother. I had always thought it meant that God was up there, that he was the all-powerful One, apart from everything else, looking down, but now I saw it differently."

I nodded. That was always my objection to it too. The idea of an omnipotent creator God never made much sense to me.

"I understood it differently," he said. "God is everything, everything and everywhere. That's what it means that God is one. And I remembered the follow-up, 'Thou shalt love the Lord thy God with all your heart, with all your soul, with all your might.'" Zeki repeated the last phrase and made a fist. "With all your *might*. I felt love for everything all around me. The way I had been holding back just melted away."

I told Zeki that he should forget interviewing me and let me interview him! "It would be much more interesting," I said. Listening to him, I knew that his take on oneness was totally in line with the Buddha, Cage, Winnicott, and the Zen poets my year of contemplation had put me in touch with. *Being* rather than doing. Oneness, not as merger with an omnipotent or idealized other, but as an infinite matrix of interpenetrating centers. Oneness, not as a place apart from it all, but as an invisible membrane encompassing everything and everyone including itself. His grandmother's affection as an expression of the love that underlies all existence. Innocence after experience. "All your might" as a stand-in for the infant's ruthless love for the mother and the soul's longing for God (whatever those words "soul" and "God" might mean!). Ayahuasca had cleared, at least temporarily, the debris from Zeki's mind and let him peer deeply into one of the great truths of our being. In loving everything and everyone, we *are* love. I thought of my patient Zach and his dream of recovering "being" while having sex. I thought of Jack like a bodhisattva healing his survivor parents, of Debby in Calcutta seeing everyone as Jesus, of Margaret peering into her mother's newly attentive eyes in her dream, of Willa making room for her uncorrupted love for her father, and of Rebecca's frozen shoulder, paralysis where once her love had flowed. Zeki was affirming all of this for me, and more: plums blossoming in a year of therapy. He was putting a new slant on the inquiry that had motivated this book. How do I filter a Buddhist sensibility into my work? By knowing that, despite our multiplicity, we are all the same.

I had only a little time left to chat, but I was curious about one thing. "There are Jews in Turkey?" I inquired. "I had no idea. Where? In Istanbul?"

"Yes," he said. "From 1492, when they were expelled from Spain, Turkey was one of the places that took them in. When the Ottoman Empire fell years later, most of them left, some to Eastern Europe and some to the Middle East, but a few remained. They are mostly traders. And they continue to speak a form of Old Spanish, among many other languages. Ladino, it is called. For almost six hundred years, that's how it went. Only in my generation has it begun to change. When we moved to Scotland," he continued, "I didn't speak the language or anything. I had to keep part of me under wraps as a result. And I always felt, even when I was relating wholeheartedly, that there was a part of me that I couldn't express, something I had to keep back. I felt that give way after the ayahuasca."

I was very moved by Zeki's account. It came as a confirmation of everything I had been thinking as I worked on this book, and it brought to mind something I first heard from the Dalai Lama more than forty years ago.

On his initial trip to America, in 1979, during which time we met with him in Dr. Benson's office at the Beth Israel Hospital in Boston, the Dalai Lama gave a series of lectures at universities and churches and museums and community centers around the country. Jeffrey Hopkins, the professor at the University of Virginia who accompanied us on our trip to Dharamsala to measure the temperatures of the heat yoga monks, served as his translator and later collected his talks into the first book published in North America by the Dalai Lama: *Kindness, Clarity, and Insight*. Because it was his first trip and because he was working hard to convey the depth and breadth of his tradition, his talks were fresh, rich, and varied, filled with the untrammeled optimism of his then forty-four-year-old self. He gave some portion of each talk in broken English but then, with Hopkins translating, launched into intricate explications of Buddhist psychology and philosophy that were vivid and compelling, and that always circled back to the central importance of kindness. As Hopkins put it in his preface, "The appeal is to the heart but by way of the mind, using reason and sense to curb selfishness and to generate deeply felt altruism." The Dalai Lama's talk at Trinity Church in Boston, given the evening before we met with him at the hospital, turned out to be especially relevant for the themes of this book.

In his talk entitled "Altruism and the Six Perfections," the

Dalai Lama used mother/infant imagery, not as a metaphor for
ultimate understanding, but as an introduction to the qualities to
be cultivated in the search for inner peace. In doing so, he made
it clear that kindness is central to both the beginning and the end
of the entire journey of awakening. Speaking to an audience
wholly unfamiliar with the intricacies of Buddhist thought, he
outlined a practice far removed from their conceptions of meditation. There was no talk of emptying the mind, watching the
breath, relaxing the body, or dealing with stress. There was only
a discussion of the kindness of mothers.

"The main theme of Buddhism," the Dalai Lama began, "is
altruism based on compassion and love." He then went on to
teach the foundational Tibetan Buddhist practice of "mother recognition": imagining all beings as one's mother.

*Again, in order to have a sense of closeness and dearness for
others, you must first train in a sense of their kindness
through using as a model a person in this lifetime who was
very kind to yourself and then extending this sense of gratitude to all beings. Since, in general, in this life your mother
was the closest and offered the most help, the process of
meditation begins with recognizing all other sentient beings
as like your mother.*

The Dalai Lama was helped by his belief in reincarnation.
Over an infinite period of time, he reasoned, we have died and
been reborn countless times, so, if we take that idea seriously, all
beings must have, at one time or another, actually been our mothers and are therefore deserving of our gratitude.

In our culture, of course, in no small part due to the influence
of psychoanalysis, mothers do not have the same universal high
regard that they seem to have had in Tibet, nor do we have a
belief in reincarnation to fall back on. The Dalai Lama himself,

removed from his mother's care early in life to be educated in a monastery, must have found it easy, and perhaps comforting, to idealize her in this way. I remember talking with another Tibetan lama, years later, about how difficult it is for some Westerners to engage with this idea because of how conflicted they are about their own mothers. "For those people," the lama said, smiling, "I always say think about your grandmother instead." He would have approved of my new friend Zeki's ayahuasca memories!

Be that as it may, the simplicity and elegance of the Dalai Lama's imagining is not to be ignored. As a foundational practice, it sets the scene for all that comes later in meditation. For just as Zeki, on his inward journey, was taken up short by his own self-ishness, so does Buddhist psychology seek to reveal our fear-based clinging to our own poorly understood and overly concretized self-concepts. It reaches for this through the practice of mindfulness, holding the mind the way a mother holds her baby: attentively, carefully, and lovingly while not exaggerating or indulging her baby's distress. The Dalai Lama's meditation on mother recognition is a way of reintroducing this essential mental posture to the mind. By seeing all beings as one's mother, one is reminded of one's own capacity, not just for gratitude but for beholding one's own self the way a new parent regards her treasured infant child.

Some people think of this mental posture simply as reparenting, but I do not feel this does it justice. It is more like applying an intrinsic parental capacity to a new developmental task rather than only repairing a developmental lapse. Our minds are like children, and mindfulness, like a good therapist or a good-enough parent, "holds" them so that they can grow up and come to their senses. With enough practice, and enough patience, break-throughs occur. These take many idiosyncratic forms but they are generally of two types.

On the one hand, there is a loosening of identification with the known self; people see their self-concepts as just concepts that have arisen and accumulated in response to the particular challenges and conditions of their lives but that have no ultimate stigmatizing reality. On the other hand, there is a return to simply "being." This is set in motion when awareness becomes dominant, when the observing mind becomes stronger than that which is being observed. As this observational capacity develops, a change sometimes occurs. Instead of one part of the mind observing another—"me" watching "myself"—the whole thing collapses and just "is." These are the Zen states of "thusness" or "suchness" that Winnicott also touched upon when he described the "is-ness" of the mother-infant connection, the replenishment of going to pieces without falling apart. Contact with this in an adult context gives access to a wellspring of positive and life-affirming energy that carries with it an inherent sense of connection.

The closest Freud ever came to probing this experience was in his thirteen-year correspondence with the French poet and Nobel laureate Romain Rolland. Rolland was influenced by the writings of the Indian mystic Sri Ramakrishna, and he was eager to get Freud's thoughts about what he called "the oceanic feeling." This feeling, Rolland wrote, was, to his mind, the origin of all religious sentiment. It gave a sense of the eternal, of no perceptible limits: oceanic, limitless, unbounded, a "feeling of an indissoluble bond, of being one with the external world as a whole." Freud took Rolland's description seriously and did his best to analyze and interpret it. Taking it solely in a regressive direction, though, he called it a restoration of limitless narcissism and a resurrection of infantile helplessness. Religious experiences, he concluded, give satisfaction by reminding us of soothing feelings we once had as infants nursing at our mother's breast. He was correct, I think, but only partially. In essence, he interpreted the oceanic feeling not as a return to "being" but as a satisfaction of primitive "oral" needs. His interpretation became the de facto one about religious experience in the psychoanalytic world, at least until recently, when the field finally moved away from the language of appetites, drives, and instincts toward one of relatedness and connection.

While there certainly are mystical or meditative experiences of merger and union that are satisfying in this way, it seems to me that Freud, in looking solely through the eyes of a needy infant, was missing the boat. Buddhist mindfulness, like therapy, is built on the cultivation not just of an infant's consciousness but also of a mother's. It would be more accurate to say that it allows a return of the underlying rapport that binds us to each other as first expressed in mother-child union. Mindfulness, if it resurrects anything, resurrects the holding environment of the good-enough parent so that our own still-primitive minds can grow out of their tendency to cling to their own misperceptions. In setting this up, mindfulness, like therapy, helps us make peace with our personal histories while encouraging us not to be overly defined by them. Holding this dual reality is what allows *being* to shine through. One does not experience this as a state of merger (in which one person or one thing dissolves into another) but rather as a state of clarity, as if the conceptual barriers of who we think we are have been lifted from the mind. John Cage had a good way of describing this. Error, he was fond of saying, is "simply a failure to adjust immediately from a preconception to an actuality." We are full of preconceptions about ourselves and are limited by them. The actuality of our being is not something we have an easy time making room for.

The actuality that Cage had in mind, at least in its formal sense, occurs when both self and other (or subject and object) shed their falsely conceived identities, allowing something more fundamental (like the sound of one hand or our essential interconnectedness or our intrinsic kindly nature) to be uncovered. Cage's vision of interpenetrating centers is a helpful way of understanding this. This inter-being is our birthright: its template is there already in our earliest intimate relationships. And as the Buddha found, this early prototype can be rediscovered, nurtured, and cultivated so that it becomes a living presence, an inner resource accessible in the midst of everyday life. Therapy, as I have seen, can open a window into this too.

That this potential exists in all of us is something that inspired Rolland, eluded Freud, and was brought home by Cage and Winnicott. It is both the foundation and the apogee of Buddhist wisdom. One of the most profound Buddhist teachings, dating from the first century AD and attributed to a sage named Nāgārjuna, states that "voidness is the womb of compassion." "Voidness" is another word for emptiness, for the lack of a fixed identity in persons and in things. Insight into the insubstantial nature of the self, this means, shows us our relational nature. This is mother recognition from the other side. Not only have all beings been our mothers but we are also mothers to all beings: the womb of compassion is there within us waiting to be rediscovered. When we realize how readily we have misconstrued ourselves, when we stop clinging to our falsely conceived constructs of how limited, isolated, and alone we are, when we touch the ground of *being*, we come home.

I had a quite literal taste of this in my final visit with Ram Dass two years before he died. It was my own version of the oceanic feeling, and it has stayed with me ever since. It had been more than twenty years since I had last seen him (when he had asked me if I saw my patients as already free) and, while I had talked with him on the phone several times, I had made no plans to see him again. But my friend Jack Kornfield called me one day and told me I should go to Maui, where Ram Dass had been living for years, to see him one last time. Ram Dass was a complicated person. He had a persona that was one thing and a character that was another, but Jack told me that things had really changed. Ram Dass was old now (he was eighty-six at the time) and had been dealing with the increasingly severe ravages of the stroke that had partially paralyzed him twenty years before. His body was in terrible shape but his mind had apparently become very free. Jack said Ram Dass had become the person he had always pretended to be and I should go to see for myself.

I was shy about reaching out. Ram Dass had been an important influence on me but we were not exactly friends. He was someone I looked up to and learned from, but I never thought of myself as being part of his inner circle. Yet Jack urged me to email and say I wanted to come, and he assured me that I would be able to stay in Ram Dass's house in his guest room for a couple of days. I wrote and before too long, in April of 2017, flew to Maui for a three-day visit at his home on the grounds of an old horse farm on the north shore of the island.

On this visit, Ram Dass did not tease me about anything. He welcomed me and was very generous with his time. When I first arrived, I waited for him on the patio behind his house at sunset, having flown fourteen hours from New York. He came gliding down in his wheelchair on a little elevator from his bedroom, the back door of the house flying open as he descended, and rolled out onto the terrace in time for dinner. There was a smile on his face as he registered my surprise at his unanticipated backdoor entrance. Three white cranes had just swooped into the yard. His speech was improved from the last time I had seen him, and he greeted me warmly. "I'm spending much more time in here now," he told me, pointing to his chest. His meaning was not lost on me. No longer performing for a sea of onlookers, he was now putting what he had always talked about into practice, dwelling in awareness or, as he sometimes put it, in his soul.

The most striking thing about being with him was how uncomplaining he was. I could see what Jack meant about him. It was really extraordinary. He needed help from various attendants to go to the bathroom, to move from his wheelchair to a garden chair, and to lift and place his paralyzed right arm and leg. He was plagued with chronic and painful urinary tract infections and recurrent bouts of diverticulitis. His speech, despite the improvement I noted on my arrival, remained halting, and he often had trouble finding his words. But his mood was lighthearted and chipper, and he was clearly an inspiration to the people who were helping him. He was a pleasure to be with and, despite his obvious and intense discomfort and fatigue, was curious about my life, my family, and my work. While sitting around the dinner table with the members of his household one evening, Ram Dass pointed at me with a shaking finger and said to the others, "He's . . . he's . . . the real thing." I had been nervous to impose for such an extended time, but his comment made me relax. I was very glad to feel his approval.

The next morning we took an expedition to the ocean for a swim. It was raining but Mondays were beach days, and the weather app promised that it would be sunny on the other side of the island. The weekly swim was a tradition I had heard about before I arrived, but I could not really envision how it was going to happen. Swimming in the sea with a partially paralyzed, wheelchair-bound eighty-six-year-old is no simple matter. But because this was something of a weekly pilgrimage, there were people waiting at the beach to help. While I headed straight into the warm Hawaiian waters, they quickly transferred Ram Dass from his SUV into a makeshift wooden wheelbarrow, maneuvered him into a wetsuit, and wrapped a life vest around him. He lay there grinning as they wheeled him into the water and released him into the ocean. Floating now, and supported by the life vest, Ram Dass paddled toward me using his good arm and leg. I was already immersed in the water and enjoying myself. Without my being aware of it, fifteen other people joined us; they were mostly Maui regulars, retired professionals or aging hippies, who obviously knew about the weekly tradition of the group swim and had come to join it.

On land, despite dwelling more and more inside of himself, Ram Dass was a prisoner of form. But in the water, freed from his body's heavy burden, he came completely alive. His eyes sparkled, his humor was infectious, and his energy was strong. He radiated happiness and playfulness. As the other swimmers circled him, Ram Dass sidled over to me in the water. "We are a pod of souls," he whispered in my ear. This was before COVID had made "pod" into an everyday word, and his use of it was new to me. But it immediately struck me as right. We were like a pod of souls in that sea, jostling like whales as the waves lapped around us. Then he pointed to one of the men swimming nearby. "He's a retired dentist," he exclaimed with a laugh. I knew that he knew that I would get the joke. All the ambition of all of our lives (a dentist!) bringing us to this moment, bobbing up and down like overgrown children in this timeless sea.

I looked around at the other swimmers. The beauty of each of them hit me deeply. They were not especially handsome, but each one of them was stunningly lovely, even radiant. I suppose it was the communal happiness that gave me that impression. I was caught up in it: the buoyancy of the sea, the lightness of our bodies, the sun's warmth, and Ram Dass's evident pleasure. It was an oceanic feeling if there ever was one. Limitless, unbounded, and eternal.

The next thing I knew, everyone was singing:

Row, row, row your boat
Gently down the stream.
Merrily, merrily, merrily, merrily . . .

The simplicity of the song made me happy. It was perfect. Soft waves were ushering us toward shore. The group was singing the verse in rounds. Ram Dass was paddling himself, smiling broadly; the rest of us were rowing alongside him. The waves were gentle as a stream. And the phrase "merrily, merrily, merrily, merrily" came spinning off everyone's tongues like one of those hoop-rolling games European children played after the war. We were indeed a pod of souls, liberated, for an interlude, from the confines of our physical selves, singing and swimming as one.

Back on shore, Ram Dass was quickly whisked out of his wet-suit. He made it clear he was taking everyone to lunch. An empty Thai restaurant in a nearby strip mall awaited us. The proprietors had clearly seen this group—or one like it—before. They were overjoyed and set a long table for twenty. I sat across from Ram Dass, and the gathering stretched out on either side of us. Everyone was back in their body, and I began to question the veracity of what I had felt in the ocean. There was much commotion as a waitress began taking orders for Thai iced tea. A few people did not want ice; others could not drink condensed milk; many preferred theirs without sugar and a few asked for Splenda instead. Some people wanted hot tea while others wanted decaf. One woman asked the group to turn off their cell phones since their electromagnetic radiation worsened her arthritis. My judgmental thoughts, refreshingly absent during my watery sojourn, began to flow freely. I shook my head. With the possible exception of Ram Dass, more interested in his lunch than in the kvetching around him, we were all swimming in our individual egos now, myself included.

In the back of my mind, though, the nursery rhyme was running on. I had been so swept up in the rowing and the stream and the delightful sound of the word "merrily" (from the Old English "myriglice," meaning "pleasantly" or "melodiously") that I hadn't bothered to finish the song in my head. But now I did. "Life is but a dream."

Ordering the iced tea was difficult enough for the group.

Imagine what happened when it came to the soup. Ram Dass ate heartily though. I was full of sour and disapproving thoughts, but he seemed oblivious to the egos flashing around him. I made eye contact with him a couple of times across the table and he gave me a slight smile. It was enough to shake me from the foulness of my mood. I had been doubting what I had felt in the ocean, as if our group's resurgence of personality negated what had seemed so real and alive, so connected and true, just minutes before. But that fleeting smile showed me where Ram Dass was really at. He sensed my distress but he was able to hold the paradox I was struggling with. Both realities were true and the one did not obviate the other. It was a therapeutic moment if there ever was one. The ocean and the restaurant, the soul and the ego, innocence and experience, relatedness and separateness: they were all two sides of one coin. All these beings had once been my mother. And they were all my children. And now here we all were having lunch together, a pod of souls in an endless stream of family get-togethers.

I see now that what Ram Dass showed me that day is what I try to show my patients: the sense that there is something magical, something wonderful, and something to trust running through our lives, no matter how fraught they have been or might become. This is another version of the oceanic feeling, not a return to infantile helplessness or primitive narcissism, but the joyful, merry, and melodious undercurrent that blesses all of our lives. As Ram Dass endlessly repeated in his later years, "I am loving awareness." But what did he mean when he said it? "*I am* loving awareness" or "I am *loving* awareness"? I guess, as with most of those other dichotomies, he meant both.

The psychoanalyst Michael Eigen, in his endlessly inspiring book *The Psychoanalytic Mystic*, came at this mysterious undercurrent from another direction. Rather than leading with anything like loving awareness, he focused on the underworld. His approach, closer to that of D. H. Lawrence's snake poem than

Rolland's oceanic feeling, emphasized the benefit that comes from fearlessly witnessing and, when appropriate, taking responsibility for one's most shameful qualities without becoming fixated on them. In a way, Ram Dass, enduring his stroke and his physical pain without complaint, was doing a version of this by bearing it all so lightly. He did not talk about this much, though, preferring to dwell more and more, as he told me upon my arrival, in his soul. Eigen, in writing about one of his heroes, the British analyst Wilfred Bion (from whose work I pilfered the title *Thoughts without a Thinker*), came around to a similar place by way of a different path. For me, the two approaches—the one from the sky of loving awareness and the other from the underworld of personal turmoil—complement each other and converge in the ocean. Eigen wrote movingly in his book of the power of psychotherapy to inculcate the faith that links these two worlds.

> *I think Bion is trying to describe the worst in us. And I think he is trying to do something more. I feel he is saying we must and can survive the worst, if we are to be truly compassionate with ourselves and each other, if we are going to be partners with the capacities that constitute us. One of the great experiences in reading Bion, I think, is that over and over, we come through the worst. We survive ourselves, build up tolerance for ourselves, make room for ourselves. . . .*
>
> *In face of the worst that he can experience or envision experiencing (including total destruction of experience), Bion maintained a faith that openness to the unknowable ultimate reality (of a session, of a moment, of a lifetime) is somehow linked with growth processes. I think that Bion must have been close to destroying every possibility of goodness in life, and that he speaks from his own experience of surviving the great destruction. I think he must have discovered for himself that life erupts in the valley of the shadow*

*of death. . . . I think Bion always had an eye on the backcloth
of destruction. He always was facing the horror of himself.
A faith that, in spite of all horrors, experience is worthwhile,
is different from use of faith to avoid experiencing. The faith
Bion fought for was linked to intensity of living and risk of
openness.*

*Winnicott . . . and Bion share a conviction that an origi-
nary, naked self is the true subject of experience. Internaliza-
tion processes are necessary for a fully developed, human
self, but something originary shines through. I think these
authors would like the Zen koan, "What was your original
face before you were born?" . . . [They both] point to and
grow out of moments of real living, in which fresh possibilities of experience uplift the self.*

If we are to be truly compassionate with ourselves and with
others, we can and must survive the worst. What could be more
true? Intensity of living and risk of openness. What could be better? As a patient of mine once quipped when speaking of how
writing her memoir had helped her deal with a sudden and un-
imaginable tragedy that had upended her life, "Writing is a much
better quality of agony than trying to forget."

The same might be said of both meditation and psychotherapy. They each encourage a willingness to face the horrors of life,
those that dwell within and those imposed from without, with a
courage and trust that can be hard to otherwise muster. We cannot erase our histories no matter how hard we try, but in learning
to face them with kindness, as so many of my patients have been
able to do, we enter the stream that flows gently, if not always
merrily, toward inner peace.

only one koan matters
you

IKKYŪ

Acknowledgments

To all the patients who so thoughtfully and graciously permitted their personal conversations to become grist for the mill of this book, thank you for your input, your reflections, your generosity, and your support.

To Ann Godoff for much needed guidance and encouragement from start to finish, and to Casey Denis for coming through toward the end; to Jonathan Cott for a stream of Zen poetry that continues to delight; to Michael Vincent Miller for innocence after experience; to Robert Thurman and Sharon Salzberg for their ongoing revelation of the profundity of the Buddha's wisdom; to Daniel Goleman and Amy Gross for reading early versions of this work; to Donna Tartt for kindly alerting me to D. H. Lawrence's snake poem; to Lili Chopra for inviting me to explore the relevance of John Cage to psychotherapy; to Jack Kornfield for insisting that I visit with Ram Dass in Hawaii; to Lucienne Vidah for gentle guidance and structural alignment; and to Andrew Fierberg for his friendship throughout the writing of this book and beyond.

To Anne Edelstein for making it happen; to Sherrie Epstein, my mom, for her forthrightness, resilience, and love; and to my family, Sonia, Will, and Arlene, for all they do and are.

Notes

Introduction

2 **"Perhaps I've been going":** For a further accounting of this pivotal event in the Buddha's life, see chapter 7 of my book *The Trauma of Everyday Life* (New York: Penguin Press, 2013), pp. 114–17.

7 **sent her a link:** Laura Lynne Jackson, *The Light Between Us* (New York: Dial, 2016).

8 **"Taking Ayahuasca When You're":** Casey Schwartz, "Taking Ayahuasca When You're a Senior Citizen," *New York Times*, October 17, 2019.

10 **That evening I read:** Gary Snyder, "Just One Breath: The Practice of Poetry and Meditation," *Tricycle: The Buddhist Review* 1, no. 1 (Fall 1991): 54–61.

12 **As Ram Dass liked:** Ram Dass and Mirabai Bush, *Walking Each Other Home: Conversations on Loving and Dying* (Boulder, CO: Sounds True, 2018).

13 **most therapists are:** Personal communication from writer and therapist Michael Vincent Miller, Fall 2017.

14 **"This is half of":** Upaddha Sutta, *Saṃyutta Nikāya*, SN 45.2.

PART 1: INTO THE MYSTIC

15 *It is too clear:* Paul Reps and Nyogen Senzaki, comps., *Zen Flesh, Zen Bones: A Collection of Zen and Pre-Zen Writings* (New York: Anchor/Doubleday, 1958), p. 22.

Chapter One: Inner Peace

21 **In the article:** Herbert Benson and Mark Epstein, "The Placebo Effect: A Neglected Asset in the Care of Patients," *Journal of the American Medical Association* 232, no. 12 (June 23, 1975): 1225–27.

24 **we took measurements:** Herbert Benson, John W. Lehmann, M. S. Malhotra, Ralph F. Goldman, Jeffrey Hopkins, and Mark D. Epstein, "Body Temperature Changes during the Practice of gTum-mo Yoga," *Nature* 295 (January 1982): 234–36.

29 **"Selflessness means seeing":** For more on this see my book *Psychotherapy without the Self* (New Haven: Yale University Press, 2007), pp. 60–64.

Chapter Two: The Path of Investigation

39 **the clear and single-minded:** See Nyanaponika Thera, *The Heart of Buddhist Meditation* (New York: Samuel Weiser, 1962).

43 **I recently read the book:** Hayao Kawai, *Buddhism and the Art of Psychotherapy* (College Station: Texas A&M University Press, 1996).

49 **Catching the Ox:** All oxherding verses from Yamada Mumon, *Lectures on The Ten Oxherding Pictures*, trans. Victor S. Hori (Honolulu: University of Hawaii Press, 2004).

51 *substance of the true person:* Chao-chou (778–897), *Recorded Sayings*, #347, in *Zen Sourcebook: Traditional Documents from China, Korea, and Japan*, ed. Stephen Addiss (Indianapolis: Hackett, 2008), p. 81.

51 **"Foreground, background, each was":** Lucien Stryk, introduction to *The Penguin Book of Zen Poetry*, ed. Lucien Stryk and Takashi Ikemoto (London: Penguin, 1977), p. 21.

52 *On the rocky slope:* Poem by Hoin in *Penguin Book of Zen Poetry*, p. 11.

NOTES

PART 2: A YEAR OF THERAPY: WINTER, SPRING, SUMMER & FALL

53 *We all hope*: D. W. Winnicott, "The Use of an Object and Relating through Identifica-tions," in *Playing and Reality* (London: Routledge, 1971), p. 87.

Chapter Three: Winter

61 *"What is meditation?"*: Chao-chou, *Recorded Sayings*, in *Zen Sourcebook: Traditional Documents from China, Korea, and Japan*, ed. Stephen Addiss (Indianapolis: Hackett, 2008), p. 75.

66 **Hakuin, the Zen master:** Audrey Yoshiko Seo and Stephen Addiss, *The Sound of One Hand: Paintings and Calligraphy by Zen Master Hakuin* (Boston: Shambhala, 2010), p. 161. I also referenced this calligraphy in my preface to the 2013 edition of *Thoughts without a Thinker* (New York: Basic Books), pp. xviii–xxii.

70 **"unobjectionable positive transference":** Sigmund Freud, "The Dynamics of Transfer-ence" (1912), in *The Standard Edition of the Complete Psychological Works of Sigmund Freud*, vol. 12, *1911–1913*, ed. James Strachey (London: Hogarth Press, 1958).

72 *Swallow Among the Waves*: Seo and Addiss, *Sound of One Hand*, p. 152.

87 **"How, in Freud's view":** Adam Phillips, *Unforbidden Pleasures* (London: Hamish Ham-ilton, 2015), p. 115.

94 *Passionate Enlightenment*: Miranda Shaw, *Passionate Enlightenment* (Princeton, NJ: Princeton University Press, 1994).

97 *We have been taught*: Adam Phillips, *Missing Out: In Praise of the Unlived Life* (Lon-don: Hamish Hamilton, 2012), pp. 58–59.

101 *If development proceeds well*: D. W. Winnicott, *Human Nature* (New York: Routledge, 1988), pp. 137–38.

Chapter Four: Spring

109 *But let a man*: D. T. Suzuki, "Lectures on Zen Buddhism," in *Zen Buddhism and Psy-choanalysis*, ed. Erich Fromm, D. T. Suzuki, and Richard DeMartino (New York: Harper Colophon, 1960), pp. 30–31.

110 **"If you develop an ear":** John Cage, "Music of Sound and Sound of Music," *Inquiring Mind* 3, no. 2 (Winter 1986): 4–5.

111 **"Suspend judgment . . . and give":** Sigmund Freud, "Analysis of a Phobia in a Five-Year-Old Boy" (1909), in *The Standard Edition of the Complete Psychological Works of Sig-mund Freud*, vol. 10, ed. James Strachey (London: Hogarth, 1955), p. 23.

112 **"We must arrange our music":** John Cage, interview with Roger Reynolds, in *Catalogue of Works and Recordings by Robert Dunn* (New York: Henmar Press, 1962), p. 47.

113 *"By what means"*: Chao-chou, *Recorded Sayings*, in *Zen Sourcebook: Traditional Doc-uments from China, Korea, and Japan*, ed. Stephen Addiss (Indianapolis: Hackett, 2008), p. 76.

121 **"In Winnicott's view, the mind":** Adam Phillips, "The Story of the Mind," in *The Mind Object: Precocity and Pathology of Self-Sufficiency*, ed. Edward G. Corrigan and Pearl-Ellen Gordon (Northvale, NJ: Jason Aronson, 1995), p. 235.

129 **the four qualities:** Lucien Stryk and Takashi Ikemoto, eds., *The Penguin Book of Zen Poetry* (London: Penguin, 1977), p. 21.

129 *Returning / by an unused path*: Poem by Bakusui (1720–1783) in *Penguin Book of Zen Poetry*, p. 126.

137 *self other right wrong*: Ikkyū, *Crow with No Mouth: Ikkyū, 15th Century Zen Master*, trans. Stephen Berg (Port Townsend, WA: Copper Canyon Press, 1989), p. 75.

137 *Barn's burnt down*: Poem by Mizuta Masahide (1657–1723) in *Penguin Book of Zen Poetry*, p. 127.

140 *One evening when I was*: John Cage, *A Year from Monday: New Lectures and Writings by John Cage*, 1st paperback ed. (1963; repr. Middletown, CT: Wesleyan University Press, 1969), p. 133.

146 **According to Adam Phillips:** Adam Phillips, *Unforbidden Pleasures* (London: Hamish Hamilton, 2015), p. 119.

146 **"What does the Freudian superego":** Phillips, *Unforbidden Pleasures*, p. 121.

NOTES

Chapter Five: Summer

156 As Samuel Beckett: Paul Foster, *Beckett and Zen: A Study of Dilemma in the Novels of Samuel Beckett* (London: Wisdom, 1989), p. 93.

159 "What is Buddha?": Chao-chou, *Recorded Sayings,* in *Zen Sourcebook: Traditional Documents from China, Korea, and Japan,* ed. Stephen Addiss (Indianapolis: Hackett, 2008), p. 82.

168 With good-enough maternal care: Adam Phillips, "The Story of the Mind," in *The Mind Object: Precocity and Pathology of Self-Sufficiency,* ed. Edward G. Corrigan and Pearl-Ellen Gordon (Northvale, NJ: Jason Aronson, 1995), p. 234.

168 In this state mothers become: D. W. Winnicott, *Babies and Their Mothers* (Reading, MA: Addison-Wesley, 1988), p. 36.

173 "a censor, a judge": Adam Phillips, *Unforbidden Pleasures* (London: Hamish Hamilton, 2015), p. 114.

177 Cry of the deer: Poem by Nakagawa Otsuyu (1674–1739) in *The Penguin Book of Zen Poetry,* ed. Lucien Stryk and Takashi Ikemoto (London: Penguin, 1977), p. 127.

184 I'm leaving— / now you: Poem by Kobayashi Issa (1763–1828) in *Penguin Book of Zen Poetry,* p. 106.

189 "Harsh, delicate, brilliant": Stephen Berg, foreword to *Crow with No Mouth: Ikkyū, 15th Century Zen Master,* trans. Stephen Berg (Port Townsend, WA: Copper Canyon Press, 1989), p. 15.

190 oh green green willow: Poem by Ikkyū (1394–1481), *Crow with No Mouth,* p. 24.

190 I didn't see one thing: Poem by Ikkyū, *Crow with No Mouth,* p. 25.

196 I was the first-born: Nobuyuki Yuasa, *The Year of My Life: A Translation of Issa's Oraga Haru* (Berkeley: University of California Press, 1960), p. 85.

197 The world of dew: Poem by Issa (1763–1828) in Yuasa, *Year of My Life,* p. 11.

204 He is suspicious: D. W. Winnicott, "Hate in the Counter-Transference," *International Journal of Psychoanalysis* 30 (1949): 72.

204 An old rabbi in Poland: John Cage, *A Year from Monday: New Lectures and Writings by John Cage,* 1st paperback ed. (1963; repr. Middletown, CT: Wesleyan University Press, 1969), p. 138.

204 The rice cakes: Poem by Issa (1763–1828) in Yuasa, *Year of My Life,* p. 138.

205 audiobook about couples: Terry Real, *Fierce Intimacy: Standing Up to One Another with Love* (Boulder, CO: Sounds True, 2018).

Chapter Six: Fall

211 A "strange sorrow": Karen Armstrong, *Buddha* (New York: Penguin, 2001), p. 66.

212 Koans show you: John Tarrant, *Bring Me the Rhinoceros: And Other Zen Koans That Will Save Your Life* (Boulder, CO: Shambhala, 2008), pp. 2–3.

213 If you are used to: Tarrant, *Bring Me the Rhinoceros,* p. 3.

214 Autumn moon, / tide foams: Poem by Matsuo Bashō (1644–1694) in *The Penguin Book of Zen Poetry,* ed. Lucien Stryk and Takashi Ikemoto (London: Penguin, 1977), p. 89.

215 "The Second Patriarch": Chao-chou, *Recorded Sayings,* in *Zen Sourcebook: Traditional Documents from China, Korea, and Japan,* ed. Stephen Addiss (Indianapolis: Hackett, 2008), p. 79.

224 I saw art not: Richard Kostelanetz, *Conversing with Cage* (New York: Routledge, 2003), p. 44.

225 It doesn't make the virtuoso: Kostelanetz, *Conversing with Cage,* p. 44.

230 In this language: D. W. Winnicott, "The Development of the Capacity for Concern" (1963), in *The Maturational Processes and the Facilitating Environment: Studies in the Theory of Emotional Development* (Madison, CT: International Universities Press, 1965), p. 76.

232 All we do in successful: D. W. Winnicott, *Babies and Their Mothers* (Reading, MA: Addison-Wesley, 1988), p. 102.

236 There is a wide variation: D. W. Winnicott, "Transitional Objects and Transitional Phenomena," in *Playing and Reality* (London: Routledge, 1971), p. 2.

237 "an intermediate area": For more on transitional objects, see Winnicott, *Playing and Reality,* pp. 1–25.

240 If you have a reason: Tarrant, *Bring Me the Rhinoceros,* p. 3.

NOTES

240 *One day, Yanguan called:* Tarrant, *Bring Me the Rhinoceros*, p. 37.

241 **"His rhinoceros," writes Tarrant:** Tarrant, *Bring Me the Rhinoceros*, p. 40.

243 **She understands the reference:** Jon Kabat-Zinn, *Full Catastrophe Living: Using the Wisdom of Your Body and Mind to Face Stress, Pain, and Illness* (New York: Delacorte Press, 1990).

244 **"It should be regarded":** Bhadantācariya Buddhaghosa, *The Path of Purification: A Classic Textbook of Buddhist Psychology*, vol. 1, trans. Bhikkhu Nānamoli (Berkeley, CA: Shambhala, 1976).

244 **This is territory:** Jessica Benjamin, *The Bonds of Love: Psychoanalysis, Feminism, and the Problem of Domination* (New York: Pantheon, 1988), pp. 86–87.

249 *In the initial stages:* Winnicott, "Development of the Capacity," p. 82.

252 *Now, emptiness is:* D. W. Winnicott, "Fear of Breakdown" (1963), in *Psycho-Analytic Explorations* (Cambridge, MA: Harvard University Press, 1989), p. 94.

256 *Never forget: / we walk:* Poem by Kobayashi Issa (1763–1828) in *Penguin Book of Zen Poetry*, p. 108.

259 *This hexagram represents:* Richard Wilhelm, *The I Ching or Book of Changes* (Princeton, NJ: Princeton University Press, 1950), p. 86.

260 *It is creative apperception:* Winnicott, "Creativity and Its Origins," in *Playing and Reality*, p. 65.

261 **"Two separate persons":** Winnicott, "Creativity and Its Origins," p. 80.

261 *Psychoanalysts have perhaps:* Winnicott, "Creativity and Its Origins," p. 81.

PART 3: THE GATE OF ONENESS

265 *"What is one word?":* Chao-chou, *Recorded Sayings*, in *Zen Sourcebook: Traditional Documents from China, Korea, and Japan*, ed. Stephen Addiss (Indianapolis: Hackett, 2008), p. 79.

Chapter Seven: Kindness

269 *It is only in recent:* D. W. Winnicott, "The Use of an Object and Relating through Identifications," in *Playing and Reality* (London: Routledge, 1971), pp. 86–87.

276 **"The appeal is to":** Jeffrey Hopkins, preface to *Kindness, Clarity, and Insight*, by the Fourteenth Dalai Lama, His Holiness Tenzin Gyatso, trans. and ed. Jeffrey Hopkins (Ithaca, NY: Snow Lion, 1984), p. 1.

277 **"The main theme":** Gyatso, *Kindness, Clarity, and Insight*, p. 32.

277 *Again, in order to:* Gyatso, *Kindness, Clarity, and Insight*, p. 33.

279 **"feeling of an indissoluble":** Sigmund Freud, *Civilization and Its Discontents* (1930), in *The Standard Edition of the Complete Psychological Works of Sigmund Freud*, vol. 21, *1927–1931, The Future of an Illusion, Civilization and Its Discontents and Other Works*, ed. James Strachey (London: Hogarth Press and Institute of Psycho-Analysis, 1961), p. 72.

280 **"simply a failure":** John Cage, *Silence* (Middletown, CT: Wesleyan University Press, 1961), p. 170.

281 **"voidness is the womb":** Robert Thurman, email message to author, August 20, 2020: "Shūnyatā-karuṇā-garbham goes back to Nāgārjuna's Jewel Rosary (Precious Garland for some) where it is part of his description of the most advanced teaching. It is coupled with advayam (nondual), gambhīram (profound), bhīrubhishanam (frightening to the timid) and bodhi-sādhanam (enlightenment in practice, or in performance). The compound can be analyzed in various ways, I translate it as 'emptiness the womb of compassion,' meaning that emptiness as nondual relativity leads to the realization of the absoluteness of the relative, hence one's total interconnection with others in an inconceivable empathetic oneness with them in mind and body, feeling both what they are feeling and deeper what they have of wisdom and love buried in deepest heart, luckily. Often the two are opposed to each other, therefore it is inconceivable to the binary conceptual mind."

281 **my final visit:** An earlier version of this trip was described in my article "Already Free: A Swim with Ram Dass Is a Dip into Egolessness," *Tricycle: The Buddhist Review* (Spring 2019). Reprinted in John David, *Meetings with Remarkable People* (Hitdorf on the Rhine, Germany: Open Sky, 2020), pp. 313–320.

287 *I think Bion is trying:* Michael Eigen, *The Psychoanalytic Mystic* (Binghamton, NY: Esf, 1998), p. 34.

288 **"Writing is a much":** Sonali Deraniyagala, author of *Wave* (New York: Knopf, 2013), quoted in Teju Cole, "A Better Quality of Agony," *New Yorker*, March 27, 2013.

Index

"absolutizing," 188–89, 190
afterlife, 193
aggression, 13, 77–78, 208–13, 215, 244, 262, 267–68
"already free," 11–12, 186, 252, 268
altruism, 33–34, 276–77
"Altruism and the Six Perfections" (Dalai Lama), 276–77
ambition, 28, 284
Ananda, 14
anatta, 180–81, 184, 188, 190
anger, 208–10, 221–22, 229, 233, 244
 in meditation, 28, 100
 mindfulness and, 118, 119
 reconfiguring, 33, 209–10
 against the self, 154–55
 Winnicott on, 203–4, 209–10, 218–19, 221
anicca, 180–81, 184
anorexia, 1, 120
anxiety, 124, 125, 170–73. *See also* performance anxiety
ascetism, 1, 5, 48–49, 209
Autobiography of a Yogi (Yogananda), 185–86
Avalokiteśvara, 65
ayahuasca, 8–9, 273–74, 275

Bakusui, 129
Banderas, Antonio, 201
Bashō, 214
Beckett, Samuel, 156
"beggarly" giving, 74
"beholding," 48
Benson, Herbert, 17–27, 30, 84
 on meditation practice, 17–27, 35–37, 111

on placebo effect, 19–20, 21–23, 37
on "relaxation response," 17–21, 31, 35, 237
beta-blockers, 92–93
Beth Israel Hospital, 276
Bion, Wilfred, 287–88
Bodhidharma, 88
bodhisattvas, 65, 67, 275
Boston City Hospital, 17, 19–20
breath (breathing), 41, 94, 178–79, 219, 237
Bring Me the Rhinoceros (Tarrant), 212–13, 240–41, 268
Buddha, 1–5, 30, 156–57, 261
 on aggression, 209
 on anger, 212, 222
 conversation with Ananda, 14
 Eightfold Path of, 78, 81
 on friendship, 14
 golden bowl of Sujata, 1–4, 5, 14, 48, 209
 on ignorance or delusion, 88, 180
 loss of Sariputta and Moggallana, 194–95
 on "mental development," 209
 metta, 127
 mother's death, 1, 4
 rose-apple tree experience of, 2, 11, 145–46, 210–12, 262, 270
 the self, 153
 on suffering, 66, 108, 125, 133, 180, 196–97, 210, 211
 three marks of existence, 180–81
  anatta, 180–81, 184, 188, 190
  anicca, 180–81, 184
  dukkha, 125, 180–81, 184
 triumphing over Mara, 144, 145

Buddhism, 210–11, 262. *See also* Tibetan
    Buddhism; Zen Buddhism
    approach to loss, 194–95
    author's engagement with, 5, 12, 14,
        29–30, 267
    conceit and, 126–27
    contemplation, 42, 48, 108
    emptiness and, 28, 29, 133, 189–90,
        195, 197, 262, 281
    finding the clinging, 66, 68, 80, 98
    four qualities of, 129
    "good-enough," 155, 156–57
    hierarchy of giving, 74
    ignorance or delusion, 88, 180
    "injured innocence," 96–98, 133, 205
    "kalyana mitra," 186
    on mother recognition, 277–78, 281
    the self and, 170–71, 202–3
    synergy of psychotherapy and, 3–4,
        5–6, 11, 13, 43–44, 55–59,
        111–12, 163–64, 185–86, 207–8,
        209, 212–13, 268–69, 272–73
    three poisons, 142
    "voidness" and, 281, 296*n*

Cage, John, 107–12, 248, 280–81
    Buddhism and Suzuki's influence on,
        109–10, 129, 224, 225
    Cunningham's dances, 107, 140, 204
    music and sounds, 110–12, 117, 133,
        211, 225
    Noguchi narrative of, 140–41
    throwing the *I Ching*, 107, 121, 122,
        259
"caretaker" self, 155
Cervantes, Miguel de, 146–47
Chao-chou, 61, 113, 159, 215, 265
childhood traumas, 64–66, 70–71, 71, 77
clear light mind, 34
clinging
    in couples, 74–75, 77, 78
    energy blocks, 71
    to inner critics, 87–88
    perpetuating suffering, 13, 66, 68, 72,
        79–80, 83, 97–98, 235
    roots of, 103, 104
cognitive neuroscience, 36–37
Columbia University, 31, 108–9, 185
compassion, 13, 22, 42–43, 65, 83,
    228–29
conceit, 126–27, 129
concentration, 19, 41, 42, 255

consciousness, 42, 154, 157
contemplation, 42, 48, 108
Corso, Gregory, 180
COVID-19 pandemic, 6, 58, 213, 273
"Creativity and Its Origins" (Winnicott),
    260–62
cuckoo, 66–67, 71, 72, 144
Cunningham, Merce, 107, 140, 204

Dalai Lama, 23–25, 29–36, 276–78
    author's private meeting with, 29–30
    author's study of Buddhism, 24–25,
        27–29
    on destructive emotions, 142
    on inner peace, 31–33, 96, 100,
        276–77
    on kindness, 276–77
    on mother recognition, 277–78, 281
    on "nonaffirming negative," 28,
        29, 190
    on nonviolence, 32–33, 37, 100
    on person wearing sunglasses, 29, 190
    on the self, 34–35, 133, 202
Danto, Arthur, 109
David-Neel, Alexandra, 23, 24, 25
death, 123–25
delusion, 88, 180
"developmental trauma," 250–51
"Development of the Capacity for
        Concern, The" (Winnicott),
        229–32, 248–49
Dharamsala, 29–30
    author's visit to, 24–28
Dhonden, Yeshi, 24, 27–28
dialectical behavioral therapy, 142
directness, 129
dissociation, 199, 250
distractions, 40
"doing versus being," 258, 260–61, 275
Don Quixote (Cervantes), 146–47, 151
Dreyfus, Georges, 27–28
drowning man, 67–68
drug-assisted insights, 8–9, 273–74
dukkha, 125, 180–81, 184

Eck, Diana, 18
ego, 5, 28, 32, 48, 87, 146–47, 156, 261
ego habit, 126–27
Eigen, Michael, 286–87
Eightfold Path, 78
Emotional Intelligence (Goleman), 18
empathy, 28, 210, 228, 237, 248

emptiness, 155, 157
  Buddhist concept of, 28, 29, 133,
      189–90, 195, 197, 262, 281
  Winnicott on, 252–53
energy blocks, 71
"environment-mother," 230–32, 258
Epstein, Franklin H., 18, 19–20, 132, 133
Epstein, Sherrie S., 6–8, 10–11
Epstein, Sonia Shechet, 182–83
Epstein, Will, 124–25, 178–80, 182–83
erotogenic zone, 234
expectations, 74, 80, 81, 115
eye contact, 247, 249

false self, 155, 171, 201–3
"Fear of Breakdown" (Winnicott), 251,
      252–53
female agency, 244–45
female arousal, 94
female/male dichotomy, 258, 260
Fierce Intimacy (Real), 205
"fierce mother," 34
food issues, 120–22, 166–69, 238
Forest Refuge, 149
forgiveness, 228, 272
free association, 2, 34, 108
Freud, Anna, 32
Freud, Sigmund, 108, 111, 146–47
  on free association, 34, 108
  on Oedipus complex, 103–4,
      125, 154
  on religious experiences ("oceanic
      feeling"), 279–80
  on resistance, 5
  on superego, 32, 87–88, 128,
      146–47, 173
  on transference, 70, 71–72, 104
Freudian slip, 130
"friendly" giving, 74
friendship, 12, 14, 126–29
From, Isadore, 189
Fromm, Erich, 109

Gerstein, Mordicai, 124–25
Ginsberg, Allen, 109
"God is one," 273–75
Goldstein, Joseph, 23, 39, 80, 111,
      150–51, 194, 195, 197
Goleman, Daniel, 18, 26
"good-enough," 33–34, 155, 156–57,
      168, 209, 230–31, 236, 280
Good Omens (TV show), 239

grieving (grief), 123–25, 174, 176–77,
      194–95, 196–97
gtum-mo meditation, 23, 24–25,
      27–28, 30, 34
guilt, 83, 118–19, 121, 242, 245, 249
gurus, 185–87
Guston, Philip, 109

habits, 8, 33, 82
haikus, 72, 129, 137, 177, 183–84, 197,
      204–5, 214, 226, 256
Hakuin, 66–67, 68, 71, 72, 144, 212
Hamlet (Shakespeare), 223
Harvard Medical School, 12, 18–19, 24,
      25–26, 36, 85
"Hate in the Counter-Transference"
      (Winnicott), 203–4,
      218–19
heat yoga, 28–29, 34, 36, 276
Heraclitus, 180
heroin, 121
hexagram, 258–60
Highest Yoga Tantra, 28–29, 33
Hinduism, 36–37, 39
holding, 98, 168–69, 232, 237, 280
Holocaust, 63–64, 66
Hopkins, Jeffrey, 24–25, 27–28, 276
Horney, Karen, 109
How to Pass, Kick, Fall, and Run
      (dance), 140
humor, 203–5

I Ching, 107, 121, 122, 258–60
id, 32, 146–47
ignorance, 88, 108
"I guess," 174–75
Ikkyū, 137, 189–90
impermanence, 51, 129, 180, 194, 197
implicit memory, 248
"injured innocence," 96–98, 133, 205
inner peace, 1, 31–33, 96, 100, 110,
      202, 277
Inquiring Mind (newspaper), 108
"insight," 42, 180
insight meditation, 14, 23, 39–41, 42–43,
      180, 201–2
Insight Meditation Society, 23–24, 150
instability, 65, 72
Institute of Buddhist Dialectics,
      29–30
introjection, 64–65
Issa, 196–97, 204–5, 256

Jesus, 90, 91, 136–37, 165, 275
Journal of the American Medical Association, 21
Joyce, James, 48
Judaism, 273–74, 275–76
Jungian analysis, 43

"kalyana mitra," 186
Kennedy, John F., 163
Kernberg, Otto, 220–21, 230–31
kindness, 221, 228, 267, 268–69, 276–77
Kindness, Clarity, and Insight (Dalai Lama), 276
"kingly" giving, 74, 75
koans, 67–68, 212–13, 225, 239–41, 268–69
Kobayashi Issa, 183–84
Kornfield, Jack, 23, 39, 80, 111, 281–83
Krishna, 27
Krishna Das, 27
Kuan Yin, 65, 67

Ladino, 275–76
"lama," 186
Lawrence, D. H., "Snake," 44–49, 71, 75, 83, 208–9, 286–87
lies (lying), 101
Linehan, Marsha, 142
"love the thoughts," 83, 84, 128, 268
LSD (lysergic acid diethylamide), 246–47

Maharishi Mahesh Yogi, 17, 19
male/female dichotomy, 258, 260
mantras, 41
Martin, Agnes, 109
Masahide, 137
masturbation, 161–62, 234
"maturational process," 209
Mecca, 86
meditation, 13, 61, 148–50, 207, 278–79
  author's engagement with, 7–8, 12, 18, 20, 29, 32–33, 35–37, 39, 55–56, 84, 169
  Benson's research on, 17–27, 35–37, 111
  brain science and, 36–37
  direction to face, 86
  gtum-mo (tummo), 23, 24–25, 27–28, 30, 34
  insight (vipassana), 14, 23, 39–41, 42–43, 180, 201–2
  instruction, 55, 58, 178–81, 182–83

investigation of self in, 98
  music and, 110–12, 117
  personal thoughts and, 86–87
  setting aside time for, 115–16
  Snyder on, 10, 11
  types of, 41–43
  unmet oral needs, 236
meditation retreats, 7–8, 23–24, 55, 121, 148, 150, 185–87, 238
Menla Mountain House Retreat Center, 185–87
mental health, 36
Merton, Thomas, 109
#MeToo movement, 82
metta, 127
Mickey Mouse Club, The (TV show), 40–41
microdosing, 247
Miller, Michael Vincent, 163–63, 167, 173, 268
Mind/Body Effect, The (Benson), 22–23
mindfulness, 13, 36–37, 42–43, 94, 156, 280
  author's engagement with, 23–24, 111, 112
  psychotherapy and, 56, 108
  "remembering" aspect of, 139, 141
"mindful psychotherapy," 56
mind object, 121–22, 128, 155, 167
  Buddhist therapy for, 133–34, 157, 181, 270
  Winnicott on, 121–22, 167, 168
Missing Out (Phillips), 97–98
Moggallana, 194
"monkey mind," 67, 77
moon, 194, 195
mother recognition, 277–78, 281
Mother Teresa, 90, 91, 137
Mountains of Tibet, The (Gerstein), 124–25
mushrooms, 107
music and meditation, 110–12, 117
Muzak, 110

Nāgārjuna, 281, 296n
narcissism, 279, 286
Naropa Institute, 107, 109
naturalness, 129
Nature (journal), 30
nervous system, 17, 30, 119
neuroticism, 108
New Introductory Lectures (Freud), 146

New Yorker, 6
New York Times, 6, 8–9
nirvana, 210–11
Nobel Peace Prize, 31
Noguchi, Isamu, 140
"nonaffirming negative," 28, 29, 190
"non-doing," 43
nonviolence, 32–33, 37, 100
nothingness, 198–99

"object-mother," 229–32
"oceanic feeling," 279–80
Oedipus complex, 103–4, 125, 154
oneness, 273–75
oral stage, 234, 235–36
Otsuyu, Nakagawa, 177

Passionate Enlightenment (Shaw), 94
Peaky Blinders (TV show), 239
perfectionism, 94, 95, 100, 101, 168, 228
performance anxiety, 92–93, 94, 242, 243
Phillips, Adam
    on Freud and *Don Quixote,*
        146–47, 151
    on self-criticism, 87–88
    on therapy and feeding grievances,
        97–98, 268
    on Winnicott and mind object,
        121, 168
placebo effect, 19–20, 21–23, 37, 268
pleasure/unpleasure duality, 120–21
Pollan, Michael, 8
prasad, 175–76
prayers, 41
profundity, 129
prostitutes, 120–21
Psychoanalytic Mystic, The (Eigen),
    286–87
psychotherapy and Buddhism, 3–4, 5–6,
    11, 13, 43–44, 55–59, 111–12,
    163–64, 185–86, 207–8, 209,
    212–13, 268–69, 272–73
psychotherapy sessions, 5–6, 12–13,
    55–59
    Anne, 76–78
    April, 170–73
    Beth, 120–22, 166–69
    Brad, 188–90
    Carol, 250–53
    Chloe, 263–64
    Corinne, 254–56
    Craig, 118–19

David, 142–47
Debby, 90–91
Donald, 201–5
Fred, 115–17
Hunter, 233–37
Jack, 63–68
Jean, 135–37, 165, 238–41
Lakshman, 82–85, 105
Linnéa, 182–84
Lukas, 191–92
Margaret, 86–89, 148–51, 246–49
Mitch, 73–75
Opal, 79–81
Rachel, 102–4
Rebecca, 138–41
Ricki, 174–77
Sally, 96–98
Sandy, 193–97
Sarah, 131–34
Shirley, 217–22
Steve, 227–32
Tom and Willa, 161–64
Violette, 92–95, 99–101, 242–45
Willa, 69–72, 198–200, 223–26
Will and Linnéa, 178–81
Zach, 126–30, 257–62

qigong, 258

Ramakrishna, 279
Ram Dass, 27, 39, 82–85, 111
    "already free," 11–12, 186, 252, 268
    author's meditations and visits with,
        11–12, 23, 84–85, 281–86
    "be here now," 261, 84-8
    Lakshman and, 82–85, 128
    "love the thoughts," 83, 84, 128, 268
    "see yourself as a soul," 83, 84,
        128, 268
    "walking each other home," 12, 272
    "you are not who you think you are,"
        84–85, 169, 171
"reaction formation," 4
reciprocity, 74
Reiki, 70–71
reincarnation, 7, 277
"relaxation response," 17–21, 31, 35,
    237
Relaxation Response, The (Benson),
    18–19
"remembering," 139, 141
resentment, 121–22

resistance, 5, 180
rhinoceros, 212–13, 240–41, 245, 268
Right Action, 78
righteous indignation, 133, 201, 202–3,
    205
Rolland, Romain, 279

sadness, 139–40
Salinger, J. D., 109
Salzberg, Sharon, 23, 39
Sariputta, 194
Schoenberg, Arnold, 110
"screen memories," 40
seasoned meditation, 42–43
"see yourself as a soul," 83, 84, 128, 268
self, 5, 29, 32, 108, 133–34, 153–56, 201–3
self-centeredness, 34–35
self-cherishing attitude, 35, 96, 133
self-concepts, 41, 136, 278–79
self-criticism, 87–88, 154, 170, 172–73,
    188–89, 199, 238–39
self-doubt, 143, 144–45, 243
self-esteem, 77, 83, 154, 272
self-judgment, 111, 128–29
self-knowledge, 261
selflessness, 29, 192, 210
separation, 74–75
sex, 93–95, 162–63, 191–92, 233–34, 235
sex therapists, 93–94
sexual abuse, 69, 70–71, 161–63,
    199–200
sexual objectification of women,
    82–84, 105
shame, 4, 83, 126, 128–29, 135–37, 238,
    240, 272
    early childhood trauma and, 69, 71,
    162–63, 199–200
Shaw, Miranda, 94
Shechet, Arlene, 9–10, 41, 69, 175, 182
shyness, 170–73, 198
Silberstein, Eduard, 146
simplicity, 129, 284
Six Yogas of Naropa, 28–29
"Snake" (Lawrence), 44–49, 71, 75, 83,
    208–9, 286–87
Snyder, Gary, 10, 11
social media, 40, 254
soul, 109–10
    Ram Dass's "see yourself as a soul,"
    83, 84, 128, 268
"sound of one hand," 67, 72, 122, 138,
    144, 212

"spiritual but not religious," 6–8, 11
Stryk, Lucien, 51
stutter, 171–72, 173
submission, 93, 186, 191–92, 244
suffering, 90, 136–37
    Buddha and Buddhism on, 66, 67,
    108, 125, 133, 150, 180, 196–97,
    210, 211
    clinging perpetuating, 13, 66, 68, 72,
    79–80, 83, 97–98, 235
    Freud on, 108
suicidal thoughts, 175
Sujata, 2–4, 5, 14, 209
superego, 32, 87–88, 94, 128, 145–47,
    172, 208, 269
    April and, 172, 173
    Buddha and, 88, 144, 145–46
    Freud on, 32, 87–88, 128, 146–47, 173
    Goldstein and, 150–51
    Phillips on Freud and Don Quixote,
    146–47, 151
Suzuki, D. T., 109–10, 129
Swallow Among the Waves (Hakuin), 72

tantric sex, 94
Target, 100, 132
Tarrant, John, 212–13, 240–41, 268
"ten fetters," 127, 128
Ten Ox Herding, 49–50
Tewari, K. C., 27
therapeutic relationship, 270–71
therapy sessions. See psychotherapy
    sessions
Theravada Buddhism, 41–42
Thoughts without a Thinker (Epstein),
    31–32, 287
Thurman, Robert, 31, 185–87, 188, 202
Tibetan Buddhism, 23–25. See also
    Dalai Lama
    author's engagement with, 12, 29–30
    author's study of, 24–25, 27–29, 30, 36
    gtum-mo meditation, 23, 24–25,
    27–28, 30, 34
    Highest Yoga Tantra, 28–29, 33
    the self and, 202–3
time-outs, 244
Torah, 274
Trader Joe's, 131, 132
Transcendental Meditation (TM), 17,
    19, 22, 36–37
transference, 70–73, 104, 155, 187,
    203–4, 218–19, 225

transitional objects, 236–37
tummo (gtum-mo) meditation, 23,
    24–25, 27–28, 30, 34
Turkish Jews, 275–76
'turn the other cheek," 136–37

University of Virginia, 24, 276
unlimited centers, 225–26, 229, 248
"Use of an Object and Relating through
    Identifications, The" (Winn-
    icott), 269–70

value judgments, 224–25
Velvet (TV show), 239
vipassana, 23, 39–42. See also insight
    meditation
visualizations, 185
vitamin B12 shots, 166
"voidness," 281, 296n
Vrindavan, 26–27

"wakeful hypometabolic state," 17–18
Wallace, Robert Keith, 17–18
whimpering, 138–39
Wilhelm, Richard, 259
Williams College, 28
Winnicott, Donald W., 33–34, 53, 250
    on anger and aggression, 203–4,
        209–10, 218–19, 221
    on capacity for concern, 229–32,
        248–49
    on children's lies, 101

"Creativity and Its Origins," 260–62
"Fear of Breakdown," 251, 252–53
on "good-enough mother," 33–34,
    168, 209, 230–31
"Hate in the Counter-Transference,"
    203–4, 218–19
on male/female dichotomy, 258,
    260–61
on mind object, 121–22, 168
on "object-mother" and
    "environment-mother,"
    229–32, 258
"The Use of an Object and Relating
    through Identifications," 269–70
on transitional objects, 237
World War II, 63–64

yearning, 143, 262
Year of My Life, The (Issa), 196–97
yoga, 185–86
    heat, 28–29, 34, 36, 276
Yogananda, Paramahansa, 185–86

Zeki, 273–76, 278
Zen Buddhism
    koans, 67–68, 212–13, 225, 239–41,
        268–69
    Suzuki on, 109–10, 129
Zen Buddhist poetry, 14, 49–52, 66–67,
    129–30
    Ten Ox Herding, 49–50
Zen of therapy, 13, 43, 269–70